VIEW OF STOCKBRIDGE
DRAWN ON THE WALL OF CHERRY COTTAGE BY HARRY HOPKINS
IN 1830

Facsimile Edition by

The Troy Book Makers
www.thetroybookmakers.com

COPYRIGHT, 1939
BY
SARAH CABOT SEDGWICK
AND
CHRISTINA SEDGWICK MARQUAND

Second Printing

ENGRAVINGS BY THE JAMES MCKINNON COMPANY
SPRINGFIELD, MASSACHUSETTS

MAP BY JAMES L. SINCLAIR

PRINTED IN THE UNITED STATES OF AMERICA
BY
THE BERKSHIRE COURIER
GREAT BARRINGTON, MASSACHUSETTS

To
The Town of Stockbridge
this book is affectionately dedicated

Acknowledgments

A GREAT deal of the material for this book has been gathered from personal reminiscences, papers and letters, and we wish to express our gratitude for the help which has been so liberally given us. Mr. Chester Averill lent us excerpts copied from the *Acts and Resolves of the Province of Massachusetts Bay;* The Reverend Albert R. Brown put at our disposal papers relating to the Congregational Church; Mrs. Raymond L. Buell made accessible the R. H. W. Dwight collection of historical papers at her house in Richmond; Miss Mabel Choate lent papers relating to John Sergeant; Mrs. J. H. Denison allowed us to quote from Esther Burr's journal in her husband's unpublished manuscript, entitled *Abigail Williams and Early Stockbridge;* Mr. David Dudley Field lent an account of the life of his father, Stephen Dudley Field; Mr. David Milton Jones, papers on Curtisville; Miss Elizabeth G. Norton of Boston, the unpublished recollections of Anne Ashburner. Mr. Henry Dwight Sedgwick and The Reverend Theodore Sedgwick and Mrs. Charles Stuart Wilson wrote personal reminiscences, and Mr. Carl Wurtzbach of Lee allowed us to use two papers he had written on Curtisville.

In addition, anecdotes and contributions have been gratefully received from Mrs. Charles Bidwell, Mr. Edward M. Church, Mr. Frank Crowninshield, Mr. Frank Farrell, Miss Daisy French, Mrs. George de Gersdorff, Mrs. Charles E. Hull, Miss Florence M. Jones, Miss Helen Kobbé, The Reverend Edmund R. Laine, Miss Anna C. Lufburrow, Mrs. Augustus H. Lukeman, Mrs. John C. Lynch, Mr. Arthur C.

STOCKBRIDGE

Monroe, Mrs. John P. Palmer, Mr. Walter E. Patterson, Mrs. Carter Richardson, Miss Alice Riggs, Mrs. Ella Edwards Rogers, Mrs. William Scoville, Miss Gertrude Robinson-Smith, Mrs. H. C. Stanton, and Mr. Allen T. Treadway.

Mr. A. M. Costello photographed the Harry Hopkins drawing fifty years ago and retouched it for inclusion in this book. Mr. Karl M. Foster generously contributed his time and skill in preparing all the old photographs used and in taking the new ones.

Mr. and Mrs. Arthur N. Bartlett at the Mission House, and Miss Rosalie Ellis and Mrs. Graham D. Wilcox at the Stockbridge Library have been unfailingly kind and helpful.

Finally, we wish especially to thank Miss Nancy Osborne for acting as our publisher. Her tireless industry and patience have made it possible to have the history ready in time for the Bicentennial Celebration of the town.

THE AUTHORS.

Contents

CHAPTER		PAGE
	FOREWORD	xiii
I.	THE MISSION	1
II.	THE INDIAN TOWN	25
III.	THE WILLIAMS RING	49
IV.	JONATHAN EDWARDS	72
V.	THE GROWTH OF THE ENGLISH TOWN	98
VI.	THE REVOLUTION	125
VII.	SHAYS' REBELLION	150
VIII.	THE FEDERALIST PERIOD	166
IX.	GOING OUT INTO THE WORLD	182
X.	THE VILLAGE BECOMES LITERARY	205
XI.	THE VILLAGE EXPANDS	225
XII.	THE RESORT	237
	EPILOGUE	264
	NOTES	283
	BIBLIOGRAPHY	293
	INDEX	301

List of Illustrations

MAP	*Endpaper*
A VIEW OF STOCKBRIDGE IN 1830	*Frontispiece*
	FACING PAGE
JOHN SERGEANT	14
THE MISSION HOUSE	32
GLENDALE WOOLEN MILLS	152
THE FIELD BROTHERS	196
CATHERINE SEDGWICK	212
THE VILLAGE STREET	246
THE BERKSHIRE PLAYHOUSE	276

Foreword

IT is impossible for me to write with maturity of Stockbridge, for I knew it only through the eyes of a child. By the same token it is difficult to be impersonal about a place that was a complete world in itself for the first ten years of my life. It bears no relationship to other places, though even then I knew that such did exist. In time I came to accept that fact, always however with a certain resentment. There was New York City, for instance, which was apparently bigger than Pittsfield; there was the Mississippi River that dared to compete with the Housatonic, and Mt. Blanc and Pike's Peak that wore snow caps all the year round, not just in winter like Monument Mountain. But for all that, Stockbridge and the Universe were synonymous to one of its least important inhabitants in those early years of the 1900's.

To a child, Berkshire seasons were like a clock where every subtle shifting of light and shade, of budding or reddening leaf, every note of fall cricket or summer thrush, marked the passing of time as plainly as the movement of pointing hour and minute hands. Unconsciously even today I reckon the seasons according to their arrival in Stockbridge, not as they have come to other places where I have since lived.

It was winter not so much when the first snow fell as when the Red Lion Inn put up its shutters, after the departure of the last city visitor, and the isinglass-eyes of the big iron stoves in the station and Van Deusen's store began to glow again. It would be Thanksgiving, we knew, when the shallow pools in the river meadows below the Indian Burying Ground had ice solid enough for skating. Christmas meant snow, of course, and Saturday excursion to woods outside town limits where we gathered ground pine to make wreaths and holiday festoons. Our mittens were frozen stiff from snowy burrowing as we bore home our greens in the dark of those shortest days of the year. Miss Wells lighted the library lamps early then and their yellow oblongs welcomed us at the corner where the watering trough was a white gothic of icicles. But that was only the prelude to Christmas Eve and the carol service at Saint Paul's Church with Dr. Lawrence stepping down from the chancel to hand out gifts of his own choosing. We could never quite live up to his annual pleas that the candy wrappings should remain intact until the service was over. So peppermint sticks, ground pine garlands and evergreen trees always mingled their scents and became forever linked with the frankincense and myrrh of the Wise Men in Bethlehem before we rustled to our feet for the last carol. Then the squeak of sleigh runners, the frosty-clearness of bells, and snow crunching under our feet as we clutched our presents and started home with the long, stained-glass windows still bright behind us. Yes, those were Christmas Eves.

Sunrise Prayer Meeting on the first morning of January stands out as another important event. I can just remember the famous one when the century came in. First, the strangeness of being wakened in the pitch dark and then the setting off with lanterns in below-zero cold to meet something of breath-taking significance that went by the name of 1900. We whispered as we climbed the stairs to an upper hall and sat on easily collapsible chairs waiting for the town to gather. All the familiar sounds of winter were outside: trees creaking with cold and sleighs that squeaked and jingled as they drove up; and inside there was that no less wintry sound in that zipperless era—the clank-clank of loosened goloshes' buckles as

FOREWORD

people filed in. All the important men in town and a few of the hardier women arose and said a few words about the new century. But only Mr. Alexander Sedgwick dared to confess in public that he had come breakfastless to do honor to the New Year. After we had prayed and sung it in in proper fashion, there followed such an orgy of handshaking that I can recall only the problem of rescuing my own goloshes from under chairs and at the same time keeping my right hand free to be wrung by larger hands reached down to me from every direction.

Others of my generation must have known the same long winter evenings by open fires or Franklin stoves with kerosene lamplight soft on the table and the rest of the room shadowy and chill. They must have known those incredible mornings after a night of sleet when icy trees in the sun could put Christmas tinsel to shame. They must have known, as I did, the wonder of County Fair and Cattle Show, and have felt the same excited responsibility of going for the mail. I can see the postmistress's fingers yet as they slipped letters and papers into the little numbered boxes. Did others know, I wonder, where the clumps of pink lady slippers made their appearance in a patch of pine woods whose secret we guarded? Did they also stand incredulous before the miracle of those migrant fringed gentians that for several autumns turned a bit of swampland by the South Lee road into pure indigo?

March was a test of skill in navigation whenever we crossed the village street and that was the time the willows by the Housatonic stood in sheets of quicksilver. Their branches took on a pinkish tinge that would change to yellow by April Fool's Day when we concocted delicious looking candies stuffed with cotton batting to be brought for recess at Miss Brewer's and Miss Byington's school. And then there were May baskets to be filled with early offerings of hepatica and violets or with the rare white and rosy stars of arbutus that hid under damp leaves in a remote clearing Bear Mountain way. We felt it a personal calamity if springs were tardy and the plentiful and unfailing bluets had to do duty instead.

Lilacs, of course, belonged to Memorial Day. It has always seemed, because of Stockbridge, a little forward of them to blossom two and even three weeks before that time in other places. Apple trees were in full bloom then, too, and usually falling in delicate showers as the little company of old men in blue and townspeople followed a fife and drum to the cemetery. The cemetery was a beautiful spot and I am glad now that no one thought it queer for children to play there as we so often did. We knew all the different family plots and had our favorites among the headstones, though the dog's statue in the Sedgwick lot was the one we loved best. He was, and still is, as real to me as our own fox terrier and the neighbors' dogs we greeted by name each day.

In those days when summer came in like a green and overwhelming tide of leaf and bloom, the Inn opened its doors wide to the summer visitors who usually returned season after season. Occasionally, too, there were couples who appeared to stroll about hand in hand in obviously new and stylish clothes. These were apt to be brides and grooms and they lent romance to the scene. Sometimes they asked the way of us and we volunteered not only to guide but to show them what we considered the points of interest of the town. There would be coaching parties, too, in summer, on the way to or from Lenox and it was a sight to see these sporting travelers alighting from the high seats to have lunch at the Inn. The call of the tally-ho horn used to sound like Tennyson's *Blow, Bugle, Blow,* to us as we heard its flourish in the distance and saw the coach appear or disappear in a cloud of dust.

FOREWORD

Yet there was another warning sound that heralded a far less popular dust cloud. This was the first automobile that I recall personally. It was always referred to as The White Terror and we children were warned to flee it as our forebears were warned of Satan himself. People swore and shook their fists at it, and if it were rumored to be "at large" our mothers debating the hazard of meeting it on the Lenox road. The owner of The White Terror had a summer place on that road and it was unfortunate because visitors must always be driven to Lenox and it took the better part of an afternoon to go there and return. Tom Carey who kept the Stockbridge livery stable learned to be almost psychic about the automobile's whereabouts and people trusted their lives to him and his horses even with such a menace in the offing.

Summer, it seems to me now, ended officially with the Laurel Hill Association Meeting in the grove behind the schoolhouse. We scanned the weather for days in advance and hoped the skies would be fair because if rain fell the meeting would be held in the Casino and there would be no room for children in its glories. For days beforehand, too, sandwiches and cakes were in preparation for the tea that followed the speeches. I can feel the hardness of those improvised benches yet, and how hot the sun felt as it shifted through the trees in the clearing, now on our backs, now in our eyes. But we never thought of this as an inconvenience and neither did the speakers who came from Boston and New York and Washington and even from London to talk in Laurel Hill about the Village Improvement Society. They all said the same thing in different words—that there was no place in the world like Stockbridge. We, of course, knew that already, but we counted on hearing it each year and I cannot remember that we were ever disappointed.

STOCKBRIDGE

It was a truly great occasion, next to the Torch Light Parade in my mind. Nothing quite equaled that for commotion and color. I am uncertain of its origin and I do not know if it has survived, but then it came with turning leaves and the first frosts of fall. On the chosen night all the young and agile dressed in costume. The street was alive with gypsies, peasants, Indians and pirates and they formed a long procession that disappeared into the woods and on into the mysterious depths of Ice Glen. The torches made glorious flares and the familiar features of neighbors took on strangeness in that pulsating light. I was considered too small to join the revelers. Only the sure-footed were encouraged to explore those caves, but once I was allowed to stay up and see the return and the dance round a tremendous bonfire. I watched fascinated, feeling vaguely awed and excited as if I were witnessing some pagan rite, so old that no one could remember its reason for being or why the heart must respond with quickened, instinctive clamor.

Did red-skinned King Konkapot hand it down as some wild legacy to his white friends and neighbors, I wonder? Did Jonathan Edwards forget his preoccupation with the affairs of the soul to take part in it with his sons and daughters? Did other generations of Dwights and Sedgwicks, of Cannings and Williamses and Fields join hands around other such bonfires? Did Fanny Kemble, perhaps catch up the folds of her riding-habit, the better to dance there, and did Hawthorne and Melville on their brief sojourns watch and remember it, as I am remembering now?

A quarter of a century, with a decade added, is a long stretch to span in the life of a person, though not so much in the life of a town. If these fragments that I have set down seem random and insignificant it is because we can never account for the memories that we pull out of the mind's

FOREWORD

clutter much as New England housewives used to turn out the contents of their piece bags. Sometimes a bright bit of cloth will recall the lost pattern of which a forgotten garment was made. And sometimes only the unrelated snippet remains in the hand. The whistle of an evening train from New York, a train that I had heard was bringing Joseph H. Choate from his years at the Court of St. James's home to Stockbridge and the house on the Hill—that is no more vivid than the call of the oriole that returned each spring to nest in our plum tree. These are the stuff of which memories are made, and so I set them down for others who know and cherish the same scene to match them as they will.

RACHEL FIELD

STOCKBRIDGE

Chapter I

THE MISSION

IN the autumn of the year 1734, the Berkshire Hills, dressed in their gaudiest and most pagan garb, looked down upon a curious scene. In front of a large wigwam, by the winding Housatonic river, stood a group of about twenty Indians. Ragged-looking, but brave in paint and feathers, they harmonized with their background and contrasted with the sober black and white of two earnest-browed ministers, who were engaged in conversation with the only Indian present who could speak English. The two chiefs of the tribe, Konkapot and Umpachene, were standing by, grave and uncomprehending, as the Reverend Nehemiah Bull of Westfield, and John Sergeant, a young tutor from Yale College, were examining this Indian on his knowledge of the Christian faith. They explained that his name was to be Ebenezer. He dramatically declared that he would like to have the rites of baptism administered immediately and that his faith in Christ was such that he would rather burn in the fire than forsake the truth. Parrot-fashion, he repeated the profession of faith: "Through the goodness of God towards me, in bringing me into the way of the knowledge of the Gospel, I am convinc'd of the truth of the Christian religion, and that it is the only way to salvation and happiness. I therefore freely and heartily forsake heathenish darkness, and embrace the light of the Gospel and the way of Holiness, and do now, in the presence of Almighty God, the searcher of Hearts, and before many witnesses, seriously and solemnly take the Lord Jehovah to be my God and Portion, Jesus Christ his Son to be my Lord Redeemer, and the Holy Ghost to be my Sanctifier and Teacher."

To Konkapot, a man of stalwart character but limited brain power, it seemed obvious that these kindly Englishmen must worship the same Great Spirit that the Indians knew, although the form of their religion was somewhat different. There was no ritual. No wampum was passed, and no sacrifice was offered, but to his simple mind the idea was clearly the same. He invited his visitors to climb over the mountain a few days later to the Great Meadow where he lived, and where Indians and Englishmen together would offer a deer to the Supreme Being. Ebenezer, acting as interpreter, would explain the ceremony.

Accordingly they set out, Ebenezer leading the way over the faintly marked trail. As they rested a moment upon the summit of the mountain, Sergeant noticed a large heap of stones on which Ebenezer was carefully placing another. He explained that this was their custom, which had been handed down from father to son through the ages. It was an expression of their gratitude to the Great Spirit for preserving them to look down upon the valley again. Sergeant gazed upon the future scene of his labors and, although his mind was not primarily occupied with the beauties of nature, and he thought the Indian custom a barbaric one, perhaps he acknowledged to himself that there was some justification for it. The mountains—hills they were by measurement but they had the bold outline of mountains—stood protectively above the Indian community that lay below them, seeming to guard it from intrusion. Nature had apportioned the village on three levels that rose in steps, one above the other: the first, a plateau of broad meadows that followed the capricious windings of the Housatonic River; the second, a plain terminated at its eastern end by a laurel-covered hill; and a third, a hill that formed the northern boundary of the settlement. Indian wigwams were scattered over hill and plain, not grouped as an Englishman would expect. The smoke rose from a single isolated wigwam, as if the Indians valued privacy.

Konkapot, who lived down by the river, had a neighbor, so Ebenezer told Sergeant, who had shared the rich intervale with him for many years. This was a Dutchman, a trader named Jehoiakim Van Valkenburgh, one of the first white men to dwell in the valley. He lived on the most friendly terms with Konkapot and the others, carrying on a profitable trade and occasionally acting as their interpreter to the English. His was a simple and practical attitude toward the Indians, Sergeant was to learn later. He interfered in no way with their customs, their way of living, or their religion, but drove the sharpest possible bargain with them and, with liberal applications of rum, quieted any objections they might have to being cheated.

As they walked down from the white-cliffed mountain on which they had been standing, Ebenezer, slipping into a reminiscent vein, told Sergeant many things which the Indians had always believed to be true. Childish and ridiculous fables, Sergeant called them later in his journal, but they were an ancient and integral part of the Indian inheritance and would be hard to uproot.

Ebenezer told him of the seven stars that were seven good Indians translated to heaven in a dance. The stars in Charles's Wain, on the other hand, were Indians hunting a bear. All spring and summer they chased it, and wounded it in the autumn, and that was why the leaves turned red. By winter, they killed it, and the snow was its fat. This melted with the coming of spring and turned into the sap of the trees.

Once there had been a prophet among them. He had descended from the sky fully equipped with snowshoes, the first they had ever seen. Striding over the countryside, he had cleared the land of monsters. He had married a human wife who bore him two mortal children. One day when he was praying with a child on each knee, he was suddenly, in a wonderful manner, raised from the ground. Just as he was about to disappear through the top of the wigwam, he paused, a child still on each knee. The Indians begged him to leave them one child to remember him by. So as the prophet continued his upward flight, his half-mortal child floated down to them, a token of his favor.

Questioned more specifically about the Indians' religious beliefs, Ebenezer was vague. Some believed God to be the sun; some that the sun was the habitation of God; others were professed atheists, believing that all things began, continued and ceased, according to the laws of their natures without any direction from an outside power.

Sergeant and Bull were received by the tribe at Konkapot's wigwam, situated by a little brook just south of the river. Van Valkenburgh was there and viewed the Englishmen with suspicion. He knew their purpose in coming over the hills into this sanctuary of the red man and, unlike the simple Konkapot, he had no illusions as to their reception of the ceremony about to take place. The offering of the deer was made with Sergeant and Bull sitting with the Indians in a semi-circle around the priest.

After the deer had been cut up according to an elaborate ritual, it was placed upon a strip of bark in the middle of the wigwam, with the skin arranged over it to make it look like a whole deer. Then the priest hallooed to God to attract his attention and spoke this prayer: "O great God, pity us, grant us food to eat, afford us good and comfortable sleep, preserve us from being devoured by the fowls that fly in the air. This

THE MISSION

deer is given in token that we acknowledge thee the giver of all things." Then wampum was passed, the deer was boiled, and everyone ate a piece, except the priest. The skin and feet, and some of the organs, were given to an old widow-woman, an act of charity that was part of the ceremony. They told Sergeant that the man who had come down from Heaven on snowshoes had taught them these things. Of course Sergeant explained to them that this sort of ceremony was not consistent with the true faith and such practices were actually offensive to God.

A hundred years before they would not have listened to him. Strong in numbers, owners of a vast territory, they could then afford to ignore the white man, his ways and his beliefs. Now they had fallen upon evil days. The great Mahican tribe was a pitifully depleted group—perhaps thirty families in all—scattered along the banks of the Housatonic. The tribe was a branch of the Algonquins and the Indian name is Muh-he-ka-neew, which means "the people of the ever-flowing waters," because at the height of their glory their principal home had been on the banks of the Hudson River. In those far-off days when the tribe could muster 1,000 fighting men, the Housatonic country had been only their hunting ground, visited at certain seasons of the year. Their possessions, extending from the Hudson River to the Connecticut Valley, reached north of Lake George and Lake Champlain. All through the seventeenth century, however, they had been greatly reduced in numbers and property by a long and murderous war with their hereditary enemies, the Mohawks, who, in forming the confederation known as the Six Nations, which included the Oneidas, the Onondagas, the Cayugas, the Tuscaroras, and the Senecas, had proved an invincible foe. By 1680 the Mahicans had been entirely driven from the west bank of the Hudson River. From the east bank of the Hudson, they found themselves gradually crowded out by the farming and commercial activities of the Dutch, so that they came, more and more, to frequent this wild tract of land, their former hunting ground. Here, perhaps, in these lonely hills, they would be free of the white man and the complications of civilization.

From the east, however, the English were pushing inland as fast as they could. The trading post of Westfield was already within the Indian territory. As the Indians expressed it: "Clean across this extent of country, our grandfather [the Delawares] had a long house, with a door at each end, one door being at Patehammoc [Potomac] and the other at Gaschtenick [Albany]; which doors were always open to all nations united with them. To this house the nations from ever so far off used to resort, and smoke the pipe of peace with their grandfather. The white people coming over the great water, unfortunately, landed at each end of this long house of our grandfather's, and it was not long before they started to pull down the same at both ends. Our grandfather still kept repairing the same, although obliged to make it from time to time shorter, until at length the white people, who had by this time grown very powerful, assisted the common enemy, the Maqua [Mohawks] in erecting a strong house on the ruins of their grandfather."

Pushed east by the Dutch and west by the English, the tribe still held this Housatonic country untouched by the white man up to the year 1722, twelve years before Ebenezer's baptism. Here the old Indian way of life went on unhampered. Rich in ceremony and ritual, it was an elaborate and serious game. On entering a wigwam an Indian never spoke before eating. Belts of wampum passed solemnly between them in confirmation of treaties, or to accompany messages. Silent and dignified, they would sit around their chief, with visiting members of some other tribe, and pass the pipe of peace from hand to hand. The women were expected to do

THE MISSION

the work. They cleared the land, felling the trees by burning them through their bases, and then cultivated their simple crops. "Men," the Indians said, "were made for war and hunting. Women and hedgehogs to scratch the earth." And a favorite saying among them was, "The Great Spirit gave the white man a plough and the red man a bow and arrow and sent them into the world by different paths, each to get a living in his own way."

With the outbreak of King Philip's War in 1675, the westward expansion had come to an abrupt halt at the Connecticut River and, for almost fifty years, Springfield, Hatfield, Deerfield, Northampton and Hadley had been outposts dotting the frontier in the wilderness. The bloody history of these years explains why the Berkshires remained so long undisturbed. One marvels, not at the lack of enterprise that kept the English from pushing farther west, but at the tenacity with which they clung to the already settled line of the frontier.

The story of the repeated massacres of Deerfield is, in a lesser degree, the story of all these towns. With half of the population deported to Canada, many others the victims of the scalping knife, and their buildings razed to the ground, men feared to go into the fields to gather their crops. The Indian war whoop—a sound once heard never to be forgotten—was the prelude to a multitude of screaming maniacs descending upon a town to demolish it. Life was lived in breathless anticipation of the next blow. For the Indians played their deadly game by rules that no Englishman could understand and always managed to catch the settlers off their guard. Then, as the English gathered themselves together to retaliate and pursue them, the Indians would melt silently and completely back into the forest, of which they seemed as much a part as the trees.

In 1722, there was a breathing space. Peace, comparatively speaking, had existed since 1713. The moment seemed opportune for the English to cross the barrier of the Hoosac mountains and to inquire of the Indians what price they put on this last lovely strip of land which separated Massachusetts from New York, and which is known today as Berkshire County. The bold thought of settling this region originated in the head of John Stoddard, who was at this time, and for many years, the master mind of the Connecticut Valley.

Stoddard was one of a series of self-appointed autocrats who grew up in the Connecticut Valley during the eighteenth century. Boston was far away, and the problems which confronted these pioneering towns had to be dealt with energetically and immediately. The River Gods, as they were called, held virtual sway over western Massachusetts. Up to the time of the Revolution, when the two sections of the state became welded together in a common cause, western Massachusetts was like a separate little kingdom, and in 1722 everything that was done, while receiving the official sanction of the Governor in Boston, was planned in the fertile brain of John Stoddard. He pointed out to his less enterprising neighbors that it was highly desirable to extend the English settlements to the west. The boundary line between New York and Massachusetts, he said, was about to be run, and as possession is nine points of the law, the farther west their settlements lay, the better bargain they would make in the final adjustment. Fortunately he did not know that the authorities in both states were to wrangle over this line down to the year 1784.

He dwelt upon the friendliness of the Indians who lived across the mountains and how important it was to conciliate them and to maintain them as allies in the war. Finally he

THE MISSION

appealed to that fallacy in men's minds which urges them always forward into the next blueberry patch. One hundred and seventy-seven bold hearts were found eager for adventure under the leadership of Joseph Parsons and Thomas Nash, and to them the first grant of land in the present Berkshire County was made in 1722.

The domain consisted of two contiguous towns, the upper and lower Housatonic townships, as they were called, of seven square miles each, running north and south along the Housatonic River. The Connecticut line formed the boundary to the south, the New York line (wherever that was to be) to the west, a line four miles east of the Housatonic River to the east, and the Great Mountain to the north, which was probably Rattlesnake Hill in Stockbridge.

The price which Konkapot asked for the extinction of the Indian title to this land was £460 legal tender, three barrels of cider and thirty quarts of rum. The Indians kept for themselves only two small reservations—one on the northern boundary of the lower Housatonic township, which they called Skatehook, and the other, beyond the mountain, Wnahtakook, later to become the town of Stockbridge. Here Konkapot lived, his group of neighbors including the rum-dispensing Van Valkenburgh, while below at Skatehook, Umpachene, second in command of the tribe, maintained the Great Wigwam, a tent sixty feet long, where all their important conferences and ceremonies took place.

As the lower Housatonic township sprouted into the town of Sheffield, the Indians looked at the large and thriving families of the English, and then back at their own depleted numbers with growing feeling of self-distrust. Perhaps if they embraced this curious and rigid religion of the white man, and learned to live as he did, they would be saved from extinction. Certainly this English settlement looked neat and prosperous enough, with the church and the schoolhouse, and the little frame houses set in rows. As Ebenezer sagely remarked, "The Indians continue in their Heathenism notwithstanding the Gospel has been bro't so near them, and they are greatly diminished; so that since my remembrance there were ten Indians, where there is now One. But the Christians greatly increase and multiply and spread over the Land; let us, therefore leave our former Courses and become Christians." Konkapot gave ear to this advice, although he objected that if they became Christians, they would probably be disowned not only by the rest of their own tribe, but by all the related tribes. Also, reflecting probably on his neighbor Van Valkenburgh, he said he was struck with the "ill conversation of the Christians." However, he was seriously disposed to consider the idea, and he sent word to Stoddard that he would be glad to discuss it with him.

Stoddard and his friends among the clergy of the neighborhood were genuinely concerned over the plight of this pathetic remnant of a great nation stranded in the rising tide of white civilization. Nehemiah Bull of Westfield, Stephen Williams of Springfield and Samuel Hopkins of West Springfield gathered together to consider how they could best effect the salvation of the souls of these heathen brethren. Governor Belcher was about to confer military titles of Captain and Lieutenant upon Konkapot and Umpachene for services rendered to the English. This honor would please them and would provide a ceremony, always attractive to the Indians. At Stoddard's suggestion, the clergymen agreed to meet the Indians at Springfield, where the titles would be given, and there they could discuss the matter.

The gentlemen also decided to write to the Commissioners in Boston, who were the representatives in this country for The Society for the Propagation of the Gospel in Foreign Parts. This organization which had its headquarters in London, had been the result of the great interest which had sprung up in 1643 after the publication of John Eliot's book, *The First Fruits of New England,* in which he told of his missionary work among the Indians. This movement had grown, money had been raised, and now the agents appointed for the missionary work in this country, with Governor Belcher at their head, were anxious to accomplish great things. Missionaries had been sent out to different trading posts and forts to which the Indians came with their furs, but the atmosphere of trade had not proved conducive to the preaching of the gospel, and they had soon ceased their efforts. However, when the commissioners heard of this tribe at Housatonic, who were at least not hostile to the idea of Christianity, they felt that here might be their opportunity. The conversion of this tribe might be the door through which they might reach all the various tribes connected with them, the Delawares and even the important and powerful Six Nations. This was a result devoutly to be hoped for, not alone from religious, but also from political, motives.

With the glittering military titles of Captain and Lieutenant as bait, Konkapot and Umpachene were induced to come to Springfield, accompanied by Van Valkenburgh. Here they sat down with Stephen Williams, Nehemiah Bull and John Stoddard to discuss, through the reluctant medium of Van Valkenburgh, the Indians' interest in the Christian faith. Bull and Williams readily agreed to Konkapot's suggestion to make a trip to the banks of the Housatonic, where they would explain to the whole tribe this scheme for the regeneration of their souls. This meeting had taken place in Umpachene's Great Wigwam in the July preceding Ebenezer's baptism. After four days of anxious consultation, the Indians had agreed that their souls should be saved and that a missionary should come to live among them.

John Sergeant had been the choice of the Commissioners at Boston, and he and Nehemiah Bull took their way over the mountains that brilliant October day of Ebenezer's baptism. As they rode along he may well have pondered on the difficulties of his situation. The trip itself was "thro' a most doleful wilderness and the worst road, perhaps, that ever was rid," and he reflected that after the snow fell it would be impossible to find the way, and "his Majesties' subjects living in these parts of the Province" would be completely cut off and unable to supply themselves with the necessary "foreign commodities."

He was young, only twenty-four, his courage was high and he was by nature peculiarly fitted for the task which he was undertaking. He was, indeed, the perfect combination of pioneer and man of God desirable in a missionary. Short, sturdy and compact of build, with lively black eyes, he had "a beautiful countenance and goodly to look to."

At this time he was engaged in tutoring at Yale where "the comeliness of his person, the sweetness of his temper, the decency of his behavior, the agreeableness of his conversation" made him extremely popular. In his early youth he had received a cut in the muscles of his left hand, while scything in a meadow, which had incapacitated him for an active life and had thrown him perforce into a life of study. Although already absorbed in the spiritual life, he could not feel that God called him to the studious and sedentary career of a clergyman in one of the many expanding towns about him. Such a life would satisfy neither his burning desire to serve God in some extraordinary way nor the boundless energy which he felt within him.

The tragedy of the Indians had always touched his heart and he had often prayed God to send him among them. In his journal he wrote: "I told the gentlemen that I was so far from being unwilling to devote myself to the service of God in so good a cause, that I was rather desirous, if none better qualify'd could be found, to improve what abilities I had in such an undertaking; tho' I was sensible I must not only lose a great many agreeable amusements of life, especially in leaving my business at College, which was the most agreeable to me that could be, but also expose myself to many fatigues and hardships, and I know not what dangers, among a barbarous people. For indeed I should be asham'd to own myself a Christian, or even a Man, and yet utterly refuse doing what lay in my power to cultivate humanity among a people naturally ingenious enough, but for want of instruction living so much below the Dignity of human nature . . . "

Sergeant had the singlemindedness that leads to success. No thought of the advantage to the English cause of converting the Indians crossed his mind, nor did he consider the possibilities of attaining riches for himself in opening up a new and fertile country. He thought of nothing but the darkness in which these heathen lived and his own opportunity for leading them to the light. His faith was simple and unquestioning, and given to action rather than contemplation. Although he studied under Jonathan Edwards at Yale and greatly admired him, it was the spirit of Edwards, not the mind, he followed. Sergeant was in no sense an intellectual, but had a mind which matched his physique—bright, energetic and practical. A vigorous little saint, he turned his back at the age of twenty-four on all worldly prospects.

His agreement with the Commissioners at Boston was that he should go to Housatonic as soon as possible and spend a few months on trial. Then he would return to Yale College to finish out the year with the pupils he was then engaged in tutoring, and, if his trial expedition had proved successful, he would return the following summer as a permanent missionary to the Mahican Indians, at a salary of £100 a year.

The offering of the deer, made in such good faith before his eyes, showed him that in spite of Ebenezer's protestations, the Indians grasped little of the meaning of Christianity, and

Sergeant set about preaching to them immediately. He talked to them long and earnestly through Ebenezer. Sometimes he was obliged to call upon Van Valkenburgh's aid, although the Dutchman continued to look upon the proceedings with great disfavor. For if the Indians stopped drinking rum, where would his business be?

Whether it was Sergeant's eloquence or the goodness of his countenance that moved them, one cannot say, but by the end of October they were building a house between the two settlements. This was to serve them as meetinghouse and schoolhouse. Around it they put up their wigwams during the winter months, although they had to move at the end of February, for then the sugar season began and they all dispersed into the woods. This was one of the joys of their life—the ease with which they could move about the countryside. They roamed as naturally as deer through the forest. A wigwam was taken down in ten minutes and they were gone, leaving little trace behind them. This they were to be taught was wrong. They must build houses and stay in them, and till the ground, and live like the white man.

It was now the middle of December, and Sergeant had to return to his pupils at Yale. So great had been his success that the Commissioners in Boston had sent up another young man, Timothy Woodbridge, to take charge of the school while he was away. By this time both Umpachene and Konkapot placed such confidence in Sergeant that they allowed him to take their two sons back with him to New Haven. This would be of great advantage to him, as well as to them, because he would thus be enabled to lay the foundation of a knowledge of the Indian language. He was to find great difficulty with it, for being composed almost entirely of gutterals it was unlike any European language. He thought it more like Hebrew than anything else. But by becoming conversant with this uncouth tongue, he became aware of the

John Sergeant

THE MISSION

way in which the minds of the Indians worked and he learned to express himself in a way which they could understand. Like all primitive people, they made constant use of simple and beautiful metaphor. Their speech clung very close to the soil and spoke in terms of the most ordinary human experience. Sergeant's letters to them, written from New Haven that winter, might have been written by an Indian.

"Knowledge is certainly good," he wrote. "It is to the mind what light is to the eye. You would think them your greatest enemies that should endeavor to put out your eyes, especially if you were traveling a difficult road. This world is like a thick and intangled Wilderness and why should not you, as well as other people, enjoy the benefit of light?" Again he wrote, "My heart is with you, tho' I am so far from you; but the greatest pleasure of all is, that you have it yet in your hearts to become Christians . . . it is more pleasing to me than cold water to a thirsty man in the heat of summer, or a plentiful meal to one almost starv'd with hunger, or good success to one who has hunted a great while in vain."

Sergeant had now definitely decided to spend his life as missionary to these Indians, and he realized, when he returned to Housatonic in the spring, that he must receive his ordination as soon as possible. Ebenezer had been baptized, Konkapot and his family were ready for baptism, and some of the others soon would be. It was important to act quickly with the Indians and he wished to follow up their enthusiasm which had been manifested in building a meetinghouse, by enrolling them as active members of the church of Christ. Appreciating the effect that ceremony and display of any kind had upon them, he further suggested, when he wrote to the Commissioners, that his ordination might take place, if possible, somewhere in their neighborhood so that they could be present. It would not only be an ordination, but a dedication of his life to the Indians.

It so happened that this could be arranged most conveniently. The Governor, with an imposing array of members of his Majesty's Council and House of Representatives, was going to Deerfield on August 25th to meet a delegation of the Six Nations and arrange an important treaty with them. This powerful confederation of tribes was in very different circumstances from their ancient enemies, the Mahicans. By banding together, they made a group commanding the respect of both the English and the French, and neither side was ever sure which way they were going to jump. They carefully pursued this ambiguous line of conduct throughout the weary length of the French and Indian wars, thus obtaining the benefits of the friendship of both parties. At this date, they appeared to lean to the English cause, and everything was being done to conciliate them. There would be several days of negotiations, with all the usual procedure of presents exchanged, wampum passed, and quantities of rum consumed. The Indians never committed themselves easily under the best of circumstances, and this treaty was of such importance to the English that neither time nor money would be spared. It would be a magnificent sight, the Indians in full tribal regalia, and the Governor and his suite in their most imposing uniforms. And it would be an excellent opportunity for Sergeant to impress his flock with the friendliness of government toward them.

The Governor's party was to spend the week in Deerfield and Sergeant's ordination was to be the climax of the proceedings. When the time came, Sergeant was unable to travel, as he was stricken with the fever which seems to have afflicted all newcomers to the valley. The Indians appeared at the appointed time and greatly enjoyed the show, and Sergeant joined them in time for his ordination. Succinctly he notes in his journal, "Lord's Day, August 31, 1735. I was ordained at Deerfield," which does little to give a picture of

THE MISSION

the scene in the Deerfield meetinghouse that August day. Fortunately there are other sidelights. The service opened with a sermon of generous length by the Reverend Nathaniel Appleton, who had come from Cambridge for the purpose. The text was appropriate to the occasion: Acts 9:15—"But the Lord said unto him Go thy way: for he is a chosen vessel unto me to bear my name before the Gentiles . . ."

After the sermon, William Williams, who acted as "moderator," asked the Governor if it was his pleasure that Sergeant should be set apart for this work. When he signified his approval, Sergeant was asked if he wished to consecrate his life to the mission as a minister to the Indians, to which he replied, "I do." Finally the Indians were asked, through an interpreter, if they were desirous of having Mr. Sergeant for their minister, and that if they were they would show "some Sign or Manifestation thereof: Whereupon they all rose up by one Consent and with grave as well as Cheerful Countenances, signified their full, and hearty Acceptance of him." It was a sort of marriage between John Sergeant and the Mahican Indians.

All the protagonists in the struggle between the Indians and English were represented in the meetinghouse at Deerfield that day and the hopeless division between the two races was shown up in a series of dramatic contrasts. Some of these contrasts were quite deliberate. The showy paint and feathers and gay blankets of the Six Nations were a definite indication to the English of the arrogance of the Indians in the wily game they were playing between the English and the French. The English, on their side, were doing everything in the way of full regimentals in scarlet and gold to impress the Six Nations with what a powerful hand they held in this game. Over against this brilliance was set the assembled clergy of the district, dressed in the black and white of their order, come to witness the solemn contract between the

Housatonic Indians and Sergeant, the important consequences of which none of them overlooked. And finally the half-clad Mahicans, looking hopefully into John Sergeant's face, believed that here was a holy man who could guide them in a changing and puzzling world.

They proudly returned to Housatonic with their minister and the work of spreading the gospel began. Sergeant preached, baptized, and married people all that winter. Konkapot and Umpachene became John and Aaron, and their wives, Mary and Hannah. Ebenezer, who always seems to have taken the first step in these matters, was the first to be married. This was a very radical step to Indian eyes. Men and women lived together and parted casually, few couples continuing together until they were old. In the case of separation, the woman kept the children and all mutual possessions, except the gun, with which the man would wander off again into the forest to seek his fortune. All this, of course, had to be changed, but it was a slow and laborious process with many backslidings and a considerable amount of drinking.

Van Valkenburgh and other Dutch traders encouraged the Indians' transgressions, for they were now becoming seriously alarmed. Van Valkenburgh's exploitation of these Indians had hitherto been highly successful and he had no intention of abandoning his position without a struggle. The Indians' passion for strong drink was the one to which he could most easily appeal, and he assured them that Sergeant was infringing upon their liberties when he told them not to drink, and that they were being used as dogs and slaves. If they wished to test the length of their chain and show their independence, they would drink. This it was not hard to persuade them to do, and a number of drunken "frolicks" disturbed the peace of this winter. They would drink themselves into insensibility and then fling themselves down in the snow to sleep it off, awakening to find all their possessions in the hands of the traders. Sergeant struggled indefatigably with this vice. "Their beloved Destruction," he called it.

The present arrangement of living was wholly unsatisfactory. The Indians were able to pitch their wigwams around the meetinghouse for only a short period in the winter. In February they dispersed to the woods for the sugar season, and the rest of the year they spent at their own settlements, Konkapot and his group retiring into the dangerous neighborhood of Van Valkenburgh, and Umpachene to the outskirts of the upper Housatonic township. During this time Sergeant taught school at one settlement and Woodbridge at the other. Woodbridge lodged with Konkapot and had a large attendance of pupils, but Sergeant writes of him at this time that he had a "tedious task of it . . . [and] lives a very lonesome life." The distance between the two missionaries was a great disadvantage, and although the Indians were all supposed to come to the central meetinghouse on Sunday, the inclemency of the weather or a Saturday night's "frolick" would often provide them with excuses used in recent times by more civilized churchgoers.

Sergeant made little in his letters to the Commissioners of the difficulties of his situation but dwelt upon the fact of forty converts in one year. Not a large number, certainly, but his enthusiasm was contagious. He wrote gaily of a further plan of sharing in the Indians' lives: "Our Indians are this week gone out to make sugar. Mr. Woodbridge and I design to go out to them next day after tomorrow and live with them, till they return if we can hold it out. Perhaps we shall be so taken with them and their way of living that we shall take each of us a wife from amongst, and sadly disappoint all other fair ones that may have any expectations from us. And indeed I am almost of the opinion that this will be our wisest course; lest if we don't disappoint them, they will us."

All this winter he had been working upon a scheme for establishing the Indians in one spot. It would be a model village established entirely for the Indians and owned by them, except for a small extent of territory reserved for himself and Woodbridge and perhaps four other English families. A few English living among them, he thought, would serve as patterns of everything that the Indians should strive to be. He had talked the plan over with the Governor at the time of his ordination at Deerfield, and the Governor had consented to lay the matter before the General Court. The Court had appointed a committee to go to Housatonic and offer the township to the Indians. Colonel John Stoddard was appointed with two other men, and in March they arrived to make the proposal. It was for a township beyond the mountain, which would be six miles square and include Konkapot's reservation. The area would also include Van Valkenburgh's forty acres in the Great Meadow and his 250 acres of upland adjoining it. All that was asked of the Indians was that they give up the land they owned at Skatehook, a small tract compared to what they were getting.

The committee expected opposition from Van Valkenburgh, but they were surprised to meet with reluctance on the part of some of the Indians. They were given a month to consider the proposition, and when Stoddard returned in April for their answer, Umpachene told him that he had been turning over a number of things in his mind and would like to ask a few questions. Although he confessed himself grateful to the English for all they had done in providing instruction in the gospel, and in teaching the children to read, and said that his gratitude for these things brought tears to his eyes, and he was convinced of the truth of the Christian religion, as far as he understood it, still a number of things "stumbled" him. Why had the English neglected preaching the gospel to them for so long, and why was this sudden favor toward them? Was it all love and good will? If so, he was thankful for it, but it was just possible there might be some other motive. Again, if the Christian religion was so good and so true, as he believed it was, why were there so many vicious Christians? Also how were they, the Indians, to establish titles to their lands? These things were not written down with them as they were with the white man, and yet their titles were quite as good according to their own law. Finally, he wondered about this large six-mile tract which was to be given them? Would there not, some day, arise contention between their children and the children of the English as to the ownership of this land?

Colonel Stoddard used all his tact and knowledge of Indians to smooth these ruffled feathers, for he was well aware of Umpachene's influence over the tribe and realized that at this late date he might upset the whole plan. He began by quoting from the charter that one of the original intentions of the white settlers had been to preach the gospel to the Indians and, not dwelling upon the neglect of this intention for twenty-six years, he extolled the labors of Mr. Eliot. He said that the Government had always been eager to propagate the gospel, but that since Mr. Eliot's time, their efforts had met with little success. As for the titles to their lands, they held their lands in the same manner as the English, and therefore could have no reason to fear that they would be taken advantage of. He agreed that the viciousnesss of some Christians was a shameful thing, but it sprang from the corruption of men's hearts and not from any defect in the religion they preached. These remarks and the authoritative manner in which they were delivered by Colonel Stoddard carried conviction to the skeptical mind of Umpachene, and he declared himself satisfied.

The committee came up against a more solid obstacle in Van Valkenburgh. He would not listen to an exchange of his lands for an equivalent elsewhere in the province. Konkapot was his friend and had given him the land, business was good, and there he was going to stay. Sergeant was much disturbed by this obstinacy, and he was obliged to pursue his plans around Van Valkenburgh, who sat immovably upon his acres. In spite of him, the Indians were established in the new town in time to plant their crops in the spring of 1736.

The clergy of the Connecticut River valley looked upon this venture of a model Indian town with much sympathy. Nehemiah Bull, Stephen Williams, Samuel Hopkins, Peter Reynold, and Jonathan Edwards (interested through his uncle, John Stoddard) all cast a kindly eye upon the Mission. These men were, in fact, the godfathers of the town and presided over its birth with anxious solicitude. It would be impossible, they felt, to send the "glorious and everlasting gospel among the Indians, among whom Satan's kingdom had remained so long undisturbed," while Van Valkenburgh, a veritable Satan, dwelt among them. The small amount of money that these gentlemen could command would be insufficient, they knew, to tempt him from his profitable trading base. It was three years after the Indians had moved into the new village that a solution to this problem was finally provided through the agency of resourceful Colonel Stoddard.

As chairman of the committee for the establishment of the town, he selected the four families who were to be introduced into the village as patterns of English life, and his first choice fell on Ephraim Williams of Newton. Williams was the typical, hard-headed pioneer who carves his way through forests, builds roads, throws out bridges and in the process rolls up for himself a handsome fortune. Stoddard considered him a man of sound common sense, with the added advantage of having a certain amount of capital to invest. Williams arrived in 1737, with his children in panniers on the sides of the horses, and various schemes in his head for becoming

THE MISSION

a large frog in a small pond. He grasped the difficulty about Van Valkenburgh and in 1739, in partnership with the clergymen of the Connecticut River valley, put up most of the money to buy him out. The plan which Williams suggested, and the clergymen enthusiastically accepted, was that they should buy the 290 acres of Van Valkenburgh, and give it to the Indians as a gift, on the understanding that the Indians would repay them by giving them 4,000 acres out of the "wild" and unappropriated land of the province. Although the 290 acres were under cultivation and the 4,000 were wild, still this bargain in real estate was clearly the work of a very fine business head. Williams well knew that it was only a short time before all this country would be opened up to settlers and land was therefore a profitable investment. The 4,000 acres adjoined the Indian township in the northeast, and Williams, as principal investor, took as his portion a 900-acre tract lying around what is now Laurel Lake in Lee. His associates had small tracts, the size depending upon the amount of their investment.

Although the Indians moved into their new town in 1736 and settled their wigwams along the winding course of the river in the Great Meadow, it was not until a year later that Williams and the other three English families arrived. They were Ephraim Brown of Watertown, Josiah Jones of Weston, and Joseph Woodbridge, the brother of Timothy, who came from West Springfield. They all settled themselves on the ridge of the hill to the north where they believed the air to be more wholesome and where the view was of surpassing loveliness. These earliest aristocrats of the valley did not have much time to think about the view, but from that day to this the cream has always risen to the top, and the largest and finest houses have been built on the crest of Prospect Hill.

Sergeant characteristically chose to build his house among the Indians at the western extremity of the village where the

Indians were soon to build the church, and where the school-house would be. Timothy Woodbridge decided to settle next to Konkapot, whose boarder he had been for the past two years.

In this same year, the General Court made a formal grant of the township to the Indians, with the exception of the small amount of land allotted to the English. A part of the grant reads thus: " . . . The Soils, Swamps, meadows, rivers, rivulets, Ponds, Pools, woods, underwoods, Trees, Timber, Herbage, Feeding, Fishing, Fowling, and Hunting, Rights members Hereditaments, Emoluments, profits, privileges and appurtenances thereto belonging or in any ways appertaining TO HAVE AND TO HOLD, the said Tract of land or Township . . . unto the said Housatannuck Tribe of Indians . . . TO their use and behoof forever . . . "

This grant embodies the impractical dream for which Sergeant and Woodbridge were to give their lives. The Stockbridge of today, swept clean of its old owners, the Indians, is the actuality which Williams and the other English families up on the Hill have built for us.

Chapter II

THE INDIAN TOWN

THIS experiment in philanthropy was now fully launched, and the Indians were like pleased children, enchanted with their shiny new toy of an English village all their own. They could not do enough for Sergeant. Clumsily but faithfully, under his direction, they built the meetinghouse and the schoolhouse. The government had allowed them some small amount of financial aid for these buildings, and the Indians, in a burst of gratitude, insisted on giving the Governor a present in return: one mile on each side of the road from Housatonic to Westfield—a not inconsiderable gift. This was accompanied by a graceful speech from Umpachene and a further present of skins. The Governor sold the skins to buy books for Sergeant and thus the compliments flew back and forth.

The Indians were determined to apply themselves to this difficult task of becoming civilized, and they worked at it as hard as their indolent natures would allow. They decided to put away from them the worst of their temptations, and imposed a fine of £40 on anyone bringing rum into the village. "The Ethiopian is really going to change his spots and the Leopard his skin," Sergeant reflected thankfully as he gazed upon these fruits of his labors. A traveler passing through Stockbridge at this time was very gracious about them in an account published in the *Boston Post-Boy:* "I have lately visited my friends in Stockbridge and was well pleased to find the Indians so improved. I saw several young women sewing; but I was in special gratified to find them so improved in learning. Some of them have made good proficiency and can read in their Bibles and several can write a good hand." Boston responded to this praise by presenting the town with an enormous conch-shell, which someone had brought back from the East Indies. This shell has become inextricably woven into the story of the mission and, long after the Indians had vanished from the scene, oldest inhabitants would tell their grandchildren about the first church bell of Stockbridge. For the Indians, to their delight, found that by blowing it like a horn, it uttered a penetrating and baleful note that quavered from one end of the village to the other. Metoxin, an Indian of gigantic lung power and dependable character, applied himself to it enthusiastically every Sabbath for many years, to summon the worshipers, red and white, to the meetinghouse.

Channels of communication ran from the little mission to Boston and from there across the ocean to the great world of London. The romantic picture of Sergeant preaching to his strange hybrid flock in the heart of the wilderness caused some passing notice in Boston. But it didn't make a very deep impression. People were thoroughly accustomed to the idea of Indians. The woods were uncomfortably full of them, and memories of the tomahawk and the scalping knife, wielded by Eliot's "praying Indians" in a peculiarly vicious manner, caused them to be skeptical about their red Christian brothers. However, Sergeant's idealism was heavily backed by the commissioners for The Society for the Propagation of the Gospel, and some of these gentlemen sat in high places. Besides Governor Belcher, whose faith in the mission was unbounded, old Dr. Benjamin Colman, minister of the church on Brattle Street in Cambridge, corresponded constantly with Sergeant, and it was he who became the

THE INDIAN TOWN

connecting link between the Stockbridge Indians and fashionable London society. Dr. Colman had spent some years in England and was well acquainted with the sympathetic interest which ladies, who sat in cushioned luxury, and gentlemen with fat bank rolls took in the sad plight of the Indians in the New World. Tragedy close at hand is apt to be uncomfortable, but at a distance it is picturesque. So Dr. Colman wrote to Sergeant of his correspondence with his London friends as early as 1735: "I have read with great pleasure your first discourse to those poor Natives, and have ventur'd a copy of it to the Earl of Egmont and the associates of the late eminent Dr. Bray at London. I have observ'd to his Lordship that yours is a proper original; and how justly adapted to the genius and capacity of the savages! May God make you a father to them, and beget them to Christ by the Gospel . . . I gave some account to the excellent Dr. Watts, of London, of the strange disposition of the Housetunnuck tribe to receive the Gospel, and of the good spirit on you to leave the College and go among them."

Money, presents of books, and letters of advice as to how to deal with the heathen in their native haunt, were proffered freely and soon beat a path between London and Stockbridge. The mission became a fashionable charity. The Society for the Propagation of the Gospel sent £300, a welcome addition to Sergeant's slender funds, for he needed ploughs and axes, clothes and books for his Indians, to persuade them that these were the blessings which the white man brought, rather than the rum and gunpowder that Van Valkenburgh had so highly recommended. Mr. Isaac Hollis of London, an eccentric Baptist minister of ample means, sent money but attached definite strings to it. It must clothe, feed, and educate twelve boys a year, and they must live in an English family. He stipulated that they must be boys. He did not care to invest in heathen girls. But Mr. Samuel Holden gave Sergeant a free hand with the £100 he contributed. Why not try boarding out the Indian girls? Here Sergeant again encountered that unaccountable obstinacy in Umpachene, who if he did not bite the hand that fed him, always had a tendency to pull away from it. The Indian girls, he declared, were modest, retiring creatures, who did not want to leave their homes. Sergeant did succeed in sending two of them out among the English, but through a childish fondness for home they did not stay long. The experiment with the boys was more rewarding, because for a year and a half he took them into his own house. He was by this time quite conversant with their language, and with sympathetic understanding he was able to reach into the slow minds and incline them to listen to the story of Christ. Like twelve little dogs they gravely went through their tricks, uncomprehending but blindly devoted. At the end of their stay they were in a state of blissful confusion as to the Savior of mankind and the savior of the Mahican Indians.

Dr. Colman received a voluminous letter from Dr. Watts, the celebrated Non-Conformist leader preaching in London at this time. He was very much interested. He was, he said, "always looking out to any quarter of the world for such Appearances. May Jesus the Head of the Church and of nations, attend your young Missionary with extraordinary assistance and success. Methinks I love him upon your report, for his courage and zeal . . . My little Catechisms to to teach ye rudiments of ye Gospel . . . is ye most proper book for his purpose wch I ever wrote." He would do the books up at once and send them on the next packet, adding to the bundle his *Divine Songs for Children* and also his *Treatise on the Mind* for Sergeant's leisure hours. But he confessed that he thought little headway would be made with the Indians without some such grand effusion of the spirit of God as should manifest itself by tongues and miracles. He was thinking of the religious revival which had taken place in Northampton not long before under Jonathan Edwards, with which he was deeply sympathetic, and he felt that if tongues and miracles were necessary to impress the "polite nations," they were imperative to stir the sluggish souls of the heathen.

A town was gradually emerging out of the forest. The name of Housatonic, which vaguely covered all the territory included in the two original townships, was too inclusive a term for a community which was being noticed in Boston and applauded in London. It was time to name and incorporate the town. Lessons in government, an important part of the educational program, could best be taught by setting up the machinery of the New England town meeting, and allowing the Indians to take their part in it. They decided to call the town Stockbridge and it is thought that the name was chosen by Timothy Woodbridge.

Woodbridge was to the Indians' material concern what Sergeant was to their spiritual. He listened to all their grievances about the white families up on the Hill, how the Joneses had appropriated to their use a much larger piece of land than they were entitled to, how Ephraim Williams had his eye on a particularly rich meadow. Woodbridge was a quiet, reasonable man, who slowly pondered on these things and gave them a fair decision. Although he himself had come from West Springfield, his family had been among the first settlers of Andover, Massachusetts, and they had been instrumental in naming the town after Andover in England. Now Andover, Hampshire County, England, is next to Stockbridge. What more natural than that Woodbridge should have chosen the name of the town neighboring his ancestral home, especially as he was now living in the County of Hampshire. The town was formally incorporated under the name of Stockbridge on June 22, 1739, and the Indians swelled with pride when they received the order from the

Great and General Court: "Ephraim Williams esqr., Capt. John Kunkapaut and Lieutt Paul Umpeecheanah, principal Inhabitants of the Plantation, in the County of Hampshire on Housatannuck River, lately erected into a Township by the Name of Stockbridge, be and hereby are fully authorized and impowered to assemble the Freeholders and other qualified Voters there, as Soon as may be, in Some Convenient place in Said Town in order to Chuse a Town Clerk and all other Town Officers . . . " At this meeting Ephraim Williams was chosen moderator, John Konkapot and Aaron Umpachene, selectmen, and Josiah Jones, constable. It seemed as if Sergeant's prayer were answered, and that the two races, so utterly different, would really be amalgamated. Here was an Indian town with an English name, the New England town meeting appointing Indian officers, and on the Sabbath, summoned by Metoxin's fervent blast upon the conch-shell, Indians and English kneeling down together in their common worship.

In that same year Sergeant married pretty, high-spirited Abigail Williams, daughter of Ephraim, up on the Hill. Her common sense, like her father's, was a useful commodity in a pioneer community, and her gaiety and elegance charmed the serious-minded missionary. He adored her, and he steps out of the rôle of saint—into which the historians have rigidly cast him—to write to his friend, Dr. Colman, as a very human bridegroom: "You will forgive me, Sir, if I think that most ingenious Woman is not the smallest gift of divine bounty that I have receiv'd since I undertook a life tho't to be so self-denying. The more tenderly I love her the more thankful I am to Heaven, who has form'd her as if on purpose for me, and giv'n her to me as if (like the father of mankind) he tho't it not good for me to be here alone." Some faded letters, a pair of satin slippers, a cookbook and the fine house that Sergeant built her on the Hill are all we have left of Abigail

Williams who, like all her family, was to stamp her personality indelibly on the community in which she lived. She found Stockbridge a struggling mission to the Indians; she left it a growing English town. Handsome and worldly, she had not come to Stockbridge to hide her light under a bushel. Her interest in converting the Indians, while undoubtedly genuine, could never have been the absorbing passion of her life as it was with Sergeant. The mission with her, as with her father, was the means to the end of developing the town of Stockbridge, and with it the fortunes of the Williams family. She had no intention of coming to terms with the wilderness. The wilderness was somehow to clear itself out of the way of those elegant little brocaded slippers with the silver buckles. Her house, preserved today as a museum and known as the Mission House, is a monument 200 years old to Abigail's taste. The handsome carving of the front door, the paneling in the parlor, with its charming scalloped recess, were touches difficult of attainment in a frontier village. Two chimneys were set in the slope of the roof, for some reason best known to Abigail. The usual house of that type had a central chimney built across the rooftree. She evidently knew what she wanted and went to some pains to get it. It is said that the carving was brought by ox team from Connecticut—surely a laborious and costly proceeding. How much easier it would have been to have built the simple log cabin of the other settlers. But Abigail Williams did not believe that gentlefolk lived in log cabins, and it was worth running even her husband into debt to achieve a suitable establishment. It is characteristic of her that long after everything else she and Sergeant stood for has been swept into the ash can of oblivion, her house should still be standing, the handsomest house in the village.

Here they led their busy lives. Abigail wove and spun the cloth for sturdy jackets against the cold Berkshire winter, baked pies, and raised her family. Electa, the first white child born in Stockbridge, had appeared punctually a year after their marriage and was followed by two boys, Erastus and John. Sometimes in an interim of household tasks, Abigail would take a hand with the Indians that flocked to her husband's study at the back of the house, smiling upon this one, snubbing that one, much as she did the children. While they waited outside the house to see Sergeant—a most congenial occupation, for they had an infinite capacity for relaxation—they would tell Abigail's children stories handed down to them from their ancestors. Long before the white man came to Stockbridge, they said, there had been a gigantic eagle who had brooded over the land. And right on their father's land, there was a rock in which the mark of his right claw could still be seen, spur and all, to prove the existence of the bird. So vast was he that while his right claw rested on the Hill in Stockbridge his left claw was in Lee, his tail in Lenox, and his head in Great Barrington. The impression in the rock is still here, a witness to the Indian tale of the days when their destinies were presided over by the miraculous and benevolent eagle.

Sergeant had no time to listen to stories. He walked with God, hurrying from Hill to Plain, now reading the Scripture, which he had translated into Indian, to a group in his study, now calling on the sick, and teaching classes even in the evening. "A Person of but few words in Generale," Abigail wrote, "and agreeable to ye beautiful Description ye wise man gives us of those yt are fittly spoken, they were like apples of Gold in Pictures of Silver." Two days a week it took him to prepare his two-hour Sunday sermon for the Indians, the exhausting climax of his week, for pronouncing Indian, Abigail said, was extremely hard on the stomach. "He was generally Exceedingly spent and tired so as hardly able to Speak after his Publick Exercises." For he had not only to

THE INDIAN TOWN

preach to the Indians but to the English, and Timothy Woodbridge says his people were not entertained with "unconnected and undigested matter but with excellent discourses." Closely reasoned and substantial, thirty-five pages of a sermon come down to us, on the *Causes and Danger of Delusions in the Affairs of Religion,* no Christianity in a sugar-coated pill, but a careful exposition of his stand on the burning issue of the day. The stone which Jonathan Edwards had thrown into the theological pool by reasserting the old Calvinist doctrines had formed ripples that were extending all over New England. But Sergeant, in his "Solitary abode in this Howling Wilderness," as Abigail dramatically overstated it, could not believe or preach such a religion. In his world, values had to be very simple and distinct, with evil painted very black, virtue very white, and punishments and rewards handed out by a reasonable Deity. The Williamses and the Joneses and the Woodbridges up on the Hill, were rough and hearty folk, hewing the town of Stockbridge out of the primeval forest, and liking their religion in good strong doses. Two hours of stiff preaching was none too much for them, but they liked to be told of God as a beneficent Father who loved them and would reward their labors in a happier world, where there would be peace for the righteous and surely a crown for John Sergeant.

David Brainerd, a pupil of Edwards, used to come over from Kaunameek, about twenty miles away from Stockbridge, where he was teaching a neighboring tribe. He came ostensibly to take lessons in Indian, but perhaps really to gain strength from the halo that Sergeant carried so unconsciously around his head. A sufferer from tuberculosis, this neurotic young man was destroyed by his faith, not upheld by it like Sergeant. Neither physically nor spiritually did he have the stomach for the Edwards creed and his journal is a heartbreaking account of sickness of the soul. "I had no idea of joy from this world. I cared not where or how I lived or what hardships I might have to endure if I might only gain souls to Christ . . . [but] to an eye of Reason everything that respects the conversion of the Heathen is dark as midnight and yet I cannot but hope in God for the accomplishment of something glorious among them." It was hard for him to see a light for the savages that flickered so to his own despairing gaze. The Dutchmen were as uncooperative at Kaunameek as at Stockbridge. "All their discourses turn upon Things of the world," he complained. "Oh what a hell it would be to spend an Eternity with such Men." Sergeant soothed and sympathized and told him that the Devil had always his temptations and instruments to promote his cause, and added that anyone who had much to do with Indians had need to fortify himself with an obstinate patience. Sergeant looked out upon the evil in the world, and with the energetic Abigail at his side, laid briskly about him to subdue it.

One bright spot that Brainerd noticed in the gloom was the Indian's fondness for music, and he arranged several prayers and psalms in metrical form and taught the Indians to sing. Some of the bottled-up wildness and love of natural beauty poured into their singing, and spontaneous bursts of song would often drift up on the evening air from the wigwams by the river to Sergeant's house on the Hill. Years later, a stranger passing through Stockbridge was so enchanted by some Indians singing in a neighboring house that he excused himself from the dinner table to listen to them. He came back to apologize rapturously to his hostess, "Do you think I can deny myself the pleasure of being in Heaven for the sake of eating?"

Sergeant now began to consider an even more ambitious scheme for the regeneration of the Indians. Their way of life, he felt, was completely hindside-before. The women shouldered the axe, planted the corn, and gathered the crops, while the men, when they were not hunting, wallowed in slothful idleness—"a seed-plot of all manner of vice" among them. The women looked up to the thrifty housewives on the Hill with admiration but with a strong conviction that such domesticated virtue was not for them. Sergeant was beginning to see that to change the habits of the older generation would be impossible, but by taking the children young enough and instilling into their minds simultaneously ideas of cleanliness and godliness, he had hopes that the next generation might be raised to the level of "a civil, industrious and polish'd people." His successful experiment with Mr. Hollis's twelve boys seemed to point the way to an extension of this idea, and the establishment of a boarding school, where manual labor would be combined with the regular studies. The Indians would build the schoolhouse themselves, a substantial building with the luxuries of a cellar and three rooms with fireplaces. From the first the children would cultivate their own crops and take care of the cattle, sheep and hogs. The girls (for it was to be coeducational in spite of Mr. Hollis's predilection for boys) would spend the long winter evenings sitting by the generous fireplaces, carding wool and spinning it for the manufacture of their own clothes. They would be under the supervision of a "faithful Mistress, who should instruct them in all sorts of business suitable to their sex." He intended to open the school not only to children from Stockbridge but also to the children of any other tribes who wished to come. Mohawks, Oneidas, and Delawares would all be gathered in, until the Lord should indeed receive the heathen for His inheritance. "I design the discipline to be used with them shall be as strict as those will bear who know nothing of government among themselves and have an aversion to everything that restrains their liberty," Sergeant wrote. With the kindest of hearts, he was building the prison walls a little higher, clipping their wings a little closer.

The only trouble was that the time and place were very poorly chosen for such a grandiose scheme. Unmistakable rumblings of another war with the French penetrated the protecting wall of hills, and even Sergeant had to admit that Stockbridge was situated right in the Indian warpath between Canada and Connecticut. With terror the white settlers gazed north, where stretched "that great and terrible wilderness of several hundred miles extent" which reached to Canada. Their own Indians were loyal, they knew, but what of the ever-vacillating Six Nations? In a conference with the Mahican Indians at Stockbridge they had solemnly declared their intentions. "The white people are about to enter into war. We only destroy ourselves by meddling with their wars . . . while they fight let us sit and smoke together." But with pressure from the French would they not yield, menacing Stockbridge with a deadly and treacherous enemy to the west?

Ephraim Williams was the first to see that this notion of Sergeant's for a charity school might be used with profitable effect as a means of protection to the town. For if the Mohawks could be tamed and brought to heel, as the Mahicans had been, they would no longer be potential murderers. The Mohawks safely tethered to the boarding school, with presents of blankets and bits of mirrors handed out to them judiciously, was a comforting thought to the anxious settlers, and Sergeant had no difficulty in raising the large sum of £115 among the eight white settlers for his school. All over the colonies went out an appeal for money in the small meticulous handwriting of Dr. Colman—to the governors of the colonies, presidents of the colleges, and any influential people that he could think of who would be interested in Indian uplift. But this eighteenth-century advertisement, a long-winded pamphlet, lay unopened on these dignitaries' desks, for the souls of the Indians was not an appealing topic. Even to such friends as Governor

Belcher and John Stoddard, the spotlight was turned off the little mission on to a larger theater of events. Governor Belcher was busy adjusting the New Hampshire-Massachusetts boundary line in such a way that a strip of territory fourteen miles wide and fifty miles long was handed over to New Hampshire. Massachusetts was indignant over this injustice, and he was recalled to England. Stoddard, in charge of the whole western frontier, had the protection of all Hampshire County to think of, and his mind was moving more in terms of forts than of charity schools. He had a scheme in his head to run a line of forts at intervals of five miles from the Connecticut River to the western limit of the county.

In comfortable London drawing rooms, the plight of the red-skinned savages, bright with paint and feathers, seemed more romantic than ever. Dr. Watts hurried around and collected £70 from his Dissenting friends. A naval gentleman, Captain Coram, who had interest at Court, wrote an impassioned plea to the Prince of Wales, who graciously put himself down for £20, and pity for the Indians was raised in such exalted breasts as those of the Lord Chancellor, the Duke of Dorset, and Lord Gower.

As for Mr. Hollis, his heart became centered entirely in Stockbridge and, in spite of the Atlantic ocean, he supervised the spending of every penny. His friends became quite worried about him and Dr. Watts wrote confidentially to Dr. Colman: "He is of so religious and pious a temper as to devote his life and all he has to the service of God and goodness, but in such a peculiar way as borders on enthusiasm, and has been many years . . . so exceedingly scrupulous that he cannot trade or merchandize . . . Tho he is a very good man, yet his excessive scrupulosity and his conduct were a matter of great concern to his relatives." He ordered a dozen more heathen boys clothed, fed, and educated at Mr. Sergeant's earliest convenience. "Pray let the gentleman that has care of the boys be desired to pray with them every morning and every night, and before and after every meal." And again a few months later, he fussed: "Please inform me how it has gone with the lads instructed at my expense some time ago. If some prove naughty, others may come to good. As to the war with France, let that not hinder the education of children at my expense. I request it may be done speedily, if there are Indian parents willing to have their children educated." He was impatient at the lack of interest shown in this country. "You at Boston might save it out of your fine Hollands, silks and laces and superfine woolen cloths, and have a school erected for heathen children," he reproached the callous Bostonians.

The Reverend Doctor Francis Ayscough, Clerk of the Closet and First Chaplain to his Royal Highness, sent the Indians a present of a brown leather Bible, large and magnificent and beautifully illustrated. This Bible made them feel a direct personal link with the Court of St. James's. It bore the following inscription on the outside in gilt letters: "To the use of the Congregation of Indians, at or near Housotonic, in a vast Wilderness part of New England, Who are at present under the Voluntary Care and Instruction of the Learned and Religious Mr. John Sergeant, And is to Remain, to the use, of the Successors of those Indians from Generation to Generation . . ." This struck some dim ancestral chord in their imaginations. So much that was intangible, legends and customs and precepts, all the baggage that they carried with them in this world, had been handed down to them from father to son, so much that was now being forever destroyed. So a present sent to them personally from the chaplain of the King, who lived far away over the great salt lake, was something to be prized indeed from generation to generation.

THE INDIAN TOWN

Many years later, when they left their old hunting ground of the Housatonic and set forth on their flight from civilization, they took the Bible with them—their most treasured possession. In 1830, after many migrations and vicissitudes, they landed upon the banks of the Fox River, in northwestern Wisconsin. An English traveler, the Reverend C. Colton, visiting them there observed their Bible, safely kept in a sort of ark at their place of worship. "Here it is a perpetual monument of their fear of God, and of their love of His word and ordinances. Their reverence for this volume and for the ark, which contains it, is almost superstitious. Nay, I had almost said—it is idolatrous." Like the Hebrews of old, they carried the ark of the covenant before them into the wilderness.

The schoolhouse, on a beautiful bow of the river, a 200-acre tract that the Indians had given, was still unfinished, but Mr. Hollis's impatience would brook no delay, so twelve boys were sent to Mr. Martin Kellog in Newington, Connecticut. He turned out to be a most unsuitable master, but Sergeant, so guileless himself, was slow to suspect guile in others. Full of trust in Mr. Kellog, he sent the boys off. Kellog was an elderly army captain, retired on half pay, who had been much in the government service as an interpreter to the Indians. His knowledge of the Indian language was his only qualification. He was illiterate and not particularly honest. The manual part of the boys' training he found highly lucrative to himself, as he employed them to work his farm, which enabled him to be absent from home a great part of the time. Far away in London, Mr. Hollis painted a rosy picture to himself, and continued to send money and pious advice freely.

In the meantime the white settlers in Stockbridge could not sleep easily in their beds at night, until every precaution was taken to secure them against invasion. That cold draft that blew down out of the north over the old Indian warpath caused them to shiver. Memories of the Deerfield massacre and the burning of Springfield were either first-hand, or at furthest second-hand, experiences. Not one of them but had some relative who had either been victim of the scalping knife or taken captive to Canada. Rumors, wild and usually unfounded, flew through the Housatonic townships. Samuel Hopkins, in Great Barrington, was wakened out of his bed at midnight, to be told by a breathless rider that Stockbridge was beset by a multitude of Indians. "This news," he wrote, "alarmed the whole house and the whole town in an instant." Even though this proved a false alarm, and the excitement simmered down, mothers looked at their children and wondered whether it would not be wiser to abandon these isolated townships. But their men possessed hearts of oak and determined to stick it out.

In such a crisis Ephraim Williams was the man to turn to and he gave the orders. Sergeant's house, as the most substantial in town, was made into a fort and sixteen soldiers were sent by Stoddard to man it. Connected by blood with all the bigwigs of the Connecticut valley, Williams, shrewd, and hard-headed, by no means confined his activities to the infant town of Stockbridge. Through the network of his Williams cousins, he was well informed as to all the important military operations. Most important from their point of view, he told his neighbors on the Hill, was the line of forts which Stoddard was building across the northern frontier— one at Colrain, another at Heath, a third at Rowe, and at the western extremity of the line, Fort Massachusetts, which was the nearest to Stockbridge. This fort would lie right in the enemy's path, a formidable rat-trap. The regular route followed by the Indians down from Canada led down from Lake Champlain and across the Hoosac River at the junction of the Waloomsac. Here they crossed by a ford which Fort Massachusetts would command. William Williams, his cousin, was in charge of the building of the forts, and during the cold winter of 1745 Ephraim Williams, sometimes accompanied by Ephraim Jr., used to ride over to get the latest news for Stockbridge.

The recent arrival home of this eldest son, brother to Thomas, now a doctor in Deerfield, and half brother to Abigail, greatly enhanced the Williams prestige. Ephraim, Jr., was an easy, affable gentleman, with a pleasant taste in reading and an appreciation of the good things of this world, which endeared him to Abigail. He had traveled extensively in Europe for a number of years, and now returned to find his father settled in a mission station, in what appeared to him to be the Far West. Not his cup of tea at all, and he at once began to look about him for a more congenial field for his activities. Stockbridge, much impressed with the air of sophistication that hung about his corpulent and genial person, sent him as representative to the General Court. Although the conversion of the Indians was not a matter of much interest to him, he was well aware that any juicy military plum in that part of the world was apt to fall his way through his large and devoted family connection. He did not have to wait long for his opportunity. It was the great year of the siege of Louisburg, and William Williams being called to the colors, a messenger from John Stoddard rode into town, appointing Ephraim Williams commander of the forts with the proud rank of captain.

Stockbridge's first success story centers around Captain Williams. The war did not mean to the town primarily the spectacular prize of Louisburg laid at the feet of the English King, for this took place too far beyond their horizon. But the star of Captain Williams's military career—as it rose, sank, and mysteriously reappeared—was a matter of passionate local pride. He seems to have combined a talent for doing the wrong thing at the wrong time, with a happy faculty of never having to pay for his mistakes, of never having it even appear very conspicuously that he had made mistakes. Perhaps his famous will, leaving the money which founded Williams College, threw a luster for posterity over his previous career, perhaps his influential family covered up his blunders, or perhaps his amiability won all hearts. It is said that he was extremely popular with his men: "He entered into the pastimes of the soldiers on an equal footing and permitted every decent freedom, and again when the diversions were over, he with ease and dignity resumed the Captain." Resplendent in his new uniform, Captain Williams rode off to his command, early in June, 1745. His duties were to go from one fort to another, supervising the supplies of ammunition, drilling the men and, through the ears of his scouts who circulated north of the forts, to listen for signs of the approaching enemy. The bait offered was £100 for every Indian scalp they brought in. With him sometimes would go the chaplain, the Reverend John Norton, or Dr. Thomas Williams, who by a curious coincidence occupied the post of doctor to the forts.

With the victory of Louisburg ringing in their ears, and the northwestern frontier guarded by their own gallant Captain Williams, Stockbridge began to breathe more easily. Tales drifted back into the hills through the Williams network, giving information of the glories of the battle, first-hand accounts from the lips of William Williams, and even from the magnificent Brigadier General Joseph Dwight of Brookfield, who sometimes rode over to Stockbridge. He had played a major rôle in the drama, and as a friend of the Williams family was not above accepting a cup of tea from the shapely hand of Abigail Sergeant. To Captain Ephraim, patroling the frontier from Fort Shirley to Fort Massachusetts, the winter of 1746 was disappointing. It was long and cold and dull. Companies of snowshoe men endlessly scouted for an apparently non-existent enemy. The troops were restive, cooped up in the wooden blockhouses on the monotonous army diet of pork and beans. As winter dragged into spring, the men looked wistfully toward Boston, where excitement was boiling up again. A French fleet had been sighted off the coast, and destruction of the city was an appalling possibility. Colonel William Williams and Brigadier General Dwight marched off again at the head of their columns, and Captain Ephraim cursed the luck which confined him to a scene as quiet as a churchyard. All eyes fastened nervously upon Boston, where the French fleet dipped in and out of the harbor. The forts had been somewhat depleted of their garrisons by the Louisburg expedition, and now again there was a call for men. There certainly seemed no harm in reducing the number of soldiers from this peaceful frontier. The August heat beat down upon those that remained. At Fort Massachusetts the low swampy land by the river was so unhealthy that the men sickened, and early in August the ever kind-hearted Williams allowed the garrison to dwindle to twenty-two men. However, he directed Dr. Williams to take from Fort Shirley fourteen raw recruits to reinforce this fort, which he well knew was the key to the whole valley below. With this order, Captain Williams seems to have disappeared into space, and he is heard of no more during the exciting days that followed. When Dr. Williams arrived there on August 15th, he heard a disquieting report from Sergeant Hawks, who was in command. Eleven of his men were sick, their ammunition was low, and through the damp stillness of the August heat ominous sounds of the approach of the enemy were heard.

Dr. Williams consulted with Mr. Norton and Sergeant Hawks and they decided desperate measures must be taken to relieve the fort. With the fourteen best soldiers as bodyguard, Dr. Williams would go to Deerfield the next day for help, leaving in the fort the Chaplain, Sergeant Hawks, eight able-bodied men, fourteen sick ones, and a few women and children. On the morning of August 16th, Dr. Williams and his men set off. They walked out of the gate and down the slope that led to the river. At that moment the Indians were so close to them that they could have touched them with the butts of their guns. Sharp, black, animal eyes watched them from the underbrush, but not a sound broke the stillness of the morning air. They were allowed to walk into a trap and out of it again, and out of earshot of the bedlam that was presently to break loose. The French, supposing the fort to be heavily manned, did not wish to apprise the garrison of their presence until their whole army was assembled. For they had a high opinion of this Fort Massachusetts, which so obstinately blocked the old Indian warpath, and had collected a redoutable army of 900 men—Indian and French—to demolish it.

Three days after the last crackle of twigs from the marching feet had died away, the air was suddenly rent by 500 savage voices, singsonging the hideous Indian war whoop. Into the clearing around the fort they danced and, down from the woods above in regular formation, marched the blue-and-white uniformed troops of General Vaudreuil. By some miracle of audacity, Sergeant Hawks and his men kept this army at bay for almost two days. Their little store of ammunition was strategically used where it would do the most good. A fatal aim at the chief Sachem broke the Indians' morale. A messenger, riding out from the French ranks to tell them to capitulate or they would all be scalped, received a telling bullet in his shoulder. But finally not a round of ammunition was left, and they were about to succumb to their fate when another messenger from the French came with an offer of truce—on condition that they go into captivity in Canada. The truce was accepted, although the militant chaplain wrote ruefully, "Had we all been in health or had there been only those eight of us that were in health, I believe every man would willingly have stood it out to the last. For my part I should." The handful of half-sick men walked out of the fort to the disgust and confusion of General Vaudreuil. The next day the French retreated into Canada with their captives. Nothing was left of Fort Massachusetts but its charred remains—with the bones of the dead men strewn about as if left by dogs. Only a note, written by Mr. Norton and pinned to a tree, told the sad tale.

Where was Captain Williams during these stirring days? Nobody knows exactly. Perhaps he was at Deerfield or Albany or even Boston. But the hard fact stares us in the face that he left his most important and exposed post insufficiently protected in time of war.

When this alarming story reached Stockbridge, the little town shook in its shoes, but the Williamses, father and son, were reassuring. The fort would be built up again in no time, and father Ephraim was dispatched to supervise the new structure. He was to have command of the new Fort Massachusetts, and would interpose his stalwart form between Stockbridge and the enemy, while the young captain would patrol the other forts more vigilantly than before. Sergeant insisted that the town, being predominantly Indian, was safe and that there was too much to do to dwell upon impending disaster. Stockbridge was here today and, on the assumption that it would be here tomorrow, the uphill work of making Englishmen out of Indians must go on.

The Indians had now built seventeen English houses, straggling along what pretended to be a street running east and west through the center of town. The trees were all cleared off it, and if the cows occasionally mistook it for a pasture, still a perceptible path could be made out between the houses. The church at the west end of town was beginning to have a settled air, surrounded by the orthodox village green, and abutted at its northeastern extremity by the graveyard where in these early years the English lay down for their long rest democratically side by side with their Indian brethren.

The only road into the village up to this time had been the rough and circuitous trail over Bear Mountain, through Tyringham, where it joined the Albany road leading into Great Barrington. In 1745 the plan of Stockbridge, much as it is today, was formed although to call the blazed trails, threading the wilderness in every direction, "roads" was perhaps an overstatement. A road led west, along what is now Church Street, which would later be punctuated by the village of West Stockbridge. This road was intersected by a second road running over the Hill and entering a highway, which led to the hamlets of Lenox and Pittsfield. The only bridge built at this time was a wooden one with high red sides, crossing the river to the south of the village, and connecting it with a road to Great Barrington and Sheffield. A grist mill, Ephraim Williams's practical suggestion, was turning steadily at the eastern end of the village, by a brook which rippled down to join the river. Encampments of wigwams still persisted in little drifts around the edges of the village, melting into the landscape as quietly as heaps of dried leaves.

The newness was wearing off the town and the Indians were finding all this tidiness and morality irksome. Konkapot, who represented their better nature, had died. One wishes that the epitaph reputed to be on his gravestone were not apocryphal:

> Here lies Old Konkapot
> Be kind to him, O God;
> As he would were he God
> And God Old Konkapot.

Umpachene had lapsed permanently into drunkenness. Abigail protested with some truth that after all Sergeant did for them, they were nothing but miserable hypocrites who returned "as ye dog to his vomit and as ye sow yt was washed to her wallowing in ye mire." Sergeant was wearing thin his slender strength with overwork and worry, for in order to finish the boarding school, to which he now pinned all his hopes, he had to borrow heavily. The Mohawks came to look over the new school with grunts of approval, and asked how much would Sergeant give them if they consented to be educated. He decided that it would be best to keep all the Mahican Indians together with the English, under their old schoolmaster, Mr. Woodbridge, and let the interesting Mr. Kellog, whom he would import from Newington, devote all his powers to the visiting tribes. Abigail could look after the girls.

The Peace of Aix-la-Chappelle in 1748 was at least a truce in the hostilities, but a greater calamity than the war was to befall the mission. John Sergeant, friend to all their little world, English and Indian alike, fell fatally ill of a fever and "canker" in his throat, in the early summer of 1749. He had been the common denominator of the town, explaining each race in terms that the other could understand, and keeping them from splitting wide apart. With a final effort of his aching throat he delivered an admonition to his Indian children, scolding them like an affectionate father. He "fear'd that some of them grew worse and worse, notwithstanding all that God had done for them . . . and there were many ways in which God could, and often did testify his displeasure against a sinful people . . . It may be that God will take me from you, and then my mouth will be shut and I will speak to you no more." These were his last words to them, and he left the church, wearily to climb the Hill for the last time. "I can call myself a most unprofitable servant," he said, as he lay dying. "God be merciful to me, a sinner." During his illness the Indians gathered together of their own accord in the meetinghouse, frightened as a flock of sheep suddenly bereft of the friendly bark of the shepherd dog, and earnestly prayed that he might be restored to them. Did he realize at the end the futility of the task he had set himself? Was a corner of the curtain of the future lifted for a moment, and did he glimpse his Indians pushed out of Stockbridge, no longer their old hunting ground, but a thriving American town in which there was no room for them? Or did he die secure in the belief that the boarding school would accomplish the miracle, guided by the capable hands of Abigail and her father?

Chapter III

THE WILLIAMS RING

"HE was a tender parent and a most kind, affectionate and obliging husband," Abigail grieved in a letter to her mother-in-law. "God was pleased to make him a distinguished blessing to the world in general, but remarkably so to this poor bereaved little flock who are incessantly lamenting this judgment upon them." These were the days when the last word was said in an epitaph. The one just decipherable on the worn gravestone marked John Sergeant, although often attributed to the Indians, does not seem in the least characteristic of them. Surely it was written by Abigail, a cry straight from the heart:

> "Where is that pleasing form? I ask; thou cans't not show:
> He's not within, false stone there's nought but death below.
> And where's that pious soul, that thinking, conscious mind?
> Wilt thou pretend, vain cypher, that's with thee enshrined?
> Alas, my friends, not here with thee that I can find;
> Here's not a Sergeant's body, or a Sergeant's mind.
> I'll seek him hence, for all's alike deception here,
> I'll go to heaven, and I shall find my Sergeant there."

But sorrow, like fear, was too costly an emotion to be indulged in in the wilderness. Somehow two Sergeant sons must be raised into men of the world and not rough pioneers, and Electa must be brought up a young lady with the proper airs and graces to make an advantageous match. These ends must be attained with no money, for Sergeant had left her only a legacy of debt. Abigail's natural zest for life soon rose to these contingencies and mercifully dulled the edges of her grief.

There were moral as well as material problems for her to face, for with Sergeant dead, the basic quarrel between the whites and the Indians flared up. It had long lain just below the surface of their common life, but during his lifetime everyone had behaved a little better than he really was—the Indian was less shiftless, the Englishman less rapacious. Complaints had traveled as far as his doorstep, to be settled with justice and finality. He had been aided, of course, by the invaluable Timothy Woodbridge, who had acted as his second in these matters. But now that Sergeant was gone, Woodbridge found himself unable to assume the leadership, which gravitated easily to the strongest, richest man in town—Ephraim Williams. This gentleman's attitude toward the Indians was purely utilitarian. He unconsciously thought of them in terms of a commodity, useful in time of war, and very troublesome in time of peace. Indians could be used most effectively as a protection to the town, and what he didn't use he could throw away. It was Abigail's problem to decide whether to accept this philosophy of her father's or to champion her husband's idealism.

Colonel Williams, back from the rebuilding of Fort Massachusetts, boxed himself up in his new house on the Hill, impervious to the rising murmur of resentment against him in the village. Stately and forbidding, The Castle was really a fort and commanded the sweep of the valley, bidding haughty defiance to the enemy on the prowl from the north. There was even a well in the cellar, so that in case of siege, those seeking the protection of its three-inch, oak-plank walls, would be supplied with water. The Indians, looking up at the house from the Plain, used it as a clock, for the first gleam of sunshine touching its bleak west side marked the stroke of noon. Its owner looked around him on the Hill at a goodly property, which he had accumulated in the past ten years by one device or another. One hundred and fifty acres had been the allowance made to him upon his arrival in 1737, but Colonel Williams had ignored the tiresome ruling which forbade the English to buy land in the Indian township, and at the time of Sergeant's death his property within the village alone amounted to over 400 acres. Sergeant had appeased the Indians by explaining that Williams did not really own this land himself, for he had disposed of lots to members of his own family. Substantial slices had been cut off and sold— not given—to his three sons, Ephraim, Elijah, and Josiah, for the Colonel never allowed sentiment to interfere with real estate. Abigail and her children now owned Sergeant's land, and unobtrusively the Williams family was spreading itself over the Hill.

John Stoddard was dead and the new River God, Israel Williams, was cousin to Colonel Ephraim. No help from that quarter, and the Indians' only hope for justice lay in the General Court, far off and indifferent in Boston. In the archives of the State House are the yellowed, dusty documents, penned by faithful Timothy Woodbridge, complaining bitterly of their white neighbors in general, but stressing the iniquities of Ephraim Williams. Complaint: "viz, about eight years ago our worthy and good minister, the Revd Mr. Sergeant made your petitioners an offer if we would pitch on any piece of land that lay common or undivided in the town clear and fence the same he would procure what part of it was fit and proper for plowing to be plowed and what part was suitable for grass he would procure grass seed to sow it. And Mr. Sergeant further observed that the more land was prepared as aforesd the better he should be pleased . . . to encourage husbandry . . . your petitioners sent about thirty men to pitch on a proper place for this business . . . and applyed to Mr. Sergeant and Mr. Woodbridge for their approbation of the suitableness of the tract we had chosen. They both agreed it was well and encouraged us to work . . . But when the petitioners had accomplished more than one hundred days work in cutting drawing timber and erecting fence on sd land your petitioners were ordered very much to their surprise to desist from going on with their design for no other reason . . . than that sd land lay adjoining the sd Williams land and is good and therefore is more proper for him than for your petitioners . . . to the sd Williams another tract of land thirty acres near the meeting-house—this taken under pretence . . . to secure stream to sd Williams which is dry almost half the year on which Williams has an old useless mill which is no manner of advantage to the town nor ever can be the stream being so small and uncertain . . . such a piece of unreasonable and unjust conduct in the actor that the great and general court will not countenance it when properly laid before them in its true light." It is hard to pass judgment on this ancient dispute, but there is an undeniable ring of righteousness to these lamentations of the original owners of the soil.

A committee was appointed to repair to the town of Stockbridge and look into the "Grievances and Difficulties" between Indians and English. Colonel Williams plausibly explained to the gentlemen that the piece of land the Indians referred to was small—but his own. It lay between other lots of land belonging to the English and it was very inconvenient that the Indians should have it. Even now we can feel the tremor of indignation that ran through the Indian community when the committee decided that the English be allowed to take up this land, as part of their property, paying the Indians £10 for their labor and disappointment. Again they complained that Colonel Williams had eight acres of the intervale which he promised after three years' improvement to exchange for upland, but he kept it still. With a shrug, Williams defended himself: He never promised it absolutely, but only in case he could spare it. Finally they complained— and here is the crux of the matter—that they had been told at first that but few families besides the minister and schoolmaster should settle with them. Now, there were many families settled in the place. Upon which the committee told them that it was reasonable to expect that, as the English increased, they would settle their children on their lands. The Indians allowed it was reasonable but said they were not told so at first.

Colonel Williams certainly led the committee by the nose, and it was decided between them that the Indians should divide their lands in severalty, that is, that each Indian should own his property. This had never been their custom. The tribe had always owned the land in bulk, and Umpachene raised his voice for the last time in recorded history to protest. But no one paid attention to him any more, for he was far gone in drunkenness and disgrace, and Timothy Dwight, a surveyor from Northampton and friend of Colonel Williams, came up to survey and divide the land. He drew a neat line through the unappropriated lands of the town and allotted land on the west side of the line to the Indians and on the east side to the English, which he believed would tend to future peace. This was fair enough, once the premise had been accepted that the township was now to be only half Indian. No Indian could own more than 100 acres, a ruling tactfully not extended to the eastern and English side of the line.

But it was not only the children of the original settlers who were taking up the land. Williams was encouraging friends from Springfield, West Springfield and Northhampton to come into the valley, and within a year after Sergeant's death the Indians were bewildered by many new English faces and names. David Pixley, Stephen Nash, John Willard, Joseph Barnard, Jonathan Devereux, John Taylor, Samuel Brown, and Elnathan Curtis all moved into town with their families, while the glittering figure of Brigadier General Dwight became familiar to Stockbridge's one street. He brought with him, as an extra dash of style, his bodyguard, Lawrence Lynch, a likely young Irishman who had been in his regiment at Louisburg. Pleasure and business were agreeably combined in the Brigadier General's visits to the village. He had recently been left a widower, and he found a solace to his loneliness in Abigail Sergeant's black-eyed sparkle, demurely set off by her widow's weeds, as he sat talking mission affairs with her father. Colonel Williams was booming the even then familiar American note of a bigger-and-better Stockbridge

He said the charity school was to be put upon a more ambitious basis, and the government at Boston, realizing the "great Advantage of securing the Indians to the Crown," was donating £500 a year for the education of the Mohawks, while Mr. Hollis's annual bounty of £160 continued to arrive with pleasing regularity. These sums were in addition to the missionary's salary paid by The Society for the Propagation of the Gospel. Dwight had been recently appointed by the General Court one of a committee of three to supervise the disbursement of the government's money. The others, Joseph Pynchon and Jonathan Ashley, seem never to have been as active as Dwight. Therefore, Colonel Williams was quite easily persuading him that a resident trustee, especially if linked to the family interests, would be most helpful. He had been made one of the Commissioners for The Society for the Propagation of the Gospel, while a nephew, Elisha Williams of Wethersfield, Connecticut, had managed to get appointed to the Board in England. Young Captain Ephraim, who found time from his military duties to be in Boston a great deal, was on confidential terms with the Governor and Sir William Pepperell. Thus the Indian mission was becoming a family affair and the old Colonel, in spite of his unpopularity with the Indians, was gathering its purse strings into his powerful hands. Although his conversation was liberally sprinkled with piety, he was not unmindful of the fact that under his management the boarding school might develop into a sound business proposition.

The Brigadier General's attentions to Stockbridge and to Abigail were flattering, for he was one of the high-lighted figures of his day. During the past ten years his record, both civil and military, had been impressive as he steadily climbed the ladder of success. He had lived for many years in Brookfield, which he had represented at the General Court. Speaker of the House of Representatives, Judge of the Court of Common Pleas, Colonel of the Militia, he had finally risen to the rank of Brigadier General in the expedition to Louisburg in 1745. The military bearing, the handsome, finely-cut features, the beautiful hands—which he rather studiously displayed in conversation — proclaimed the gentleman *par excellence,* as his granddaughter, Catherine Sedgwick, was to remember years later. It is not surprising that Abigail was unable to resist all this magnificence laid at her feet, nor that eighteen months after Sergeant's death she sailed up the aisle once more. Sergeant was put away in the top drawer of her heart, along with youthful idealism, and if her views on the Indian mission were seen to undergo a change in the years that followed, they were more consistent with her character. It had been rather forced for her to strain quite so persistently heavenward as she had in the years of her first marriage. She found herself agreeing with her father that the mission, as Sergeant had envisaged it, was a lost cause, and that it and the town must now be established along more practical lines.

Two parties were forming themselves in the village, as they have so many times since in the 200 years of its life. The Williams school of thought was upheld by Dwight and the powerful Williams clique, while Timothy Woodbridge, the new English settlers, and the entire Indian population formed the opposition. They clung to the old ideal of Stockbridge for the Indians. The Mohawks had settled their families on the land allotted to them around the charity school, in the hope of giving their children an English education, and were deeply disappointed in the methods of the indolent Mr. Kellog, whom Williams had insisted upon retaining. They began loudly to complain of the unruliness and disorder of their children. They were "neither being dieted, clothed or instructed in industry or any other useful knowledge as they had expected when they delivered their children to be instructed by sd Kellog." Disgruntled, they began to move away, taking their children with them, while Woodbridge and his party pointed accusing forefingers at the Williams faction on the Hill. The charity school was mere fiction, they said, for which elaborate machinery was being constructed, less for the purpose of educating the Indians than for bringing money into the Williamses' pockets.

For almost two years the town limped along in this way, for it had been difficult to find a minister to fill Sergeant's place. Samuel Hopkins, of Great Barrington, unanimously approved by both parties, had been called. But either he did not care to handle a situation so filled with dynamite or he wished to secure the position for his old teacher, Jonathan Edwards, for he refused to come, recommending Edwards in his place. Various strings had tied this celebrated divine to the mission for the past ten years. It will be remembered that he was one of the clergymen who, taking a paternal interest in the new town, had joined Williams in buying out Van Valkenburgh, so that since 1739 he had been owner of a considerable tract of land just outside of Stockbridge. Then David Brainerd, on his deathbed in Edwards's house, had talked to him of Sergeant and his Indians, and Samuel Hopkins had been another link keeping him in touch with the mission.

It was a long step down in the world for the famous preacher of Northampton, from a large and prosperous congregation in an established town to a mission station in the wilderness. To an intellect engaged in laying the cornerstone of a faith so compelling that it was to revolutionize the churches of New England for the next hundred years, the salvation of the Indians' souls must have looked like an elementary Sunday school. But, after the defeat and disappointment that the Northampton years had brought, Stockbridge promised a subsistence for his wife and large family, and the solitude he needed for his intellectual life. Here in the quiet hills, with these docile children of the forest and a small English congregation, he would be at peace.

At the time when Edwards went to Northampton, twenty-four years before he enters this history, the church was slipping comfortably down the road to a slack liberalism. The vision of a church and state run in perfect harmony by God's elect, which had brought the Puritans to the New World, was gradually fading. Originally church membership had been confined to those who could give actual proof of personal religious conversion. But as early as 1663 the Halfway Covenant was introduced, broadening the basis of church membership to include all those who intended to lead a sober and godly life. In fact, after the rigid asceticism of the first generation had passed away, religion came more and more to terms with the exigencies of pioneer life. Discipline relaxed, and the struggle for existence on the frontier tended to obscure and soften the lines of the Calvinist doctrine.

Northampton, when Edwards first came to it, was a merry, full-blooded community, living agreeably off the fat of the Connecticut River valley. Riding to church on the Sabbath, full-bosomed mothers perched on pillions behind their sturdy husbands. They came to render a dutiful service to God, while not acutely repentant of their sins. But when Jonathan Edwards succeeded his grandfather, Solomon Stoddard, in the ministry, he immediately began to preach a gospel which arrested people's attention. A tall, shadowy presence, he stood motionless in the pulpit, and without a rising inflection of his voice, without a gesture, he quietly told them his conception of Christianity. He clothed the harsh Calvinist doctrines in light and color, as he showed them the snowy mountain peaks on which the spirit united with God might dwell, and pointed downward at the yawning abyss of hell waiting to suck in the souls of the unconverted. Backed by a relentless logic, he explained the glory of heaven in terms of the horrors of hell. For how, he asked, could you explain evil except by the fact that God was angry with His children and a majority of them were doomed? "It would be a wonder," he said, "if some that are now present should not be in hell in a very short time. And it would be no wonder if some persons, that now sit here, in some seats of this meeting-house, in health, quiet and secure, should be there before tomorrow morning."

An agony of repentance swept over the terrified farmers and their wives. Wave after wave of emotional excitement broke upon the town, swelling into the Revival of 1735, and into the Great Awakening of 1741. "There was scarcely a single person in the town, either old or young, that was left unconcerned about the great things of the eternal world," Edwards wrote. "All other talk but about spiritual and eternal things was soon thrown by; all the conversations in all companies, and upon all occasions, was upon these things only, unless so much as was necessary for people to carry on their ordinary secular business." The ferment spread throughout the length and breadth of the Connecticut valley, and Edwards was acclaimed as a prophet, as people everywhere attempted the superhuman leap from sinners to become saints. But religious revivals always have their violent reactions, and nerves, stretched to the breaking point by the high pitch that Edwards had keyed them to, were bound to snap. "The Spirit of God was gradually withdrawing from us," he wrote, "'and after this time Satan seemed to be more let loose, and raged in a dreadful manner. The first instance wherein it appeared, was a person's putting an end to his own life by cutting his throat . . . After this, multitudes in this and other towns seemed to have it strongly suggested to them . . . to do as this person had done . . . as if somebody had spoken to them, 'Cut your own throat, now is a good opportunity. Now! Now!'"

When Colonel John Stoddard, Edwards's uncle and his supporter, died in 1747, Northampton turned against Edwards. Colonel Israel Williams of Hatfield, who had never been in sympathy with Edwards, succeeded to Stoddard's authority as unofficially-crowned king of Hampshire County, and the powerful Williams clan gathered behind him. In Wethersfield, Elisha Williams rose up and denounced him. In Lebanon, Solomon Williams, Israel's brother, joined the hue and cry, while uncle Ephraim, far away in Stockbridge, heartily endorsed the sentiments of his relatives. They and their cohorts were all in at the death when, in 1750, the culmination was reached in the dismissal of Edwards from the Northampton church.

It must have been with a sense of relief that he looked forward to the life in Stockbridge, the boarding school attended by fifty eager Mohawks instructed by the capable Captain Kellog, and the day school for the Housatonic Indians and white children in the hands of Timothy Woodbridge, and the whole mission financially well-oiled. There would surely be many hours free from the practical administration of his duties that he could spend in study and contemplation.

During his first visit to Stockbridge in the winter of 1751, he picked out Sergeant's original little house on the Plain. Here his wife, the saintly and capable Sarah Pierpont, would stow away the eleven children and pinch and contrive to make both ends meet. The salary from The Society for the Propagation of the Gospel would be eked out by £6.13s.4d. from the English congregation, and Indians and whites together engaged to supply him with 100 sleigh-loads of wood, not half enough for the big family. He was badly in debt but by rigid economies they could get along. Mrs. Edwards and the daughters would continue to paint landscapes on fans and send them to Boston for sale, and Edwards would write his sermons on discarded patterns of ladies' caps to save paper.

It was, however, with grave misgivings that the Williams faction saw the austere and unyielding figure of Jonathan Edwards approach Stockbridge. They were beginning to consider it entirely their private game preserve. The management of the mission funds would not square with the rigid Edwards code of ethics, besides which they were sincere believers in the easier way to salvation represented by the Halfway Covenant. Had it not been endorsed by their own John Sergeant? On the other hand the Woodbridge group was eager to have Edwards, the Commissioners at Boston stood behind him, and unexpectedly the support of the Brigadier General tipped the scales in his favor, for Dwight had long been an admirer and friend of Edwards. It was hoped that he would not stoop to such mundane affairs as the management of the mission funds, but would be content to leave business where it belonged, in Williams's hands. They counted heavily upon his reputed vagueness. He did not even know how many head of cattle he owned, they told each other. Absent-minded professor stories went the rounds. It was said that one day, as he was riding through a pasture, he met a boy who civilly doffed his cap and opened the gate for his horse. Edwards courteously thanked him and asked whose boy he was. "Cooper's boy," laconically came the answer. Edwards, returning home through the same pasture a little later, found the child still there. Again he lifted the gate, doffed his cap, again Edwards responded with thanks, and again asked the same question. "Why, sir," the boy said in bewilderment, "I'm the same man's boy I was fifteen minutes ago."

Young Captain Ephraim, believing it was an ill wind that blew nobody any good, expressed his opinion in a letter to the Reverend Jonathan Ashley of Deerfield with admirable frankness:

" . . . Mr. Edwards has lately wrote to Mr. Woodbridge of Stockbridge, who informs him he has not heard from them dont know whether they desire he should come among them, and that he hears I have done all I can to prevent his coming. I am sorry that a head so full of Divinity should be so empty of Politics. I would not have him fail of going for 500 pounds, since they are so set for him, not that I think he will ever do so much more good than an other, but on acct. of raising the price of my land. Its true when they first talkd of settling him I was against it gave my reasons, & sent them to him like an honest fellow . . .

1. That he was not sociable, the consequence of which was he was not apt to teach.

2. He was a very great Bigot, for he would not admit any person into heaven, but those that agreed fully to his sentiments, a Doctrine deeply tingd with that of the Romish church.

3. That he was an old man, & that it was not possible for him to learn the Indian tongues therefore it was not

likely he could be serviceable to the Indians as a young man that would learn the tongue . . .

    4. His principles were such, If I had rightly been informed, I could by no means agree to, that I had taken pains to read his Book, but could not understand it, that I had heard almost every gentleman in the county say the same, & that upon the whole I believd he did not know them himself.

    The above reasons I sent to him by Lt Brown, who has since told me he deliverd to him verbatim, which I believe did not suit him.

               I am Sir your most Humble Sert

                            Eph Williams Jun"

Besides the Captain's shrewd guess that the presence of such a celebrity in the town would raise the value of his land, there was truth in his catalogue of Edwards's defects for a position of missionary. He lacked the common touch, the ready smile, the hearty handshake of the successful missionary. He was out of scale with his parishioners, dwarfing the fussy pretentiousness of Colonel Williams, the elegance of Dwight, and even the square dependability of Timothy Woodbridge. Only with Monument Mountain, thrusting its baldpate above the passing scene, was he on neighborly terms.

The scholarly quiet of which Edwards had dreamed was not to be his. In the month of June, before he had even settled his family, it became apparent that the Mohawks, who were the pivot of the government's interest in the mission, were leaving in large numbers. Hendrik, the chief, in disgust at the filth and disorder of the boarding school, had already gone, and every day saw the departure of another disgruntled family over the Albany trail. The representatives of the Massachusetts government passed through Stockbridge on their way to Albany, where they were to meet with representatives of the Connecticut and New York governments, and the chiefs of the Six Nations, for the purpose of arranging a treaty. They persuaded Edwards to accompany

them and to try his hand at coaxing the Indians back to
Stockbridge. Something in his calm eye seemed to reassure
them, for Hendrik consented to give the mission one more
chance. His people would like to be educated, he said, but
they were tired of Mr. Kellog and his broken promises. He
asked the commissioners to promise nothing this time but
what they would certainly perform. The incompetency of
Mr. Kellog was agreed upon by all concerned, and the Commissioners appointed a new schoolmaster with every qualification to spread a satisfactory veneer of English culture and
piety upon the little savages. So confident was Hendrik of a
new deal in the mission that he persuaded his brothers, the
Oneidas, and also a few Tuscaroras, to return with him. Full
of hope they all trailed back to Stockbridge.

A new instructor was duly installed, a Mr. Gideon Hawley,
guaranteed for his virtue and learning, and Edwards sat down
at his desk and composed an elaborate plan for the education
of the Indians, which he sent off in a letter to his friend, Sir
William Pepperell. His ideas on methods of teaching have
a modern emphasis. "In the common method of teaching,"
he wrote, " . . . children, when they are taught to read, are
so much accustomed to reading, without any kind of
knowledge of the meaning of what they read, that they
continue reading without understanding, even a long time
after they are capable of understanding, were it not for the
habit of making such and such sounds, on the sight of such
and such letters, with a perfect inattentiveness to any meaning." But his notions of geography and history show him to
have conceived of a world safely bounded by the Old and New
Testaments. "Thus," he suggested, "they might be taught
how long it was from the Creation of the world to the Coming
of Christ, how long from the Creation to the Flood; how long
from the Flood to the calling of Abraham . . . And with like
ease, and with equal benefit, they might be taught some of the

main things in Geography: which way the land of Canaan lies from this; how far it is; which way Egypt lay from Canaan; which way Babylon lay from Jerusalem, and how far; which way Padan-Aram was from Canaan; where Rome lay from Jerusalem; where Antioch . . ."

The new master, Mr. Hawley, reported Edwards to be a very plain and practical preacher to the Indians. "His sentences were concise and full of meaning and his delivery grave and natural." "Upon no occasion," Mr. Hawley insisted, "did he display any metaphysical knowledge in the pulpit."

Disconcertingly it dawned upon the Williamses and Dwight that Edwards had no intention of remaining a massive figurehead, safely lost in clouds of speculation. If the Lord called him to run a Sunday school for savages in the wilderness, at least its morals would be measured by the same rigorous yardstick that he had used at Northampton.

It soon became evident that, although the Mohawks were delighted with Mr. Hawley and were eagerly availing themselves of his instruction, Williams and Dwight refused to acknowledge his existence. Kellog was the master of the boarding school, they persisted in claiming, and daily they dispatched him to interfere busily in every possible way with Mr. Hawley. The result was confusing to the simple minds of the savages.

Woodbridge had warned Edwards of the Williams clique from the first, but his confidence in Dwight was such that he was slow to suspect him and his relations by marriage of being involved in such a shady affair. By February, they had fairly laid their cards on the table. Dwight was in full charge of the boarding school, and in the fullness of time Mr. Kellog would retire from his duties, and Dwight's own son would become master. A store had been built in the village with government funds, and there the Indians bought liquor while the proprietor, Colonel Williams, looked the other way. A new schoolhouse was to be built for the girls, the land for which was part of the Sergeant property. It was to be sold to the government at a high price by Abigail, thus netting the Dwights a neat profit. Abigail herself would be mistress for the girls. Four of their children were receiving their education at the boarding school, and their servants' wages were paid out of the mission funds.

The feeble protests of Woodbridge and the other white settlers on the Plain, and the resentful backs of the Mohawks, huddled in their blankets, and obviously contemplating another removal in the spring, had no effect upon these questionable methods. Edwards in his wrath was another matter. He had met the Williams tribe before on the field of battle in Northampton, and had gone down to defeat, and it is supposing him to be utterly devoid of human nature to imagine that he did not sniff the air of combat with some degree of satisfaction. He decided to make an issue of the appointment of Abigail as mistress of the girls' school. There he would put his foot down. In a letter to the Commissioners in Boston he explained that Abigail was an unsuitable choice, for she was the mother of three growing families—the Sergeant children, Dwight's children by his first marriage, and a new Dwight family on the way. Moreover, she would be accountable for her actions solely to her husband, who wrote the annual report of the school for the Legislature. He further disclosed the state of affairs in the mission, the iniquity of Colonel Williams, and the unaccountable change that had come over Dwight since his marriage. He urged the Commissioners to come to Stockbridge and judge for themselves. "I have been slow to speak," he wrote. "My disposition has been, entirely to suppress what I knew, that would be to the disadvantage of any of the people here. But I dare not hold my peace any longer."

With the first thaw of the snow-clad hills and the appearance of the early pussy willows, the Mohawks turned their faces definitely westward again, leaving a scene which was degenerating into *opera-bouffe*. The elaborate machinery of the charity school now housed four of the faithful Housatonic Indians and one reluctant Mohawk under the unpopular Kellog, while in another building Mr. Hawley still continued the instruction of a group of Oneidas. One of the Williams faction, during a visit to Hawley's school, lost his temper and struck the son of the chief sachem of the Oneidas on the head. A terrible tumult ensued, which Dwight as trustee was called upon to settle. He adroitly fastened the blame for the incident on Mr. Hawley, but when the Oneidas to a man said that they would leave if Hawley did, Dwight was obliged to change his tune. He ended by paying the outraged sachem a large sum of money to keep his child in the school. One night, a little later, Hawley's school was mysteriously burned to the ground. Hawley escaped with his pupils, but lost all his books and furniture.

These events were proving too much for the aged nerves of Ephraim Williams. He was beginning to find Stockbridge extremely uncomfortable. In his fortress on the Hill he was securely buttressed by the properties of his own loyal family, but when he descended to the Plain on business or pleasure bent, he was met with dark looks and his greetings were scarcely returned. The white settlers and the Indians were a solid bloc of unfriendly opposition and Williams decided on desperate measures. If Edwards went, then Hawley would automatically go with him, and Dwight was bending every effort, as he knew, to concoct a report that would completely discredit Edwards. But what was needed was an even more thorough housecleaning. If all the disgruntled settlers who sympathized with Edwards and

Woodbridge could be bodily removed, and their places filled with settlers friendly to Williams, all might yet be well. It was a bold plan, and early one morning before the break of day he proceeded to the Plain to put it into execution.

He hurried from one house to another, calling the farmers from their beds. He offered to buy their farms himself, at large prices, cash down, if they would leave town immediately. One sleep-befogged landowner actually closed with him, and before noon he had visited every house on the Plain. By this time the astonished farmers were thoroughly awake to Williams's nefarious plot, and they indignantly repudiated his offers. Was the old man really mad to think he could buy up the whole town? Even his own family admitted that it was very peculiar and, as Edwards said, "were glad to lay this conduct to distraction." Ephraim then started coursing about the countryside in a way that alarmed Abigail, for she wrote in a letter to her brother in Deerfield: "He went away from us about three weeks past for Wethersfield. Promised us he would go nowhere Else. But ye first News we had from him was that He Rid all one Day in a bad Storm, got to Wethersfd late at Night. Sett out Next morning for Newhaven, rid all ye Day in a hard South westerly wind, there he got in ye Notion of meeting with their General Assembly Day after Day on Indian affairs, then returns to Newington, there writes us He is going to Stonington, then to Deerfield, then to Boston . . . it will vastly disserve our Public affairs & I know not but intirely ruin us . . . by one wile or other . . . I beg you Do all in your Power to get him in ye mind of Coming Home as Soon as may Be, if you have any love for him or us."

Home was none too wholesome a place for the old gentleman and it was at last decided that the wisest plan would be for him to uproot himself from the homestead on the Hill and move to the safe distance of Deerfield. This he did, selling the house and all his property rights in and about Stockbridge—a lordly demesne of 1,505 acres all told—for the sum of £1,000, to his son Ephraim. For good measure he threw in "my negro servant Moni, my negro boy London, also my Negro Girl Chloe—the latter not to be for his use or service until after my own & my wife's death."

Letters, an admixture of shrewdness and homesickness, found their way back to the sons who were to uphold the family banner in Stockbridge. "If I shod not come back to live at Stockbridge," he wrote to Elijah, who had leased the farm in Ephraim's absence, "he is to Remember I must have an Equivelent for all my Privelidges. (viz). the House Room, a Horse allways kept, firewood fitted at the door; and allso Two acres of land at the door: all which will undoubtdly be worth one Hundred Pounds pr year old tenor . . . I would now tell you if it be possible gett buck wheat Straw of the Indians . . . and lay a good Cock Round each Tree; but dont lett the Straw come within two foot of the body of the trees lest the mice bark the trees . . . you Cant Conceive the benefitt of it, you never need to plow up your orchard any more in case you practice doing so . . . " The prudent farmer ends upon a nostalgic note: " . . . I am more sencible of the want of aples than perhaps you may be aware of . . . " It was cold in Deerfield, "I want the Red Jackit & blue millatary Britchis & the Green old winter Jackit some good chease & the shrubb . . . also the thing I put over my head to keep my Ears warm which I button under my chin . . . "

With the indiscretions of the old man out of the way, the younger generation fell upon Edwards tooth and nail. Cousin Elisha Williams, arriving opportunely from London, hurried to Stockbridge, and asserted his authority over Edwards, as one of the directors of the Society in London. He would be sorry, he said, in the tone of a schoolmaster to a refractory pupil, to hand in an unfavorable report of the missionary to the Society, but this he would do, if Edwards did not at once approve the appointment of Abigail as mistress of the female boarding school. Edwards refused to be bullied and referred him to the Commissioners of the Society in Boston, to whom he had explicitly stated his reasons for disapproving of this plan.

Dwight then launched a broadside in the form of a report to the Legislature, attacking Edwards, and accusing him of "intermeddling with what was none of his business." He claimed that Edwards had taken advantage of his absence to introduce Hawley into the school, that Edwards was wholly incompetent and too old to learn the Indian language. He also wrote a letter to his old commander at Louisburg, Sir William Pepperell, asking for the immediate removal of Edwards. In Boston, young Ephraim busily whispered insinuations and accusations against the minister.

However, virtue was to prove its own reward. The integrity of Edwards towered easily above this petty intrigue. In a letter to Sir William Pepperell he rested his case, he said, with "every man, woman and child in Stockbridge, that had any understanding, both English and Indians, except the families of the opponent of Mr. Woodbridge and of the author of the Report."

The Indians' backs were up. If the boarding school was to be a place of "contention & confusion" they would like their land back. In a lengthy petition they gave vent to their grievances: " . . . so long as the persons that are upon [the land] retain their dispositions, which are we apprehend to deprive us of our liberty and privileges, as free Subjects of the government, and rather than not bow and buckle us to their schemes, would overturn & bring to an end, all the designs of promoting Christian Knowledge among us . . . we waited on Coll Dwight soon after his return from Boston, desired him to give us his reasons for engaging so zealously to remove the minister . . . but he treated us with contempt and told us we came in an odd manner ,and upon an errand as odd, and that he was not obliged to give us his reasons . . . and we have great & just reason to complain to the Honorable court of the conduct of these Gentlemen whose restless, haughty, and selfish conduct, we veryly think to be the foundation of all our difference, and the calamity we suffer thereby . . . "

To the practical legislators in Boston, this was the point: The final contest for the prize of North America was approaching, and the rumors of war that had rumbled for five years beneath the patched-up Peace of Aix-la-Chapelle were about to break out into actual hostilities. The legislators had poured money since 1750 into the Stockbridge mission solely in the hope of adhering the Six Nations to the English cause. If the Indians had confidence in Edwards and Woodbridge, and distrusted Dwight and the Williamses, there was no more to be said. Edwards was put in undisputed charge of the mission funds from the Legislature and The Society for the Propagation of the Gospel. Even benign Mr. Hollis, when he was given proof that his draft of £160—the money for an entire year—had been pocketed outright by Kellog, wrote that his money must be hereafter administered solely by Edwards. Kellog withdrew to his native Connecticut, able to retire, it is to be assumed, in comfortable circumstances. Abigail immersed herself in domesticity, and Dwight, remembering that he was, after all, a Brigadier General, directed his not inconsiderable talents to the approaching conflict.

Israel Williams wrote to him that it was imperative that the Stockbridge Indians should not be in collusion with the enemy or even neutral, but must declare themselves definitely on the English side. Dwight wrote back that it was difficult to raise in them much enthusiasm for the English cause, because of the insults and abuses they had suffered at the hands of the soldiers. He did not mention certain other abuses which would have struck nearer home. However, by February he had persuaded most of them to enlist, and wrote to Governor Shirley that, as there had been no formal break between them and the Canadian Indians, they would be useful as spies. He dispatched three of them to Crown Point to learn the movements of the enemy. Dwight also had other irons in the fire. Only a year before, as Chief Justice of the Courts of Hampshire County, he had been instrumental in obtaining from the General Court an act incorporating the township of Pontoosuc, so-called until 1761, when it was rechristened Pittsfield. To a man of such active interests the unfortunate mission incident must soon have been lost in the shuffle of larger affairs.

Edwards had been left to pick up the pieces of the mission. He discovered to his amazement that young Ephraim's famous charm had been exercised upon the Mohawk chief, Hendrik, with great success, and that, despite the antipathy that existed between Williamses and Mohawks in general, Hendrik was in the habit of slipping into town when Williams was there, to swap army stories with the genial captain. This was a valuable connection, and perhaps contributed to the fact that the winter of 1754 saw a small number of Mohawks, Oneidas, and Tuscaroras return to Stockbridge. There were also a few of the Schaghticoke tribe lurking upon the outskirts of the village. And thereby hangs another tale.

Chapter IV

JONATHAN EDWARDS

THE peace that was so soon to be shattered on the national stage was broken almost simultaneously in Stockbridge. As George Washington engaged in the first skirmish of the war at Great Meadows in Virginia that spring, and the colonies under the leadership of Benjamin Franklin were preparing to meet in an attempt to present a united front to the enemy, a small but angry gun went off right under Jonathan Edwards's nose. It was at the height of the spring sugar season when an incident occurred which threatened to have far-reaching consequences. Two Schaghticoke Indians, father Waumpaumcorse and his son, were gathering sap in the vicinity of Tyringham. It was the same spot where John Sergeant had camped out with the Indians so many years before. Hearing a crackling of branches, they looked up to see two white men rapidly making off with some horses. As these had no saddles and wore bark halters, they supposed them to be Indian horses and started in pursuit. The white men, turning on the Indians, shot Waumpaumcorse dead. Deep was the wrath of the Indians over the murder, for such they felt it to be. An elaborate, ritualistic and purely Schaghticoke funeral took place and Indians of every persuasion defiantly attended. The two white men were brought to justice in Springfield, but one received only a slight punishment for manslaughter, while the other was entirely acquitted. An unwholesome quiet brooded over the town. In May, Edwards wrote anxiously to the Governor, stressing that this was a matter of importance not only to Stockbridge but to all New England. The Schaghticokes were a mischievous and more than commonly unreliable breed of Indian, and this unavenged murder of Waumpaumcorse was a snowball that would gather momentum. If their resentment spread to the Mahicans and thence to the Mohawks, no one could foretell the consequences, for the French would be quick to take advantage of their disaffection. Already there was an ugly rumor abroad in the village, instigated by the French, Edwards said, to the effect "that the English had made fools of [the Indians], had pretended to show kindness, instruct 'em, they had but deceived 'em, that they were only opening a whole mouth to swallow 'em up when there should be a convenient time." Edwards strongly advised a large subsidy to be applied at once to the wounded susceptibilities of the relatives of Waumpaumcorse. The Legislature procrastinated, and finally sent a small sum of money—£20—to the Schaghticokes. They remained in a sensitive frame of mind.

One Sabbath morning that summer as Edwards, with calm and deliberation, was expounding the Gospel to his congregation, the door of the meetinghouse was flung open and a man plunged down the center aisle, disheveled and hysterical with fear. The congregation gathered around him to hear, they felt sure, the worst. He had been hurrying over the Hill late to church, he told them. As he passed neighbor Chamberlain's house, he had seen an Indian slinking out the door, concealing something he was dragging after him. Thinking it to be one of the Stockbridge Indians robbing Chamberlain's house, he hastened to overtake him. It proved to be a Schaghticoke, with one of the Chamberlain children, whom he promptly tomahawked on sight of his pursuer, and then fled into the forest. The man entered the house to find an infant in its cradle brutally murdered by another Indian, a servant dead upon the floor, and Chamberlain and two little boys, half dead with fright, cowering under a bed in an adjoining room. The second Indian evaporated out of the house and away, before the terrified witness had caught his breath. Later that day word came that the Schaghticokes, making off up the footpath that was the road to Lenox, shot from the bushes a Mr. Stevens, who was hastening toward Stockbridge. Word of the Chamberlain disaster had already reached the few families that constituted the hamlet of Lenox. With these murders the price of the death of Waumpaumcorse had been exacted.

Panic seized the town. Those who lived in outlying districts, such as Lenox and Pontoosuc, crowded into Stockbridge for protection, while the Stockbridge settlers, feeling any spot safer than home, had a tendency to rush to Great Barrington. The Dwight family moved out bag and baggage, Abigail not even stopping to put shoes or stockings on little John Sergeant, and leaving hurried instructions to the colored servant, London, to bring along the three-year-old Pamela Dwight. A paroxysm of fear caused the servant to drop Pamela in a raspberry bush beside the road and take to his worthless heels. Larry Lynch, carefully escorting the family silver an hour later, discovered the child and, tucking her under his arm, restored her safely to the arms of her mamma.

The story of the Chamberlain massacre, traveling eastward on horrified lips, lost nothing in the telling. Israel Williams, commander of the western Massachusetts troops, and veteran of frontier warfare, realized the strategic position of Stockbridge. He agreed with Edwards that, if the Schaghticoke distemper spread to the Stockbridge Indians and thence to the Mohawks, the war was lost. When the French had secured the Six Nations to their interest he wrote: "Farewell peace & prosperity to New England, yea to North America."

There was, however, comfort in the fact that the Stockbridge Indians were just as much surprised and frightened by the Chamberlain incident as the rest of the community. Nevertheless, in view of the fact that the settlers were obliged to raise their bread in exposed places in the town and that "fearful apprehensions ever attend them," a large number of soldiers were detailed to protect Stockbridge. A fort was built around Edwards's house, and the entertainment of the soldiers fell upon his shoulders. In October, the expenses of such hospitality became crushing, and he was obliged to cry to the General Court for mercy. He had provided "800 meals of victuals, pasturing 150 horses, and 7 gal. of good West Indian rum" as well as food for "all poor people driven from their homes above thro fear." One of these panic-stricken ones, Aunt Cooper, née Jemima Woodbridge and niece of old Timothy, seems to have been an early American village character. She lived just over the Lenox line at the eastern end of town, and declared that she for one could stand such isolation no longer. One day a gentleman caller had assured her that she was greatly blessed. When she asked why, he told her that in every prayer those at the ends of the earth were always remembered, and he was sure that she and her family were the persons alluded to. She bustled into the middle of town and, with an eye to profit, decided to take boarders in a house of three ground-floor rooms, admitting only gentlemen who could pay well.

The soldiers, beside being a heavy drain on the hospitality of the town, proved to be a hindrance rather than a help. So eager were they in the performance of their duty that they entirely misunderstood the nature of the gentle Stockbridge Indians and accused them of the Chamberlain murders. Two blundering soldiers even exhumed the body of a dead Indian from the graveyard and removed the scalp. It was a tribute to the long-suffering patience of the Mahicans that this insulting and barbarous behavior was not rewarded by their razing the village to the ground.

Word came that summer that old Ephraim, in his retreat in Deerfield, had passed on to his somewhat doubtful reward. His children were deeply attached to the warm-hearted old reprobate, and they stood around his grave to hear him embalmed for posterity in the usual bombastic funeral oration of the day. "He always bore a testimony against vice," pronounced Jonathan Ashley, "and held a disposition to terrify the workers of iniquity; he was a lover of good men and esteemed them to be the excellent ones in all the earth; he held a great value for the Ministers of the Gospel, and was always ready to give them double honours . . ."

Young Ephraim was now the head of the family, but he was such a man of the world that Stockbridge did not see much of him. He flitted from Fort Massachusetts to Hatfield to Boston, where he was Israel Williams's confidential agent, and hobnobbed with Lieutenant Governor Phipps, Governor Shirley, and the rising young George Washington. He leased his land and The Castle to his brother Elijah, who had just returned from a Princeton education and proposed to settle down on the family acres. Josiah, a lesser light, owned the neighboring farm, and the Dwights had returned to the beautiful Sergeant house after their precipitate flight to Great Barrington.

The local feud which had so shaken the town for the past four years suddenly sank into insignificance, as the familiar nightmare of the French and Indians blackened their world. This time they had had an actual taste of bloodshed on their own doorstep. There was the old sickening suspense of waiting for news. Indian marauders molested the entire northwestern frontier, and Dutch Hoosac, a village not ten miles west of Fort Massachusetts, went up in flames. To the west the French and Indians were sweeping down the Ohio valley. If Fort Massachusetts—their only protection to the north—were to fall, the fate of all the Housatonic townships was sealed.

Lumberingly the machinery of the English offensive was put into motion from the Court of St. James's. Benjamin Franklin had failed in his intelligent attempt to unite the four New England colonies and New York, Pennsylvania, and Maryland under one leadership. The King felt that this would give the colonies too much power, and anyway they were unable to come to an agreement as to what had best be done. Three mammoth expeditions were planned in which the British Lion was conclusively to assert his supremacy. They were to take place in a rambling and somewhat disjointed manner under separate commands. General Braddock was to attack the French at the fork of the Ohio River; Governor Shirley was to strike the French line farther down at Niagara, while it was hoped that General William Johnson would capture the fort at Crown Point on Lake George. This was of strategic importance, as it controlled the best route from New York to Montreal.

The winter of 1755 saw Stockbridge torn between pride and fear in the forthcoming expedition. Sir William Johnson, the eccentric Irishman who lived up the Hudson, with Hendrik's sister Molly as his mistress, was a familiar name in town, his relation with the Mohawks being of an intimate if not uplifting nature. Hendrik and his men would certainly follow Johnson's banner to the north. Hampshire county was to provide one of the three Massachusetts regiments for the expedition, and Stockbridge's white-haired boy, Ephraim Williams, raised to the rank of colonel was to lead it. Israel Williams assured Governor Shirley that only Ephraim's popularity could raise the requisite number of men. The

Governor wrote to the new colonel: "I desire there be none, but right good men enlisted, and not under five feet five inches without their shoes, unless they are young enough to grow to that height, and none above forty years old." Stockbridge, Pontoosuc, and Fort Massachusetts emptied themselves eagerly of every soldier who met the specifications, and Hendrik promised 300 Mohawks. The staff of young Ephraim's regiment was inevitably composed of Williamses. They were Dr. Thomas Williams of Deerfield as surgeon; Rev. Stephen Williams, chaplain; Perez Marsh (Israel Williams's son-in-law), surgeon's mate; William Williams (son of Colonel William Williams of Pontoosuc), surgeon's mate's assistant; another William Williams, quartermaster. Brother Josiah contented himself with enlisting as an ensign.

It appears that Colonel Ephraim's usually bounding spirits drooped as the day of departure drew near. His letters of this period show that despite a scarlet suit made for the occasion, his mind dwelt much upon the mutability of human affairs and presaged a gloomy outcome to the campaign. He was to lead his regiment to Albany to rendezvous with the other regiments and their commander, General Johnson, and proceed northward.

Arriving in Albany early in July, delay and confusion attended the assembling of the troops. It was hard to get supplies over the wretched roads, and in the sizzling heat the men fell sick. News of Braddock's death and defeat filled Colonel Williams's heart with dismay. "It is to be feared that General Braddock is cut to pieces and a great part of his army . . . The Lord have mercy upon poor New England," he wrote. The Mohawks, feeling the shift in the wind towards the French, failed to turn up in the numbers expected. "The defeat of Braddock has had such an effect on them that their has not yet above sixty joined us, tho' more are expected & all tho' they say they are our Brothers and will live and die with us, I should not choose to venture my life with much dependence on them, for anything but intelligence, unless we could raise in them some confidence of success."

The canker of private disappointment was gnawing at his heart for, if tradition is to be believed, Elizabeth Williams, the daughter of Israel, had turned him down just before he left Hatfield. Crossed in love, it seemed improbable that there would be children and grandchildren to trot upon his knee, while he told them of the dangers and glories of Crown Point. Indeed, with the persistent dark cloud that seemed to hang over the expedition, it seemed improbable that he would be there to tell the tale at all. It would be prudent to prepare for the worst, settle his accounts, and make a will before he left Albany. His father's sins rested heavily upon his conscience and, in a letter to his executor, Israel Williams, he desired him to look into the affair of the Stockbridge Indians, and see that any wrongs inflicted by his father were righted. "I have changed my mind since I left your house," he wrote, "for reasons, as to what I designed to give (which should have been handsome) to one very near you." The unyielding Elizabeth was left only £20, the same amount as her sisters, with a small personal bequest, wistfully reminding her of the domesticity he had missed: "Item. I give and bequeath to my loving cousin, Elizabeth Williams . . . my Silver Cream pot and Tea spoons."

His private life thus disposed of, he turned to posterity. Military exploits and a bouncing family of Williamses were not to be his, but his final gesture of generosity has earmarked him a small corner of immortality. The bulk of his estate by his "will and pleasure and desire" was left for the maintenance of a "Free School (in a Township west of Fort Massachusetts commonly called the West Township) forever, provided the sd Township [is given] the name of Williamstown." The West Township, shut in to the east by the steep barrier of the Hoosac range, and looking south to Greylock towering above the valley, and north to the lofty ranges of the Green Mountains, was a tract for which his father had made the original plan in 1739. Old Ephraim had then remarked that it was "very accomadable for settlements." The Williamses had now stamped it indelibly for their own.

A campaign, which should have been pushed with dispatch and energy, was conducted by the leisurely Sir William Johnson with indecision and a lack of knowledge of border warfare. He loitered at a point halfway between Albany and Lake George for almost a month. The French commander, Baron Dieskau, was able, through the myriad eyes of his swift Indian scouts, to estimate accurately the size and strength of of the English army. Early in September, Johnson advanced to the foot of Lake George, while Dieskau circled around him to the south. The expected clash occurred on September 8. Johnson got wind of the French army camped along the road his men had just traversed, a road they had hewn out of the forest. He detailed Colonel Williams with 1,000 men, and Hendrik with his Mohawks, to reconnoiter and find out just how the enemy lay. At the council of war the night before they were to start, the wise Hendrik shook his head. He picked up a stick which he broke easily, and then picked up several together which he could not break. "If they are to be killed, too many, if they are to fight, too few," he commented laconically. Johnson persisted, and the party set out the next morning. After about two hours' march, they walked straight into a carefully prepared French ambush. Indians scattered the hillside which ran up from the road, one behind every rock and every tree, while the French army waited in a bloc, a little ahead of them. Hendrik lifted up his fine old head. "I smell Indians," he sniffed, and a few moments later the first shot sang through the air. Fortune did not favor the brave that day, for imprudent, gallant

Colonel Williams and Hendrik, who had been the only one to see the folly of the expedition, were spotted as the leaders by the enemy, and were shot down as easily as ninepins. As his army swept up in pursuit, the ranks "doubled up like a pack of cards," Dieskau said later. But the day was saved by the rest of the English force arriving in reinforcement to give the French the stiffest fight of the year. Honors were even as the French retreated to the unmolested possession of the Crown Point fortress, while the English settled down for the winter in their newly-built Fort Henry at the foot of Lake George with Dieskau as their distinguished prisoner.

Stockbridge did not gainsay the opinion of Hendrik, which was that of the whole of New England: "If they are to be killed, too many." Dr. Thomas Williams wrote home several days after the battle, "Last Monday, the 8th instant was the most awful day that my eyes have ever beheld, & may I not say, that ever was seen in New England . . ." Two months later Abigail wrote to her friend, the merchant Abram Bookee in New York, to order a supply of tea and coarse Irish thread. She digressed from business to criticize sharply the way military affairs were being run. The death of Ephraim, flower of the flock, stung her to acid indignation. "There was perhaps not a gentleman in the whole army who could have been less easily spared," she wrote. She went on to analyze the situation with masculine clarity of mind. What if they had taken Crown Point at the loss of thousands of precious lives? They would not possibly have been able to hold it against Canada's whole force. If they had burned it, the French would have built it up again in a month. "Upon ye whole it looks as if our Councils were Darkened, wisdom in a remarkable manner hid from those yt Should be Wise." A rational plan of attacking Canada on all fronts, so that the enemy's force should be divided, might have some hope of success. Then the men would "fight Ye Common Enemy rather than their own men or Ye trees." At the end of the letter, after competently disposing of her business with Mr. Bookee, she confessed that a change of scene would be agreeable. "I long to be with you Eating Lobsters Crabs & Oisters & Drink lemons: But must Content myself with Small Bear & Country fires & yet is to good for me Since I am Suffered to live when So many of my Dearest friends are gone to ye Dead."

The French war was to drag on for almost three years longer, and western Massachusetts had frankly lost the stomach for it. A generation had been born, grown to manhood and sunk into its grave on a constant diet of fear. Was the new generation to suffer a similar experience?

The year 1756, succeeding the doubtful victory at Lake George, was the darkest Stockbridge had seen. One sergeant and five privates had been left for the protection of the town; the blockhouse which had been established at Pontoosuc was equally weak. An occasional Indian carrier, running in with news from the outside world, did nothing to reassure the settlers. It was said that while the new commander, Lord Loudon, who had been sent over from England, sat at Albany with his army, the enterprising Montcalm had marched on Oswego, where after a short attack he had succeeded in raising the French colors. The soldiers at Fort William Henry were sick and demoralized by the new ruling that no colonial officers should hold a rank above that of captain. Nearer home, the two commanding officers at Fort Massachusetts, on a hunting expedition ten miles from the fort, had been seized by Indians and treated to the usual horror of scalping and tomahawking.

Dr. Bellamy, an old pupil of Edwards, who had the parish at Bethlehem in Connecticut, begged him to bring his family down there. The town was no longer safe. Edwards, who lived in a world entirely independent of the success of the British arms, refused to leave Stockbridge, but sent the six remaining children of the boarding school down to his friend. Thus finally closed the long and troubled chapter of the Mohawk school. A conviction of its failure must have crept even into the sanguine heart of Mr. Hollis for no more is heard from him. The small number of Mohawks who had finally turned out for the Crown Point expedition—the mission pushing on one side, Sir William Johnson pulling on the other—had caused the Legislature to drop the whole scheme.

So serene was Edwards in the face of danger that he even allowed his daughter, Esther, who was married to President Aaron Burr of Princeton, to come and pay him a visit that September. She left at home in the nursery a little two-year-old son, who was named Aaron after his father, and who was later to make a place for himself in American history. Esther Burr, arrived in Stockbridge after the wearisome and dangerous journey from Princeton, found it difficult to rise to her father's metaphysical calm. Her diary written at this time is an argument between the flesh and the spirit: "September 2: Almost overcome with fear, last night and Thursday night we had a watch at this fort and most of the Indians came to lodge here. Some thought that they heard the enemy last night. . . . O how distressing to live in fear every moment . . . September 3: I proposed when I came from home to tarry here till the Second week in October but believe I shall shorten my visit since things are so ordered and I am so distracted with fears . . . September 4: Sabbath heard 4 excellent Sermons tho so ill for want of sleep that I am hardly mySelf . . . I hant had a nights Sleep since I left New York. . . . Since I have been here I may say I have had none. September 5: I grow worse and worse, more afraid than ever . . . if I happen to drowse I am frighted to death with dreams, as for sleep, tis gone, and I shall go too if things dont alter . . . September 8: I want to be made willing to die in any way God pleases, but I am not willing to be butchered by a barbarous enemy nor cant make myself willing . . . The Lord Reighns and why ant I sattisfied, he will order all for the best for the publick and for me, and he will be glorified let all the power on Earth and Hell do their worst . . . September 11: Proposed to my Father to set out for home next week, but he is not willing to hear one word about it, so I must tarry the proposed time and if the Indians get me, they get me, that is all I can say, but tis my duty to make myself as easy as I can . . ."

Battle, murder, and sudden death during these crowded Stockbridge years had not kept Edwards from the clockwork regularity of thirteen hours of study a day at his six-sided table. With the works of the liberals spread before him upon its revolving surface, he waged war against an easy Christianity, the religion of a benevolent God. *The Freedom of the Will* and *Original Sin* were written at this time. They were great boulders of logic that were to stand guard before the backwater of Calvinism, against the rising tide of liberal thought, for almost a hundred years. In the extradimensional world of the spirit—the only world of clear-cut reality to Edwards—the great drama of the soul was enacted. In *The Freedom of the Will* he establishes that men are utterly dependent for action on God. This led him into the contemplation of original sin. If God was in complete control, why was He not then the author of sin? This problem, that has puzzled the philosophers through the ages, Edwards handled with dexterity. Sin was the absence of God, the withdrawal of God, like the sun hiding itself behind a cloud.

Although a God "that holds you over the pit of hell, much as one holds a spider or some lothsom insect over the fire" is revolting to modern thought, still He controlled the lives of the Congregationalists as late as 1850. The fear of hell provoked the hope of heaven. The wrath of God gave shape to human life, and under the preaching of Edwards's disciples, who worked out in mathematical formulas what with him had been the inspiration of the spirit, all natural spontaneity and effervescence were carefully ruled out. So-called Puritanism, that dread taint that has clung to New England ever since, was the practical result of those years of merciless thinking that Edwards spent in Stockbridge.

It was with a sense of relief that the more intelligent listened to the preaching of William Ellery Channing at the end of the first quarter of the nineteenth century. It was the beginning of the return swing of the pendulum. Eagerly they again embraced the idea of God as a loving Father. Straying sheep would be gathered into the fold, and the repentant Prodigal Son was sure of forgiveness. Christ upon the Cross faded into the less compelling figure of Christ as a moral teacher. The emphasis slowly shifted from the perfectibility of man with the grace of God to the perfectibility of man with the willing help of God, until in our day it has become the perfectibility of man without God at all.

The pendulum has swung away to its logical conclusion. To modern Stockbridge the flight of Edwards's mystical poetry soars very wide of the mark: "To go to heaven fully to enjoy God, is *infinitely* better than the most pleasant accommodations here. Fathers and mothers, husbands, wives, or children, or the company of earthly friends, are but shadows; but the enjoyment of God is the substance. These are but scattered beams, but God is the sun. These are but streams, but God is the fountain. These are but drops, but God is the ocean. Therefore it becomes us to spend this life only as a journey toward heaven . . ." Edwards transmuted the green and blue and golden texture of a summer day in Stockbridge into terms of the spirit: "The beauties of nature are really emanations or shadows of the excellency of the Son of God. So that when we are delighted with flowery meadows and gentle breezes of wind, we may consider that we see only the emanations of the sweet benevolence of Jesus Christ . . . the green trees and fields, and singing of birds are the emanations of His infinite joy and benignity. The easiness and naturalness of trees and vines are shadows of His beauty and loveliness. The crystal rivers and murmering streams are the footsteps of His favor, grace, and beauty. When we behold the light and brightness of the sun, the golden edges of an evening cloud or the beauteous bow, we behold the adumbrations of His glory and goodness; and in the blue sky, of His mildness and gentleness . . ."

These passionate words have lost their meaning to a generation intent upon raising itself by its own bootstraps. They are like some beautiful but archaic music. And upon the exact spot where they were written, doctors with infinite patience, kindness, and industry are teaching men to live in a Godless world. Jonathan Edwards must often turn in his grave.

In 1757, with the Williamses reduced in number, Stockbridge again seemed to offer peace to Edwards. The Ephraims, young and old, were in their graves, and the Dwights had moved to Great Barrington. Here in a house finer and more pretentious than the Sergeant house, they lived in great elegance and dignity until Dwight's death in 1765. No one was left in the old Williams stronghold on the Hill but Elijah, a still youthful figure, and Josiah, sickening to an early death from a bullet wound received at Crown Point.

The Mohawks and the storms that had raged over them had gone forever, and the town was composed for the most part of sad, gentle-faced Mahicans. Little Jonathan Edwards, only six years old when his father moved to Stockbridge, never talked English outside his own house, for all his playmates were Indians. Even now, after twenty years of settlement, the total number of courageous souls who dared risk life and limb on this exposed frontier consisted of eighteen white families in all.

With Woodbridge to take most of the responsibility of the Indians, Edwards's ministerial duties were not heavy, and a serene and studious old age seemed just within his grasp. He was gathering himself for his mightiest, most monumental effort, *A History of the Work of Redemption,* when events occurred which were to alter his life completely. His son-in-law died suddenly at Princeton, and to his horrified amazement Edwards found himself elected to succeed him.

In vain he pleaded with the Princeton authorities that he was the wrong man for the position. His constitution was, he said "in many respects peculiarly unhappy, attended with flaccid solids, vapid, sizy, and scarce fluids, and a low tide of spirits; often occasioning a kind of childish weakness & contemptibleness of speech, presence & demeanor . . ." He was better at the written than the spoken word. A council of ministers was convoked at Stockbridge to deliberate as to whether he should stay where he was or go to Princeton, and they decided he should go. When he heard the unwelcome news, he buried his face in his hands and burst into tears. Failure at Northampton, failure with the Indians, failure finally to complete his life work here, blended to produce this burst of emotion.

A few days later he stood in the rough wooden pulpit for the last time, bending a strangely prophetic gaze upon the congregation, one third rough, burly pioneer, two thirds vacillating, shifty-eyed Indian. He began the Twentieth Chapter of Acts in his quiet, even voice: "And now brethren, I go bound in the spirit into Jerusalem, not knowing the things that shall befall me there . . . For I know that after my departing shall grievous wolves enter in among you, not sparing the flock . . ." He read to the end, and then preached his last sermon on the text, "We have here no continuing city." A prescient glance into the future showed him that the grand experiment was at an end that had drawn so many and such diverse characters, for as many reasons, to give time, money, and energy to this border village. It was a brave roster that had engaged in making a silk purse out of a sow's ear: John Sergeant, John Stoddard, Governor Belcher, Mr. Hollis, His Royal Highness the Prince of Wales, Isaac Watts, Brigadier General Dwight, and Ephraim Williams. Now twenty years had passed and Edwards, bidding the Indian town good-bye, knew that it could be "no continuing city."

His own career was to be checked summarily a few weeks after his arrival at Princeton, by a fatal smallpox inoculation, and he was not to see the fulfillment of his prophecy for the Indians. Even Timothy Woodbridge was inclined to be pessimistic about them, feeling that some fatal magnet drew them to all the bad in civilization. They retained an abiding affection for him who had been their patient schoolmaster during all these years. Since 1750, when the land had been divided in severalty, he had brooded over their property like an old hen and, up to the time of Edwards's departure, had been fairly successful in keeping it intact. There is a touching demonstration of their affection for him in a petition to the General Court to be allowed to make him a present of 350 acres "for his continued kindness and care . . . for upward of 20 years."

The peace that was established between England and France in 1761 was to encourage enormously the western migration. Stockbridge had its share of pioneers, who were intent on staking out farms and building houses for themselves, and who did not pay much attention to the Indians. Johannes Metoxin still blew hopefully upon his conch-shell, and he and King Ben (Konkapot's successor as sachem) were selectmen, as well as on the committee for seating the church.

But these were empty honors. Although elected to office by necessity—for it was illegal for the English to function without them—they were not called upon to act. In the old days with Woodbridge as selectman "who gently and gradually . . . lead our people into the Knowledge of government and benefits of the English laws," the Indians "went on lovingly with our English brethren" in the management of the town. Now no one called upon the Indian selectmen or asked their advice about village affairs. Their deepest grievance was the election of Elijah Williams as representative to the General Court in 1763. The Indians wailed like unjustly punished children that they hadn't understood that it was necessary to bring their votes on bits of paper. Nobody had explained. Now, by bringing in strangers from out of town to vote for him, they claimed, he had gotten himself elected. "He has made a party in town," they concluded on a familiar note, "endeavoring to get not only all power but all our lands." Elijah was clearly a chip of the old block.

The inevitable sale of the Indian lands had begun. How could it be otherwise? The pioneer from the east had money in his pocket. The Indian, with a perpetual hole in his, was lacking also in that staple New England commodity—character. All that he could call his own was the land, the shaggy green hills, the ample meadows bordering the river, where he loved to sit and watch the speckled backs of the shad and trout flash in the sun. As he was constitutionally unable to do anything to all this richly agricultural landscape, to plough it, to till it, or to fence it, it was taken away from him by those who could.

To sell land in the Indian town of Stockbridge was illegal without the sanction of the General Court, but the need was pressing and the smaller sales seem to have gone through without permission from Boston. An appeal to Elijah Williams runs: "Plase to Let Me have Som money for which

I desire that you take 50 Eacors of Land for Which I will Give Good deed I am allmost dad for Want of Provetion and I Prey Let Me have fore Pounds of Money Out my Land My Brother Jacob has already said something to you About it and Let My Brother Jacob Aukenock have 4 Pounds out of my Land for Me.—No More at Present & but Remain yr Humble Servent Abram Aukenock."

A year later, in 1763, a clean sweep was made, giving the title to all remaining land in Berkshire County, with the exception of Stockbridge, to the General Court for the price of £1,800. Stockbridge was left an Indian island in the sea of white occupation, only precariously intact. Now there was a bill due Dr. Erastus Sergeant for doctoring an Indian, to be paid in land. Or Samuel Rowley, in consideration of his liberating Jacob Unkamug from prison by paying £37, received 100 acres. An Indian, who accidentally killed an ox belonging to William Goodrich, gave land in payment.

Finally, in 1765, upon their "pressing application," the General Court decided to recognize a situation which existed anyway, and allowed the Indians to sell their lands for payment of debt. Larger and more generous slices were lopped off the Indians' property. In 1766, Rattlesnake Mountain went for £150 to "Josiah Jones, Joseph Woodbridge yeomen, Elijah Williams esqr. Joseph Jones Junior gentleman and Erastus Sergeant phycisian."

Dr. Stephen West had succeeded to Edwards's pulpit. Hurrying to serve the needs of his growing white congregation, the Indians fitted nowhere into the scheme of his life, and he did not have time even to try to understand them. In 1774, their old friend, Timothy Woodbridge, died. His last act was a recommendation to the General Court that a committee of white men be appointed to be guardians of the money that the Indians received for their lands. Enoch

Woodbridge and Samuel Brown were chosen by the Indians as agents in all their financial dealings.

A new generation of whites was now dealing with a new generation of Indians. Enoch Woodbridge would not protect their interests with the devotion that Timothy had. Timothy Edwards, returning to town in 1772 to start a store, would be more preoccupied with his merchandise than his father had ever been with metaphysics. It was a cold world, with less room in it for Indians every year that passed. But the new generation was to produce one friend of the old stamp. In John Sergeant, Abigail's son, survived a single spark of the missionary zeal which had founded the town thirty-six years before. A gentler, less incisive John Sergeant, he had grown up with the sheep-dog instinct strong within him. For a number of years he had been studying theology under Dr. West, and had gradually assumed the Indian services. In 1775, Dr. West was thankful formally to hand over to him this responsibility, for which he received a salary of $400 from The Society for the Propagation of the Gospel.

The split was now complete between the Indians and the whites. They each had their own ministers, attended separate schools, and the Indians were perched forlornly on the outskirts of the town. King Ben lived at the western extremity in a little frame house. Tradition claims that he sold it to Electa Sergeant before he died in 1781, at the advanced age of 104. King Solomon, who succeeded him, pitched his wigwam across the river from Laurel Hill, on a piece of land that for the moment he could call his own. Here he held around him what shreds of independence and dignity he could. The empty form of the old town government, half Indian, half white, persisted until 1779, which was the last year that an Indian held office in the town.

Their hour had clearly struck. The hunting ground which had been theirs time out of mind belonged to the white man.

They must gather up their mongrel inheritance, neither English nor Indian, and depart. Their removal to a tract offered them by the Oneida tribe in Madison County, New York, in the year 1785, was to be the first of many and, like old trees with their roots struck deep in the native soil, they stood up badly under transplanting. With each removal, as they traveled gradually farther west, the sap ran less freely, their vitality diminished. Color and character fail to emerge from the dry statistics of the missionaries as they labored painfully on decade after decade. The picture they give of the Indians presents a discouraging uniformity from beginning to end: intemperance, sloth, and broken promises to reform—always one step forward and two steps back. Occasionally the dull pages are enlivened by the interpolation of an Indian speech, some Chief melodiously lifting up his voice to lament the tragedy of his race. For they were always to retain this grave dignity of utterance, no matter how low they fell in the world.

The new territory under the protection of the Oneidas was hopefully called New Stockbridge, and there, between 1783 and 1788, the Indians—about 200 in number—gathered. Sergeant traveled back and forth between the new Stockbridge and the old, rounding up the stragglers until 1796 when he and his family settled permanently in the Oneida tract. Everything that could be thought of was done to uplift and sustain. His daughter even started a Female Society for Promoting Good Morals, Industry and Manufactures among the women of the tribe, and monthly concerts were instituted. The land was rich, well watered with lakes and streams. Under the wing of the Oneidas they were more isolated from the whites, but it was no use. In 1796, The Society for the Propagation of the Gospel making its rounds, sadly shook its head over New Stockbridge. The Oneidas, it seemed, were undesirable neighbors. "The indecency of the males, they being universally sans culottes is not a favorable symptom and hard treatment the women receive from their husbands does not indicate the prevalence of Christian principles to any great extent." In a flash of clear-sightedness the report stated that the Stockbridge Indians seemed insensible to the advantages offered them and unaccountably "attached to their ancient habits which are now become impracticable. They must lay aside the character of hunters, because their game is gone, & its haunts are rendered infinitely more valuable by cultivation. They cannot be warriors, because they have no enemies to contend with. If, therefore, they continue to despise husbandry, the only remaining source of opulence & independence, they must either retire to some distant region of the American forest, or live as spendthrifts on the price of their lands; or become strollers & beggars . . ."

By 1808, it had become evident that their tenure on New Stockbridge was as insecure as it had formerly been on the original Stockbridge. Characteristically they pleaded with the Governor and Council of New York to "buy a part of their Dish" in order to enable those who so wished to be on their way again. A tract on the White River in Ohio near the border of Indiana had been given by the Miami tribe to the Stockbridges and the Delawares, who were already established there. Aware of the pressure to sell, to which the Delawares were being subjected by the whites, the older members of the Stockbridge tribe were reluctant to move, but the Delawares wrote reassuringly: "When we rise in the morning, we have our eyes fixed toward the way you are to come, in expectation of seeing you coming to sit down by us as a nation." In 1818, a group of sixty or seventy bold hearts set forth, armed with Scott's *Commentary* and a farewell address of Sergeant, which he enjoined them to read at least once a year. But the best-laid plans of Indians could be guaranteed to go astray. Before they arrived at White River, news reached them that the

Delawares had sold their land. Disheartened, they scattered, some to return home to New Stockbridge, some to hang on in Ohio, dumbly and hopelessly waiting for the United States government to restore them their lands.

As time went on, and a land company in New York became anxious to get hold of the rich Oneida territory, it became evident that this nation, "scattered and peeled, and trodden under the foot of others," as one of their teachers described it, must move on. Starting in 1822, for nine years they slowly trailed westward. A new tract had been secured for them near Green Bay, Wisconsin, on the Fox River. They took their Bible with them this time—a sure sign that New Stockbridge would see them no more.

Here in a depth of wilderness so unbroken as not yet to have evolved itself into the state of Wisconsin, they built another New England town, rough as a child's drawing, but clearly recognizable in its outlines. John Metoxin, descendant of the conch-shell Metoxin, and his wife established in this territory the first Puritan church. It was complete with two tithingmen, who wielded their switches over the heads of the irreverent, and a Sabbath School, run along orthodox lines. The Sabbath began at sunset on Saturday evening, in the old fashion. John Sergeant and Timothy Woodbridge would have glowed with pride. They had learned at least a part of their lesson well. Religion always walking hand in hand with education, the first free school in a yet unborn Wisconsin soon followed, started by another Stockbridge Indian, Electa Quinney.

Before they were fairly settled, a blow fell upon them in the death of their old pastor, John Sergeant, far away in New Stockbridge. His last strength had been spent persuading a few lingering and ingrained New Stockbridgians to go west. His death accomplished what his efforts could not, for without him New Stockbridge became an alien land. Bewildered, they declared that their "sun was setting and did not know but darkness would succeed." Shivering, the last of the tribe turned west. If they hoped that Fox River, Green Bay, Wisconsin, was to be a resting place, they were disappointed. Only three years later they were on the road again. It was the same story. Their presence on the Fox River interfered with the whites' monopoly of the water power. Again church, school, sawmill, and pathetic frame dwellings were thrown into the discard, and the tribe moved on. This time the new settlement, on the east side of Lake Winnebago, received the old name of Stockbridge.

The Indian memory was long, reaching easily over time and distance. During these years of wandering, occasionally a solitary Indian, homesick for a sight of the happy valley, would turn up in Stockbridge. One day, after the removal to Lake Winnebago, an ancient survivor of the old days was found seated on a slope above the town, gazing sad-eyed at the familiar outline of hill and valley. What was he thinking of, sitting there in wooden immobility? The words of another member of his tribe may have described the current of his thoughts: "Where are the twenty-five thousand in number and four thousand warriors who constituted the power and population of the great Muh-he-co-new Nation in 1604? They have been victims of vice and disease which the white men imported. The small-pox, measles and 'strong waters' have done the work of annihilation . . . One removal follows another and thus your sympathies and justices are evinced in speedily *fulfilling the terrible destinies of our race* . . ." A grandson of the original Sergeant was delegated to question him. Yes, he had come all the way from Winnebago, and wanted to see the town once more before his own departure from this world. He was not communicative but gravely accepted as his right and without thanks the hospitality that was offered him. He lingered several days, revisiting his ancestral countryside, and then disappeared as he had come, silently and alone.

Another story of this period concerns the local blacksmith. One day he ran out of coal, and an Indian—for there were a few who had never left—volunteered to go and get him some. He came back with a load of anthracite coal, which he said he had found on Monument Mountain, somewhere on the Stockbridge side. No one since has ever been able to find the place, for the Indian refused to tell his secret. It was a very small retaliation from the underdog.

The Reverend Cutting Marsh, missionary to the Stockbridge Indians in Wisconsin for fourteen years, finally gave up in 1848 in a mood of deep discouragement. "The trials which the Rev. David Brainerd experienced among the Indians 100 years ago are the trials of the missionary at the present day," he said. "Even now in the 3rd or 4th generation which has risen up since the first introduction of the Gospel amongst these Indians, fickleness, want of integrity of character, want of principle . . . want of love of truth, aversion to mental effort and an unconquerable one to restraint are amongst my severest trials . . ."

The sale of their property at Lake Winnebago followed in 1848, the same year that Mr. Marsh left them. In 1850 the American Board of Missions gave up supporting them and, with the departure of Mr. Marsh, their spiritual leadership was taken over by Jeremiah Slingerland, a somewhat unreliable half-breed, who had the distinction of having received an education at Dartmouth College. They now moved to Shawano County, Wisconsin, between the years of 1856 and 1859. Abandoned by the American Board of Missions, the old church lapsed. Mr. Slingerland obligingly became a Presbyterian, as that was the prevailing church of the neighborhood.

Gradually the years were erasing all traces of their remarkable history from the Stockbridge Indians, and they became more uniform with the other remnants of the great Indian tribes, who drag out a half-civilized existence on a reservation somewhere in the west. The wonderful Bible, that high-water mark of the Christian experiment, was mislaid and finally found by an enterprising Indian—in the rubbish heap! He pulled it out and dusted it off and it became his most cherished possession. Finally he consented to have it kept in the church in a safe, of which he alone knew the combination.

The Indians have bowed their heads to their inevitable tragedy, with their customary dignity. The following was written in 1810, but would fit any year in the last two centuries: "Brothers, with sorrowful hearts we now desire to look back a little, and view the ruins of our mighty trees—you can scarcely find where they are fallen—scarcely find any stump or roots remaining but if you look down near your feet, you will see the remnant of your brethren like small bushes, who now looking up speak to you, for you are become very great, you reach to the clouds you can see all over this island, but we can scarcely reach to your ankles.".

Chapter V

THE GROWTH OF THE ENGLISH TOWN

THE breathing spell which came after the French and Indian War was one of burgeoning for early Stockbridge. No longer did its citizens feel the menace of possible Indian descents. Now that Quebec had fallen, and with it the power of France in North America, the Joneses and the Woodbridges could take a firmer grip on their axes and lead their cattle to pasture with a peaceful heart. The raging wilderness of earlier days was assuming settled contours.

William Williams, Grand Panjandrum of the twenty log huts which called themselves Pittsfield, could write to his brother-in-law in the eastern part of the state, urging immediate immigration. Of the climate he could speak highly. "Languor, Sickness and Excruciating Pain were my Portion," he wrote, "while I . . . was Obliged to Tabernacle in the narrows between the West and East Mountains of Deerfield. Since I removed to this place I challenge any man in the Government to compare with me for Health and freedom from Pain. All my doctor's bill has been a gallipot or two of Unguent for the Itch . . . No Man or Woman that ever came and got settled among us wished themselves back. The air suited them and they felt frisk and alert." "This salubrious air," he claimed, "makes barren women bring forth men," and he went on to point with pride to his fellow citizens. "Look at Colonel Ephraim Williams in Stockbridge and Joseph

THE GROWTH OF THE ENGLISH TOWN 99

Woodbridge. They started poor and now they are exceedingly well off." This was, of course, all for the benefit of a brother-in-law who might be induced to buy some of the lands in which the family of Williams had so heavily invested. His long complaints to the General Court about his own embarrassed finances present a reverse side of the coin.

The picture William Williams painted was more than mere sales talk, however. There was plenty in the wooded hills and grassy meadows to attract settlers from the more civilized sections of the east. The soil had not yet become exhausted by recurrent crops. Wheat could be grown until the ground became too poor, then barley and rye, and finally beans. There was pasture for cattle and sheep, and brisk little streams on which to set up grist and fulling mills. What to John Sergeant had been a wilderness was now a possible real-estate development, and the citizens of Massachusetts were in enterprising mood. For over 100 years they had been in the New World and in the recent struggle with France the colonists had won their spurs. It had been their struggle, fought and won upon their own soil, and so intimately was it their affair that they even resented being taxed for the British soldiery they themselves had asked for. The surrender of Quebec was like a diploma to a graduating class. The colonists for the first time surveyed their untapped resources maturely. Were these to be exploited for their own benefit, or used to swell the revenues of a king thousands of miles away? As more and more immigrants moved into Berkshire and cut down the forests to build their log cabins, the future was big with that surmise.

In 1761, the County of Hampshire was divided and Berkshire incorporated. Of the new county Stockbridge was the most important settlement. As the century went on turnpikes were laid down, the road map of western Massachusetts came out of the rough, foreshadowing its modern shape. Just where the Great Barrington road crossed the Plain going up to Pittsfield, stood Stockbridge's first public house. It was called the Red Lion Inn, and its large signboard sported a rampant red lion with a fine green tail. Silas Pepoon, a man of substance, owned it. There were eight bedrooms and a large ballroom upstairs, where all the Stockbridge functions took place. Later on, this ballroom was to become famous in Berkshire history, but at first it was probably used mostly for country dances, when from miles around the farmers' girls arrived on pillions, seated behind their beaux. The parties lasted till long after midnight. "There was dancing and merrymaking among the young people," mildly deprecated Mr. J. E. A. Smith, Pittsfield historian. "The ladies sipped wine and cider and . . . the more seductive flip, while the gentlemen indulged in even more fiery and exciting beverages."

When the parties were not going on, Pepoon handed out hot punches and rum toddies over the bar in the public room and discussed the terrible condition of the roads. The end of Main Street had a way of disappearing under water when the meadows flooded. The biggest item in the town expense account for years to come was to be the repairing of highways and bridges. Those who could not afford to pay highway taxes were allowed to make them up in work, at the rate of three shillings a day, if they were fortunate enough to own a team.

Cater-cornered to the Red Lion stood the village store. It belonged to Timothy Edwards, and had a fine porch running along its front, quite a fancy step for the Stockbridge of those days. The store part was towards the east, and the family lived at the other end of the house, so that Timothy, by merely going from one room to another, could change from village potentate to shopkeeper. Down the street on the village green, near the burying ground, the meetinghouse demanded attention, and alterations were being suggested. Stockbridge was growing steadily and needed more church room. New pews were put in, the building was reclapboarded and new windows inserted. Their church was the core of life to the early settlers and the marks of its care the sign of their vitality.

Meanwhile people were moving in. The same names took turn and turn about as selectmen, fence viewers, tithingmen, hog reeves, and sealers of leather. Lawrence Lynch, Stockbridge's first Irishman, worked off his indenture to General Dwight and bought fifty acres of land at the foot of West Stockbridge Mountain, which is still known as Larrywaug. His first house soon proved too small for his fourteen children, and in 1800 he built another near by that has been the property of his family ever since.

Larry, so the story goes, had had a proud past in the old country, for his father was a baronet and owned a castle near Galway. But the young man had not liked his stepmother and enlisted under General Wolfe. There was little at the foot of West Stockbridge Mountain to mar the peace of growing old, save possibly the quiet depredations which went on in the vegetable garden, for the old Indian who had sold Larry the property could not bear to move away. He remained, a wistful neighbor in his tepee close by, occasionally helping himself to the Lynch cabbages.

The incoming English tide corresponded with the outgoing Indian one. When a dispute arose as to where the new meetinghouse should stand, its removal to a site halfway up the Hill, although nominally a compromise between the citizens of the Hill and the Plain, was in reality the sign of English domination.

Although there may have been difficulty in deciding where to put the new meetinghouse, there was none about the building itself. Even the repairs to the old edifice could not compass Stockbridge's swelling pride. The town wanted "a decent and honorable house." It felt intensely respectable and wanted its respectability to shine before men. In 1782, £1,000 was voted for the building, which could be paid in money, grain, or neat cattle, as the case might be. In succeeding years more money was appropriated for the same purpose. When finally the meetinghouse was finished and topped off with a fine weather vane in the shape of a fish, it took all the equipages in town, its two coaches and Madam Abigail Dwight's chaise, a long time to get there. Lines of carriages came over the meadows from Curtisville. Sometimes they tipped over going up the Hill, as the road was without a railing. Sometimes the dreary treeless stretch of what is now Church Street made the younger churchgoers so thirsty that they had to be excused in the middle of Dr. West's sermons to get a drink at the near-by spring.

Perhaps the minister wanted to make things easier for his flock. At any rate, he gave up the orchard ground which lay between his house and the meetinghouse, so that a road might be cut from the church over the Hill, sloping diagonally to meet Plain Street at the east end of the town. Even "the pedestrian villagers" used the new road, enjoying "its continuous views" and preferring it to "the burning sands of the plain." To accommodate them there was a long horse block outside the church and sheds for the horses. Sometimes the horses were tied to the fence at Asa Bement's near by. Tall pines grew in front of the church and there, always on time, was Dr. West, ready to greet his congregation. Inside the church, he bowed to the first families, seated in order of dignity in the pews just behind the choir, for the world was not left outside the door. Then he would read Dr. Watts's hymn, *Ye nations round the northern sea,* before climbing into the pulpit to begin his two-hour sermon.

The church was ugly enough, made of huge timbers and rickety shingles and painted white only on the outside. You could enter by three doors, from which stretched three aisles crossing each other at right angles. Another aisle ran clear around the church. There were three galleries and the deacons sat almost under the pulpit. As a special concession, the crotchety old bachelor, Dr. Partridge, who took care of Stockbridge for upward of sixty years, was allowed a pew of his own, which irreverent youth called the "partridge nest." It was a large open box, hung high over the central gallery, where he could keep his eye on the whole congregation. He was instructed to encourage singing as much as possible without going to the expense of hiring a teacher.

There were no carpets. No stove appeared for thirty years. Outside the winter winds blew so hard that the whole building shook and rattled, and the steeple had to be rebuilt on a smaller scale. When the next church was erected, the Hill church was torn down and carted away, so that nothing remains today but a few pine trees to tell the tale of so many years of pious Stockbridge going to its prayers.

Close by the meetinghouse was the town pound "to take care of strays," a necessary adjunct to any farming community where foals and yearling rams were constantly turning up in people's yards. A common pasture housed the village cattle, so people were careful to have their own particular mark. You could tell Josiah Jones's cattle anywhere by their "swallowtail, a hollow crop on the near ear, and a sloping piece cut off the top of the back ear." His son's marks were just the other way around, while Dr. West's stamp was a "short crop on both ears" of his cattle, sheep and hogs. These differences were important, for horses and cows had a way of getting out of the pasture, preferring the richer grasses of the unfenced burying ground and, in spite of town regulations, the swine would run at large.

By 1760, there were so many more whites than Indians in Stockbridge that an English school was necessary. Six pounds and ten shillings was voted for the purpose. By 1763, the selectmen were asked to find a teacher, and money appropriated supported the school and teacher as long as it lasted. To eke out expenses the teacher lived in the community, first with one family and then with another, teaching in return for his board. A committee visited the school every once in so often and heard the children's examinations.

From now on money was voted conscientiously each year for the maintenance of the schools with a continuous upward trend, so that by 1800 the sum had reached $750. In 1764, the town ordered two schoolhouses, and wished also to "procure a suitable person to keep an evening school in town for instructing in psalmody." In course of time three school districts were established, one on the Plain, one up the Hill in the northeastern section of the town, and another in the northwestern section.

There was little or no opportunity for an elaborate education when the practical side of life demanded so much attention, and the early citizens of Stockbridge were men of all trades. A justice of the peace, who was also a member of the Legislature, who was also a speculator in land, who was also a trader, who was also a church warden, had scarcely time for the amenities. Even so, among Elijah Williams's papers, sandwiched between sheriffs' suits, accountings for the sale of iron, receipts for Indian land, and notices for the purchase of negro servants, are found several notebooks, full of early English and Roman history. How large a part Tarquin and Queen Boadicea filled in the life of this frontier businessman it would be hard to say, but there are the pages in close, fine handwriting about battles and the principal events of the Roman Republic.

Looking back upon the early town is like looking at the present one through the large end of a telescope. A definite social, economic, and political foundation is there, but in embryo. It is as if the Williamses, the Dwights, the Woodbridges and the Joneses carried upon their stout persons all the implications of the civilization that was to be. The stage had so few actors that those few had to play all the parts. The same figures appear again and again, doers and done-by, in the scene. There is hardly a paper signed in the town for any purpose whatsoever where the names of Samuel Brown, Josiah Jones, Elnathan Curtis, Asa Bement and Timothy Edwards do not appear. They appoint each other, arrest each other, excommunicate each other, trade with each other, and pretty well manage to keep the wealth and executive and political power of baby Berkshire in their own firm hands. When in 1761 Governor Bernard was faced with the appointment of four justices to the Court of Common Pleas, no one was in the least surprised that Joseph Dwight, Timothy Woodbridge, William Williams and John Ashley were chosen. Elijah Williams was made sheriff, then a post of considerable dignity. It was a family party—nearly everyone related to everyone else. By marriage as well as by ability, the persistent minority kept themselves on top.

The trading of the day, like the social system, was in miniature. It was compact, closely welded together. Dominating it, emerging from yellowed account books and bills of sale, is the figure of Elijah Williams, son of Colonel Ephraim. As a boy at college, the letters he had received from his father, urging him to make good use of his time, to improve himself while he had the opportunity, must have borne some fruit. From the passage in which old Ephraim urges complete dedication to God, shortly followed by the statement that he had "a vastly better scheme" for his brother "than buying in the Jerseys," young Elijah must have absorbed that mixture of piety and shrewdness which is New England's acknowledged contribution to the world. Elijah quickly discovered a business future in the little settlement of Queensborough, named for King George's queen, on the other side of the mountain, west of Larrywaug. There he founded some iron-works, opened a store, and saw to it that roads were built and the minister paid. In 1774, he obtained its incorporation as the town of West Stockbridge from the General Court and carried the deed home from Boston in his pocket. Years afterwards it was difficult to establish whether West Stockbridge was a town at all, for Elijah had lost the Act of Incorporation. Small wonder, since he had so many things to do!

His trading must have begun even before that, for in 1762 we find a bill from him to David Van Schaack for "rum, coffee, sugar, pepper, nutmeg, indigo, tea," and two years later Van Schaack in his turn asks for money upon Elijah's account, and we find that he has bought "linen, one handkerchief, pipes," and, among other items, "blue coating, 5 yards. 3 dozen buttons, which you may return if they don't suit. I expect others next week."

Now, for the first time, the Van Schaack brothers loom large in Stockbridge affairs. They, too, were gentlemen traders, solid Dutchmen who lived at Kinderhook and were to suffer during the Revolution for their Tory sympathies. Henry afterwards bought a house and settled down in Pittsfield.

Trading was interspersed with polite intercourse and gave an excuse for passing the time of day. Henry Van Schaack insists upon inserting stockings with other goods as a present to Elijah; Mrs. Van Schaack asks for a saddle of venison and cranberries from him in return.

Elijah's financial transactions carry us out of the world of dollars and cents into a child's arithmetic book. Actual money being scarce, trade was carried on by a process of barter, so Robert Hefflin asks Elijah for cloth for one pair of trousers "and you shall have the ashes as soon as I can get them to you." Elijah exchanges a yoke of oxen and a cow for fifty acres of land. Another of his accounts with David Van Schaack places upon the debit side "buttons, wheat, gloves, tea, locks, rings, tape, thread, ale, molasses and nails, sugar, chalk and garters." And upon the credit "oxen, and an English plough, appletrees and currants." So buttons and currants, garters and frying-pans were bandied about in a sort of ring-around-a-rosy of mutual benefit, the complex needs of human beings squeezed within the narrow margin of what a single trader could supply. "A cask of as good a hogshead of Antigua rum as ever was sent to your place" comes to Elijah, while Van Schaack writes, "Your curtains are finished." Theodore Sedgwick complains, "wrote for the black britches Patern and not Drawers. You sent the Drawers but not Trimming which beg you would send." And Elijah charges Nicholson, "to making a shirt for Indian Henry 5 shillings." Credit was easily obtainable. Bearers of notes to Elijah ask to be paid a certain amount upon account, often some one else's. Accounts were settled every once in so often in goods or land, if actual money was not available.

Elijah dealt not only with the neighboring Van Schaacks, but with the world outside Berkshire. His West Stockbridge iron was sold in London; his potash also found a market there. Iron was priced at £20 per ton. Nathaniel Hazard of Philadelphia, between arranging shipments of this commodity, gives advice as to how to grind flour "so as to make it white and lively." William Imlay, in trade in New York, writes that he is anxious to serve the West Stockbridge magnate, offering to take no commission if he is paid in goods. He sends ingratiatingly "a piece of Tear Nought for Tryall, which we think must suit you as you employ a great number of laborers." But Elijah was not merely interested in his laborers' clothes. This homespun manufacturer in a pioneering town got his woolen goods from England. "It is of importance to stores in the country," writes Nathaniel

Hazard, "to have their coarse woolens, such as coatings, bearskins, friezes, baizes, as early as possible in the fall." He expected his consignment shortly and "nothing but the loss of the ship can in reason disappoint us."

But Elijah, magnificent as he was, had his difficulties. Mr. Imlay has to dun: "The very great disappointments we meet with in collecting our debt really distresses us. I therefore make no doubt but that you will exert yourself as much as possible to give us all the assistance you can. We flatter ourselves that from the great crops in your neighborhood that your remittance will be very considerable." This hope however, was destined to disappointment. Other letters follow: "We cannot extend our credit more than one year." And the year following: "We can hardly hold our heads above water." They were in a "truly distressed condition."

Imlay's distressed condition did not prevent Elijah from buying land in Pittsfield that same year, also "one black mare with a white face . . . and one black horse, white face, no white feet." Nevertheless, though his mind may have been upon his live stock, Elijah really did sell his land to pay his debts, and succeeded in paying nearly all of them. He kept an account book in his pocket of those who owed him money, and in justice to him it should be remembered that that account book includes nearly all of the names in Stockbridge at the time.

From the midst of fusty business transactions, Elijah's private life stands out in relief, dealt with in the matter-of-fact fashion of the eighteenth century, upon which the glasses of the present day focus so much more naturally than lenses dimmed by the sentimentality and blurred by the disapproval of the century which comes in between. Mr. Smith, in all the conscious morality of the Victorian era, deplored the degeneracy of the times. "With the amelioration of manners," he wrote, "went the decadence of morals."

THE GROWTH OF THE ENGLISH TOWN

In this connection, there may be a sinister coincidence: In 1762, Elijah bought a gold necklace from Paul Revere, which cost him £18, and two years later one Mary Willson complained in the Great Barrington court that she was delivered of a bastard male begotten by Elijah Williams, and sued for his support. What is more, she got it; which is one case where intrenched privilege did not work, for Elijah was a powerful man. Whatever happened to Mary and the bastard male is lost in the shuffle of more important events, but there is a chance mention of Widow Mary Willson's house in Stockbridge and perhaps she ended her days in a spurious respectability. Elijah went on his way unabashed. A suit for which the materials billed were "scarlet cloth, shalloon, gold vellum lace, fustian, two pairs of leather pockets and lining for breeches . . . velvet for the collar, and a pair of gold straps," the whole amounting to £12. 3s. 9d., did not exactly hide his impenitent light behind a bushel. Later Imlay refers to an order of "cloth for a suit," and hopes that his (Elijah's) "wedding will be productive of the most perfect felicity." So apparently Elijah forgot about Mary and let us hope she forgot about him.

Moral emphasis changes with the centuries. There was little fuss made over Mary Willson, yet David Crocker "Unnecessarily travelled on the Lord's day by setting out in the daytime on horseback to go to Lee and rode through a part of West Stockbridge, all of which is contrary to law." And among Elijah Dwight's memoranda there is a warrant of arrest "for hitching up a horse upon a Sabbath."

The community was a patriarchal one. Planting, reaping, herding of sheep and cows, taking the corn to be ground at the grist mill on Yale Hill followed upon each other's steps in dutiful round. Hazard might tempt Elijah with woolen goods imported from England, but these were unheard-of luxuries for most of the village, where all the work of clothing the family was done at home. Only the tailoring was sent out—very often to the "she tailors" whose business it was to cut and sew. Frontier democracy early made itself felt in the difficulty of obtaining domestic servants, and most women did a good deal of their own work. There were the great awkward pots to put on the cranes in the big fireplaces, the unpainted floors to keep clean, the candles and soap to be made. When physical work was over, there was the ever-present question of saving one's immortal soul. Dr. West, who was just beginning to be well known, gave all his time to this matter.

When summoned to Stockbridge, Dr. West was chaplain of Fort Massachusetts. One of the Williamses, perhaps, had heard the young man well spoken of, and suggested his taking the place Jonathan Edwards's call to Princeton had left vacant. West had come originally from Tolland, Connecticut. He had graduated from Yale in 1755, and after that had taught school and studied theology at Hatfield. He was licensed to preach by the Association of Ministers in Hampshire in 1757, just a year before he came to Stockbridge.

West was not an impressive figure, being small of stature and plain of face, but he never rose to preach without trembling, and there was great fire of eloquence in his words. His boots were always shined, his collar with the white band adjusted as it should be. His one weakness—a pride in his legs, which were firm and shapely—made him wear the old-fashioned knee breeches long after most people had discarded them. He stood very straight, all the five feet of him, and "his eye was ever ready to flow with gentle pity and tender sympathy."

Upon his arrival Dr. West found himself in a delicate position. His kindly nature led him towards Arminianism, a doctrine which softened Calvin's hard and fast rule of predestination, by admitting the possibility of conditional salvation. The tradition of the Stockbridge church was now of the more orthodox Edwards brand. Arriving at his new parish, and anxious as always to do the right thing, conscious too of the extremely prickly skin of New England congregations (they were taxed for their minister, gave him firewood and intended to get their money's worth), West doubtless cast about for orientation. In his quandary it was natural for him to turn to Dr. Samuel Hopkins. He took to driving over to Great Barrington in his two-wheeled top carriage. His hat and whip were always laid out for him the day before, that he might not be a minute late in starting. The Reverend Dr. Hopkins returned the visit, his large ungainly form the only unordered object in West's immaculate study. St. Bernard and pug dog, they spent hours discussing the weighty theological abstractions of the times. Could church membership be claimed by the children of church members? Dr. West, always charitable, hoped that it could, but Hopkins was adamant. To allow "meer membership," as opposed to "believing membership," to entitle you to the benefits of grace was opening the door of the Pandora's box of theological troubles, which he and Edwards had had such a time stamping out.

So the long afternoons wore on. Phantasms of heresies, Arminianism, Socinianism, Pelagianism, and that new horror, Unitarianism, beat their wings in the good doctors' faces, while they gave all the weight of their trained minds to hairsplitting questions which were to lose all their meaning for the generations to come. The more Dr. West talked to Dr. Hopkins, the more strongly he fell under his relentlessly logical conception of God. There was no sentimental sloppiness about this doctrine and West was careful to be exact in everything.

As Hopkins's theories gained ground upon the little doctor, he grew more and more humble. He was convinced of his own depth of sin and walked from the Plain to the Hill and back again, wondering why, when he had undertaken the charge of others' souls, he had so neglected his own. The conflict of his spirit became agonizing. Perhaps his stubborn human nature took a long time to accept gladly the belief that he would probably burn forever after his ministry had ceased. He had not reached the stage where he could understand why, under the circumstances, God was so particularly merciful. Of what avail is punctuality, the neatness of his ways, and the kindness of his heart against the fearful odds of his ultimate undoing?

But at last he received "a good hope through grace." One Sabbath, a pious old woman in the village remarked that Dr. West was a new man, and he himself dated his conversion from that moment. Perhaps he lifted up his eyes unto the hills. From Bear Mountain and Monument came his help. He experienced the identification of his will with God's, whose service is perfect freedom, which constituted the psychical phenomenon of conversion.

He dates the improvement of his character from then on. How wicked, one wonders, was he before? And it is strange that the wholesale adoption of such a horrible doctrine could have a softening effect upon his soul. "I dreaded him," wrote Catherine Sedgwick, "and certainly did not understand him in my youth. He was then only the dry, sapless embodiment of polemical divinity. It was in my mature age and his old age that I discovered his Christian features and found his unsophisticated nature as pure and gentle as a good little child's."

Probably most of the boys and girls sitting on hard pews in front of him felt the same way. He was not going to let his kindly nature interfere with his solemn duty. New England lived on sermons, and sermons Dr. West determined they should have. His Thanksgiving and Fast Day discourses were ready weeks ahead. His rhetoric was certainly effective.

Young Albert Hopkins afterwards maintained that Sunday after Sunday he would go to church in a cheerful frame of mind. As the minister stated his text and went on to take up the various headings of his sermon, point by point, the boy began to tremble. At the end of the afternoon service, hope had left him and he departed from the church a doomed man.

When newspapers came few and far between, doctrine absorbed the intellectual life of even a farming community. Congregations bristled with local ecclesiastical pride or criticism. Theology was carried out of the pulpit to the counter at Timothy Edwards's store, to the bar at Silas Pepoon's. The portentous John Bacon, just moved to Stockbridge, who had gone into farming and politics and become a country gentleman, had been dismissed from the Old South Church in Boston because he had differed from his parishioners about the doctrine of the Atonement, and the Halfway Covenant. He was a dogmatic fellow and argued violently with West. "These are my sentiments on the subject," he would thunder, thinking by mere avoirdupois to down his adversary.

Dr. West was a match for him, well aware of the responsibility of his position. Like Samuel Hopkins, he had reduced the metaphysical poetry of Edwards to a system of rules and regulations. Stockbridge was "well indoctrinated," says one of its historians, as if it were well inoculated. His sermons touched many subjects, and that upon Moral Agency made him famous. He preached on marriage and on the impotency of sinners. Upon infant baptism his ideas were possibly a little lax. He was inclined to think that children were not necessarily damned because they had not been baptized. Fathers and mothers who had dedicated themselves to the Lord by means of conversion, if they so dedicated their children, might nourish some hope of their receiving grace. On the whole, in spite of this slight wavering, West's views were as sound as Hopkins or Edwards could have wished. He maintained,

"Christian parents feel that they themselves are sinners, that they merit to be sent to hell. They feel that they have been the wicked instruments of communicating a sinful existence to their offspring . . . If God, therefore, visiting their iniquities upon their children, should destroy them forever, they know that neither they nor their children would have the least reason for complaint."

Young men came to Stockbridge to study under Dr. West and boarded in his house. They were called the School of Prophets. Even young women came for instruction, and eventually he delivered a regular theological training course, where themes were written and questions given out. Young brains stirred the caldron of controversy. Darwin was as yet unborn, and the time when all this learning would be reduced to uselessness still remained far away.

The minister, as befitted his rôle, was a man of regular habits. Every morning as soon as he was dressed, he said his prayers. His breakfast toast always had to be of the same size. At seven o'clock in the evening he measured with his finger the exact amount of meat his housekeeper was to cook. Day after day found his routine unchanged. His two wives, even though the first was a Williams and Abigail's sister, scarcely interrupted him. Two pipes he allowed himself in the evening, then summoned his family to domestic worship, and after that, bed. Year after year melted into one another, as he instructed his pupils. He was serenely impervious to the strange new forces that were creeping in even to little Stockbridge, and the strange new thoughts passing through the minds of some of the well-indoctrinated boys and girls in front of him.

Stephen West was the servant as well as the pastor of his flock. The records of the Stockbridge church show it to be an entity with definite views of its own. The conception of a state in which the church ruled according to laws expressly set forth in the Bible, lingered in church affairs long after it had actually been severed from things temporal.

Sometimes the church was a court of law, and in this capacity it proved itself no respecter of persons. As in the past the Holy Roman Emperor had been subject to rebuke by the Pope of Rome, so even the social hierarchy of Stockbridge was humbled by the awful power of its church. In a dispute between Samuel Brown and no less a person than Timothy Edwards, the latter was discovered to be wrong.

In 1782, the very year the new meetinghouse was built, Sylvia Morgan was excluded from membership in the church for "associating with vain, light and airy company, & joining them in dances and frolicking, and accompanying with a man on Saturday night," which she herself admitted to be holy time. David Pixley was accused of taking the name of the Lord in vain, as well as of quarreling. For these sins he was excluded from the church, which generously gave him a chance to retrieve himself. A year later, however, he added the sin of "drinking spirituous liquors" to his other misdemeanors, and the church's patience became exhausted. The charge against him was supported and it was finally voted "that he be laid under the censure of the church . . . he continuing obstinate and impenitent under the means and measures which have been taken with him to convince him of his wickedness." The next year he was solemnly cut off. He enlisted as a soldier during the Revolution and distinguished himself, having found at last a suitable outlet for his erring ways.

The church tribunal consisted of the deacons and elders and no fault was too private for its accusing forefinger. Daniel Hutchinson was accused of unchristian conduct towards his neighbor in "refusing to suffer him to take water from a spring in his lot when he had plenty," while George Deming came under a charge of "undutifulness to his parents and unkindness to his family, indulging in idleness." Forgiveness was not granted until the accused had walked up the "broad alley"—the middle aisle of the church—and made his confession so that the whole congregation could hear.

There was one time, however, when this prying morality bit off more than it could chew, and brought down upon the village a tempest of controversy which became state-wide. The winds of doctrine blew furiously, the storm centering upon the rather valiant figures of one Mrs. Lavinia Deane, a young widow of amiable character and probably a pretty face, and Mr. John Fisk, keeper of one of the district schools. Mr. Fisk boarded with Mrs. Deane. He made himself as useful and as charming as possible, and before long wrought havoc in her exposed and susceptible heart. Gossip had it that they were to be married. Unfortunately, Mr. Fisk, in his short stay at Stockbridge, had not made a very good impression. It was not that he had done anything actually wrong, but he had been heard to say "I swear," and "damn it," and upon several occasions had used expressions that "savored of the language of the camp." Mrs. Deane had two little children, whose immortal souls, not to speak of her own, were in jeopardy under such an influence, and the church felt its clear duty was to take a stand. Deacons Curtis and Wilson were accordingly appointed a committee to "admonish Mrs. Deane to desist from marrying Mr. Fisk," until they could rest easy in their minds regarding him. Another committee was also appointed to look into Mr. Fisk's morals as well as his language. Their findings have been withheld from our sophisticated eyes but, whatever they were, they sufficed to make the brethren of the church decide that "it was inconsistent with the rules of the Word of God for Mrs. Deane to join in wedlock with the said John Fisk"—a person "openly immoral and profane."

In vain Lavinia Deane struggled to do the church's bidding. We can see her in the small house so narrowly separating her from her ardent and unregenerate lover, trying to interest herself solely in her children's concerns and the management of a manless household. She wanted to continue in the church, both for her own and her children's sakes. Climbing the Hill to the meetinghouse, in good standing with the congregation, was a necessary element to social security; and was Mr. Fisk's manly figure worth the price she had to pay? Surely it was better to be approved of by the church elders, to have Mrs. Elnathan Curtis smile at her across the aisle and earn the kindly nod of Dr. West, than to be the outcast wife of a handsome sinner. Yet she could not help arguing: Of what, exactly, had Mr. Fisk been accused? It was true that he swore, but she had spoken to him about this, and he had promised to be more careful. True, also, he had used "a few airy words," but he had *done* nothing wrong. Again true, he didn't seem to care very much what the brethren thought of him. As for the question of eternal salvation, he had been a soldier and did not understand such matters. All he wanted was Lavinia. Alas for morality, her struggle was shortly over. In the same month in which she had been "admonished" she married John Fisk. The church at Stockbridge promptly excommunicated her.

Mrs. Fisk was a woman of some spirit once she had made up her mind. Marriage evidently made her agree less and less with the church in regard to her husband's character. She determined to ask the advice of a council. Dr. West threw up his hands at the idea. He foresaw all the endless arguments, "unfriendly to our discipline," this entailed. The old quarrels about qualification for church membership would crop up if Mrs. Fisk secured the help of the churches she wanted. A great many of these, be it said to their shame, held that persons "visibly impenitent" could be admitted to communion and therefore, needless to say, to marriage with the elect. The Halfway Covenant was bound to rear its ugly head again, and West felt that he had settled that question once for all. If Mrs. Fisk would ask the ministers of all other orthodox churches, she was welcome to the council, otherwise not. Finally Mr. Fisk took a hand in the matter. There was a fight on and his blood was up. He suggested a council of six ministers, three to be chosen by his wife, three by the church. This proposal was agreed to and in 1779 the council met. Four clergymen and four laymen were in attendance. It adjourned and met again for two days with eleven clergymen and nine laymen. Then it again adjourned and again met for another two days. The little red schoolhouse in the northwestern district of the town—upon what is now the Harder property—was packed to the doors. Buzzing crowds whispered sinister rumors. What exactly had Mr. Fisk said? Mr. Whittlesey had seen Mr. Fisk and his stepson go by in a sleigh, the little boy holding the whip. He had distinctly heard, "God damn that whip, and God damn your soul to hell."

Now, if ever, a definite verdict was to be given these enormities. Ears strained to hear it. Then, lo and behold, before the solemn council West quietly begged the question. Out of consideration for the character of Mr. Fisk, he wished to get off personalities and to restrict the whole discussion to the "grand point" to be contested, "whether it be consistent with the rules of our holy profession for Christian churches to tolerate members marrying profane and immoral persons."

But Fisk, now thoroughly aroused, insisted upon keeping the council's nose off theological scents and on to the grindstone of his character. He was determined once and for all to know what they had against him. Thus directly challenged, the second session of the council considered the charges "lame and deficient."

Dr. West, however, was sure that such a mistake could be righted. He was sure he could produce the necessary evidence, and he did. The church called in the neighbors. Quite naturally the council was shocked and West was supported. Once again, and this time forever, the unfortunate Mr. Fisk was pronounced a person "openly immoral and profane."

At this juncture, however, help came from an unexpected quarter. Dr. Joseph Huntington of Coventry arrived upon the scene. He delivered a long plea before the ecclesiastical council, the modernity of which stares out from yellowed pages like an electric-light bulb in a candle setting. The Stockbridge church, he maintained, regarded marriage as a bond between Christ and His church, whereas it was in reality based upon the carnal fact that "a man loves a woman and a woman loves a man." "Marriage has nothing of a spiritual nature in it, but is merely a civil, social connection and relation." All this talk about only converted people being able to marry each other was little short of nonsensical. Saving grace may make the best husbands and wives, but to say it is essential to the marriage relation is "wild talk indeed." "The law of nature is the law of God."

Poor Dr. West! It was shocking that such sentiments should be uttered in the town he had struggled so hard to keep pure. It was shocking that a minister should be guilty of such feelings. But Dr. Huntington went even further. He said that sometimes persons without saving grace make better rulers, parents, husbands and wives, than other persons who are the true children of God.

In West's seventy-one-page *Vindication of the Principles and the Conduct of the Church in Stockbridge* which followed Huntington's plea, we cannot but admire his unswerving loyalty to his beliefs. He maintains that even though marriage is a civil and temporal affair, "in all our concerns we are to consult the glory and good of the Kingdom of Christ." If Christ's interests are not watched in this most important of all relations, where indeed will they have a place? Will not Dr. Huntington's comments on marriage, wherein he stresses the importance of sex, or, as Dr. West more properly puts it, "the mutual tendencies of the different sexes to each other," encourage a "too general indulgence" among the "bucks and debauchees" of the age?

And what of Mrs. Fisk herself? She had two children, "whose complete happiness in heaven or unutterable torment in hell greatly depended under God on her conduct toward them." How could her behavior be consistent with a "proper benevolent concern for the eternal salvation of the offspring of her own bowels?"

The little doctor—it is almost a relief to know, so touching is his sincerity—had a staunch supporter not only in the ecclesiastical council, but in the imposing person of John Bacon. Bacon followed West's *Vindication* with an *Appendix*. West may have had his own differences of opinion with Bacon, but in this instance they stood as one.

After this, the contest waged more hotly than ever. Huntington entered the lists with a brochure containing a reference to John Bacon, "a droll, a deist and a Master of Arts, gently reprimanded." Bacon, on the other hand, was heard to say that Huntington had "a brow of brass." So the clerics chased each other around and around, very much like the tigers in *Little Black Sambo*. And whatever became of John and Lavinia Fisk? Did he swear himself into his grave? Did her children turn out the worse for their early surroundings? Did Lavinia Fisk, in the happiness of her marriage, feel herself repaid for all she had gone through? We hope, somehow, that she did, and that after all, to use Mr. Fisk's own expression, "Stephen West, Tim Edwards and all the divils of hell" were powerless to stop their "settling together."

The council's verdict was a triumph for Dr. West, and his ministry continued comparatively undisturbed for some time afterwards, certain years, like unusually high tides, bringing in more souls "to Christ from the world" than others. Those saved numbered 384 in all.

It was not until the latter part of his life that the Lord whom he served so faithfully saw fit to bring upon His minister sore affliction. Dr. West, moderate in all his ways, occasionally enjoyed a glass of wine. His second wife was prescribed spirits for her health. Advancing years had made it necessary to have an assistant, Seth Swift by name, a Uriah Heep of a man, who wanted to curry favor for himself in the village, and accordingly went about spreading the story that the minister and his wife were drunkards. Enough new people had moved to town, since Dr. West's light had been dimmed, to listen to gossip of the sort, and before long many of the village had turned against their minister. Two afternoons' inquiry sufficed to support the charge against Mrs. West, and her husband called the advice of a council. The ministers of surrounding towns, even Dr. Moore, the President of Williams College, drove solemnly over to witness their colleague's shame. The pious Edwin Dwight, grandson of the brigadier, wrote to his mother: "I suppose Aunt West is excommunicated—is the good doctor's heart broken?" If Stockbridge did not have a care, he considered, the fate of Sodom would descend upon it.

Mrs. West was a nervous, trembling, little old lady. Like her husband, she always wanted to do the right thing. She was willing to admit that perhaps she should have left off taking spirits for her health a little sooner, but she could not confess to what she had not done. A thin slip of paper covered over with a fine wavering hand is her testimony: "Considering the unhappy state of this church and feeling myself to be the occasion of it, (although I do not feel myself to have made an intemperate use of strong drink) yet if, as far as I have given reason to any candid member of this church to believe . . . that I have made a too free use of strong drink, I do cheerfully and sincerely ask their forgiveness, and I do entreat every member of this church, if in future they should have any such report of me, that they would immediately come to me and give me an opportunity to clear myself, or confess my fault. Still further, considering my weak and poor state of health and apprehending that I would feel the necessity of stimulants, I freely confess that I may at times have made such a use of spirits as that my appearance and conduct would excite in others a belief that I was guilty of intemperate drinking."

After this she was left alone. Her innocence and her humiliation were so apparent that even the council was touched. After "affectionately" hearing all the evidence brought before them, it was unanimously voted that the censure upon her be removed. But the charges against her husband were not yet cleared up. As a badge of disgrace he had to yield his place at Communion to his assistant. "My heart was near to breaking, my comfort all destroyed at the sight," wrote Abigail Dwight (the first Abigail's daughter-in-law), to her son, Edwin.

At last a witness was procured whom Mr. Swift believed was going to turn the trick. He was a dusty old parson who had lived in the Wests' house and knew their ways, and was such a doddering fellow that West's friends were terrified lest Swift should have corrupted him. On the day upon which he was to testify at the meetinghouse, everyone was tense. The judging clergy sat in a semicircle. The older families fidgeted in their pews. The newer arrivals, impartial and critical, ready to believe the worst, waited for the show.

At last the old gentleman got up. He had been with Mr. Swift two or three years ago, he told them, and Swift had said that Dr. West and his lady were guilty of gross drinking. In fact, the parson had a mug beside him and drank it every night.

"Were you at the Wests' at the time?"

"Yes," was the answer.

"Did you believe it?"

Dead, nerve-racking silence in the church. Was Dr. West's God indeed deserting him? Stockbridge's heart came right up into its mouth. The old man spoke slowly:

"Not—one—word—of—it, sir!"

"A low murmur of shame and disappointment ran over the assembly," while exclamations of delight came from West's few devoted friends. Their beloved doctor was safe.

As time went on, Stephen West figured less and less in the life of the community. Yet he lived on, feeble in strength and largely confined to his house. The world was becoming too much for him. He had bridged the gulf between the eighteenth century and the nineteenth. He had represented the convictions of his contemporaries. He was a stuffy Fundamentalist to many of the younger generation. Reason—that daughter of Belial imported from France—was breaking the world down, dissolving the old solid beliefs. His friend, Theodore Sedgwick, whom he used to consult about parish affairs, could die in the Unitarian faith and still be considered respectable. William Ellery Channing was not only tolerated, but adored. The world was becoming too big and too complicated. There were no longer just the Williamses and the Dwights and the poor ignorant savages to look after. The old colony had become a thriving new state. New roads were bringing new people to Berkshire.

As he grew older the little doctor sought refuge more and more in the consoling doctrines of Grace. His views upon infant damnation underwent a softening change. That fellow Swift had spoiled the end of his ministry. He even doubted whether his congregation had ever understood his sermons.

But the spring was lovely on the apple trees and his garden looked well in the sun. His older parishioners still loved him. "I doubt if we have seen anyone so sanctified," wrote Abigail Dwight. If the story of the little boy who used to murmur, "Old Dr. West, old Dr. West," to keep off evil spirits when passing through the woods with his cows after nightfall, did not reach the minister's ears, something of the feeling it implied must have penetrated through all the turmoil of his parishioners' quarrels. So as the years went on, he could dwell quietly upon God's tender mercies.

Chapter VI

THE REVOLUTION

IN July of the year 1774, the ballroom of the Red Lion Inn was crowded. The first Congress of the state had met to consider the alarming condition of affairs, and to take a definite stand concerning them. Events for the last fourteen years had been slowly shaping themselves towards this eventuality. Circumstances had funneled the community together into a common cause, and this meeting was not the mere feverish expression of a passing excitement but the climax of a long series of changing attitudes and needs. Removed as Berkshire was from the rest of Massachusetts, it had not remained entirely aloof from what was happening in the eastern part of the state. The insulation of hills and forests had not deadened its ears to clamors which were daily growing louder, though the slowness and self-sufficiency of back-state agriculture was less at the mercy of British policy than Boston trade.

Like all rural communities, Stockbridge was behind the times. For a while the Joneses and the Woodbridges were too busy putting crops in their cows' ears and repairing their fences to pay much attention to the complaints of Boston merchants or the rantings of Samuel Adams. Both were part and parcel of that greater and slightly over-civilized world beyond the rim of hills. Even the slogan, Taxation without Representation, had lost much of its echo, coming from so far.

The Williamses and the Dwights, however, knew what was going on. Since the close of the French and Indian War, England had adopted a new policy. She was feeling poor and wanted to recoup her losses at the colonies' expense. Henceforth the Americans were to be taxed, not merely for regulating trade, but for purposes of revenue. The Sugar and Molasses Acts, the Stamp Act, the Townshend Acts were signposts along the road.

This policy, disturbing as it might be to Massachusetts, did not seem to the Williamses as alarming as the reaction against it. William Williams, Chief Justice of the Court of Common Pleas, and for many years representative to the General Court, was still drawing his pay as a retired colonel in the British army. He had always been one of the men upon whom Tory Governor Bernard could rely. To him taxation without representation was less to be feared than Samuel Adams, who, he considered, was compensating himself for his personal failure in life by fanning the mob spirit in Boston. Although King George's recent policy might be an encroachment upon personal liberty, it was not as dangerous to the peace of the community as the hanging of Peter Oliver in effigy, the unnecessary attack upon redcoats by a mob, which resulted in the much-dramatized Boston Massacre and, finally, worst of all, the wholesale destruction of a shipload of good East India Company tea.

Nevertheless even the Williamses and their friends were gradually to learn that times were changing. In Stockbridge the domination of the Hill was challenged. The new people who had moved to the Plain were inclined to be intractable. Building their own houses, wresting their living from the soil, had disciplined them to self-reliance, and liberty was as taken for granted as the air they breathed. So long as King George was a faint, mythical figure, they accepted him as part of their universe. However, when they had to pay him a percentage every time they indulged in the luxury of white sugar, when molasses went higher, and when he must make a profit on every legal document they signed, he took tangible form and became an uncomfortable intrusion in their lives.

They were busy enough paying their own debts after the French and Indian War. Massachusetts had been taxed more than twice as much as the other colonies. Why should she be taxed for England's debts besides? It was all very well for the Williamses and the Dwights, who had money and held all the good positions, to preach subordination. Through the meager pages of the papers that reached them from Springfield, the Plain put out tentacles to hear what Sam Adams was saying. The underground sympathy of class sharpened their ears for the reactions of what their presiding Tories called "the popular mob."

Even as early as 1764, Berkshire had been conscious of the rise of the popular party. Dr. West, married to a Williams, may have had a conservative slant, but in Pittsfield the vociferous Thomas Allen every Sabbath preached a mixture of athletic Christianity and rebellious patriotism. In Sheffield, John Ashley's constituents had severely criticized him for being one of the seventeen rescinders who voted to withdraw the circular letter appealing to the other colonies for aid against English aggression. When the Stamp Act was enforced, Colonel William Williams, who could be trusted to know which way the wind was blowing, was too ill to hold the Probate Court at Pittsfield. Afterwards he wrote to Elijah Dwight in Great Barrington that his state of health had prevented him from attending to any kind of business; but "the Stamp Act being repealed and being some better" he was miraculously able once more to announce the sitting of the court in Stockbridge. No doubt he advised his kinsman Elijah not to complain too loudly about the fact that Boston merchants had put an embargo upon the sale of potash. There was no knowing how high the tide of popular resentment might rise. The Whig, or popular, party was gaining ground every day.

There was one angle of the question, however, upon which everyone agreed. A common fear as well as indignation drew Hill and Plain together—the fear that Canada would be given back to France and the old insecurity return.

Made up of varying shades of public opinion, the Stockbridge Congress was a patchwork quilt which emergency had pieced together. Not only the principal towns of the county, but the small villages—among them Richmond, Egremont, Alford, Hancock, Becket, New Marlborough and Tyringham—had all sent delegates.

When Dr. West opened the proceedings with prayer, he spoke rapidly and his voice trembled with emotion. On hard benches, or grouped together in corners, his listeners bowed their heads; some of them wholly absorbed in commending themselves to God; some of them letting their minds wander to the possible consequences of the step they were taking. John Ashley of Sheffield, who had been chosen president of the Congress, was thankful that people seemed to have forgotten all about that unfortunate rescinding affair. Like his friend William Williams, he had managed to tightrope rather skillfully through the past stormy years and at the time of the Congress he could proclaim himself loudly an ardent Whig. Timothy Edwards, the first of the Stockbridge delegates to the convention, may have foreseen the sacrifices he was to be called upon to make. To date he had been a prosperous merchant and had numbered sometimes as many as forty or fifty laborers on his place. He traded his merchandise for wheat which he sold elsewhere at a good price. Now, with a possible war in the offing, who knew what might happen to the currency?

THE REVOLUTION

Jahleel Woodbridge, Timothy's nephew, also a delegate from Stockbridge, reluctant as he had doubtless been to subscribe to any of the tenets of the liberal party, considered that since Britain had now actually abrogated the Province Charter and ordained that all executives and military officers should be appointed by the Governor, things had definitely gone too far. Dr. Erastus Sergeant, another delegate, allowed his thoughts to wander far afield. He was probably thinking of some medical duty he had had to postpone, for he performed all major operations for thirty miles around.

The clerk of the Congress was a man from Sheffield named Theodore Sedgwick, who was just beginning to make his way in the world. His family had fallen upon evil times and he had determined to retrieve their fortunes. He had studied law under Mark Hopkins, a brother of Samuel, and one of the few lawyers the state boasted. Although Sedgwick was innately conservative, he resented high-handedness of any kind, and for the moment threw his weight on the popular side.

After proclaiming a day of fast to be celebrated on July 14th, the assembly proceeded to draw up its protest:

> "Whereas the Parliament of Great Britain have of late undertaken to give and grant away our money without our knowledge or consent; and in order to compel us to a servile submission to the above measures, have proceeded to block up the harbor of Boston; we do, solemnly and in good faith, covenant and engage with each other:—
>
> "I.—That we will not import, purchase or consume, or suffer any person by, or for, us to import, purchase, or consume in any manner whatever, any goods, wares, or merchandise, which shall arrive in America from Great Britain from and after the 1st day of October, 1774, or such other time as shall be agreed upon by the American Congress, nor any goods which shall be ordered from thence, after this day, until our chartered and constitutional rights shall be restored.

"II.—We do further covenant and agree that we will observe the most strict obedience to all constitutional laws, and authority, and will at all times exert ourselves to the utmost for the discouragement of all licentiousness and suppression of all mobs and riots.

* * * * * * *

"IV.—As a strict and proper adherence to the present agreement will, if not seasonably provided against, involve us in many difficulties and inconveniences; we do promise and agree that we will take the most prudent care for the raising and preserving sheep for the manufacturing of all such cloths as shall be most useful and necessary; for the raising of flax and manufacturing of linens. Further, that we will by every prudent method, endeavor to guard against all those inconveniences which may otherwise arise from the foregoing agreement.

* * * * * * *

"VI.—That if this or a similar covenant shall after the first day of August next be offered to any trader or shop keeper in this county, and he or they shall refuse to sign the same, for the space of forty-eight hours, that we will not, from henceforth, purchase any article of British manufacture from him or them, until such time as he or they shall sign this or a similar covenant."

These resolutions were unanimously adopted and shortly afterwards Timothy Edwards, upon whose judgment everyone depended, together with Erastus Sergeant, Dr. Lemuel Barnard and Deacon James Easton, framed an agreement for the non-consumption of British goods, to be sent to the different towns in the county. The resolutions above quoted and the league formed were the first of their kind in Massachusetts and among the first in the colonies, although they were shortly followed by many others. From now on, events throughout the state and nation followed each other with accelerated inevitability. According to one of the Boston papers, "the whole country was inspired by one soul and that a vigorous and determined one."

Berkshire was planning an even more portentous step. Just before the Court of Common Pleas, acting under the new

British regulation, was to have met, a petition was preferred, "asking the Honorable Court not to transact any business that year." Then the petition "humbly sheweth:

> "That whereas two late acts of the British Parliament for superseding the charter of the Province, and vacating some of the principles and invaluable privileges and franchises therein contained, have passed the royal assent, and have been published in the Boston paper, that our obedience be yielded to them.
>
> "We view it of the greatest importance to the well-being of this Province, that the people of it utterly refuse the least submission to the said acts . . .
>
> "In order in the safest way to avoid this threatening calamity, it is, in our opinion, highly necessary that no business be transacted in the law, but that the courts of justice immediately cease, and that the people of this Province fall into a state of nature until our grievances are fully redressed by a final repeal of these injurious, oppressive, and unconstitutional acts."

Just how long this "state of nature" was going to exist no one at that time could possibly foresee.

Notwithstanding the petition, the court decided to meet as usual. When the judges reached Great Barrington, however, they found a crowd of 1,500 people awaiting them. It was a well-ordered crowd enough, but it managed to take up all the space in the courtroom and to fill even the judge's seat. Elijah Williams came forward with all his native arrogance. The position of High Sheriff became him, and he cut an imposing figure as he called, "Make way for the Court." He was told, however, that the people "knew no court or any other establishment than the ancient laws and customs of the country," and what was more, they would not give way to any other authority, upon any other terms. The Williams world, the world of early Berkshire, was turning upside down. Angry as he must have been, Elijah had to consent to parley with the crowd and he told them that the court would maintain business under the old laws as the new acts had not yet been received. The silent, unarmed crowd remained unimpressed. They knew that the judges' commissions were already revocable at the pleasure of the Governor and that the new acts might be put into execution at any minute. They had left their farms and their businesses at considerable trouble to themselves and they were determined to have their way.

Elijah no doubt would have been glad to use strong-arm methods, but what could a handful of ponderously arrayed officials do against 1,500 men? The judges quickly realized that the game was up. As they walked slowly out with as much dignity as possible, order was maintained. Only a rowdy element upon the outskirts could not bear to go away without a fight. They carried off David Ingersoll, "a particularly obnoxious" Tory, and treated him with the roughness they felt he deserved.

Berkshire's action in obstructing the courts had not gone unnoticed. "A flame sprang up at the extremity of the Province," wrote Governor Gage to England. "The popular rage is very high in Berkshire and makes its way rapidly to the east." A little later he wrote, "Civil government is near its end, the Courts of Justice expiring one after the other."

By October, the first Provincial Congress had met at Concord, to which Thomas Williams went as delegate from Stockbridge and West Stockbridge. The condition of the army was inquired into and committees formed to ascertain the population, commerce and manufactures of each town. The first Provincial Congress was followed by two others. Samuel Brown was Stockbridge's representative to the second and Timothy Edwards and Jahleel Woodbridge to the third. Committees of correspondence were set up in every town. At first these were supposed merely to communicate with the other towns on matters of war and government, but as the years went on they became the real power of the county. Timothy Edwards complained to Boston of their arrogance and Theodore Sedgwick considered them unduly radical, but from this impartial distance, they seem to have been efficient guardians, trained by habits of self-dependence, during a stormy time.

Stockbridge's patriotism was not restricted to holding congresses. Two companies of minutemen were raised by voluntary enlistment. So many young men sent in their names that there were not enough arms to go around and the town had to borrow £20 for their purchase and voted £50 to buy tents. Stockbridge youth drilled up and down the village green, no doubt full of hope that Britain would continue in its course so that all these preparations would not be in vain.

These hopes were not destined to disappointment, and the news of April 19, 1775, must have come almost as a relief. Orders had arrived from over the seas to arrest Adams and Hancock, and the British troops which had been sent to seize them at Lexington met a line of fifty minutemen who refused to disperse upon command. "If they mean to have a war, let it begin here," exclaimed Captain Parker. This was at daybreak of a Wednesday and news of the ensuing battle reached Stockbridge on the following Friday.

To arrive too late seems to have been Stockbridge's fate, if not its fault, throughout the Revolution. As quickly as possible on Saturday, April 22, the Berkshire regiments were called. Muskets were whipped out and all uniforms available put on. The only certain piece of news which had reached the soldiers was that an expedition had been sent to Lexington, so that when they finally started out along the road to Tyringham they did not know what their fate might be. When they reached the end of their journey, Lexington and Concord were already history and the British army had been driven back into Boston, which was in a state of siege.

The sight of 16,000 men, similarly recruited from towns and villages, settling down before the state's capital, must have been an invigorating one. Like streams gathering to the sea, the American army was gaining force. Together, beyond the barrier of separating hills and rivers, the colonists realized how many of themselves there were. Vermont's homespun hero, John Stark, was already in Cambridge, with his first New Hampshire company. Upon hearing the news of Lexington, the veteran, Israel Putnam, ploughing his model farm at Pomfret, had rushed to Cambridge, and ordered his minutemen to follow. From Connecticut came Benedict Arnold, heading sixty governor's guards and picking up recruits along the way, with a characteristic flourish, while easy-going Governor Gage was surprised at the number of improvised besiegers who had sprung up from every quarter to hem him in.

At Boston, the two Berkshire regiments were reorganized and separated. That of Colonel Patterson, the tall, sedate officer from Lenox, went to Cambridge and took its place in the great semicircle enclosing Gage from Jamaica Plain to Charlestown Neck. Soon, however, they were set to work building a fort in Charlestown, which was later to protect the rear of the Americans in the Battle of Bunker Hill. In this action Stockbridge's fate again overtook it, for Patterson's was one of the three regiments held in reserve in Cambridge, and sent to relieve the Americans too late. It received a consolation prize, however, when the newly appointed American Commander-in-Chief, George Washington, arrived upon the scene and praised Patterson's men for briskly repulsing a marauding party at Lechmere, and thereby cutting their military teeth.

The other regiment under Colonel Fellowes dug in at Roxbury. It seems to have played a less picturesque part, both now and later, than Colonel Patterson's. The months dragged, although much was happening around them, and Generals Howe and Burgoyne had come to Gage's aid. It was not until nearly a year from the time they had set out from Stockbridge, that Fellowes's regiment helped Washington besiege Boston from Dorchester Heights, by which maneuver he forced the British out of the town.

During this time, the siege had not been to everyone's liking, and some of the more adventurous spirits in the Berkshire regiments, attracted doubtless by the brilliant audacity of Benedict Arnold, had enlisted to go with him to Quebec. From Patterson's regiment Jared and Elkanah Bishop and Thomas Williams, of Stockbridge, volunteered and some of Fellowes's men also joined their ranks. The long march up the Kennebec River was enough to take the starch out of anyone. As the regiments cut their way through the wilderness, their shoes were torn to ribbons. There was scarcely any food, and Williams was one of the men who, under Lieutenant Colonel Enos, turned back to avoid starvation. Enos was later court-martialed for his retreat but succeeded in acquitting himself honorably. The Bishops meanwhile kept on, although Jared's only regular food for a fortnight was one sea biscuit. When finally the weariness of the march was ended and Arnold's battered army climbed the Heights of Abraham and challenged the garrison either to surrender or come out and fight, the climax of intrepidity had been reached. The Bishops were never to forget the day when they had come so near to capturing Quebec.

Back in Boston, Fellowes's regiment and a part of Patterson's which had not gone to Canada, as well as that which had come back, were ordered to New York. When they arrived, the fate of Patterson's was once more a march to Canada, and once more defeat. On their way up, Thomas Williams, now a lieutenant colonel, died at Skenesborough. Before the rest reached Montreal, they heard that, although Montgomery had captured that city, Arnold had failed at Quebec.

He was now defending the American station at the Cedars, where reinforcements were rushed to his aid.

The news the Stockbridge soldiers wrote home was depressing enough. Arnold was forced to surrender at the Cedars, ingloriously, it was said, despite the fanfare of his personality. No one could hope that the Americans would conquer Canada, when even he had been forced to capitulate. Letters may have mentioned the web of intrigue which already was weaving itself about the American command, the feud beginning between Arnold and John Brown, the hero of Pittsfield, and Arnold's ambitious schemes. More likely they simply stated that the regiment was ordered to Newtown, Pennsylvania, where they were to join Washington. As the Berkshire men sailed down the Hudson, the thought that their hills were still menaced by British and Indians was galling to their souls.

A discouraged nucleus showed up at Newtown. Only 200 of the 600 men who had originally set out for Canada had lived through the barrage of disease and starvation whose casualties were far heavier than those of battle. Fellowes's men were there to greet them and had hardly better news to tell. They had been caught in the panic at Kips Bay, had skillfully evacuated New York at the approach of Lord Howe (Elnathan Curtis all the time exclaiming, "This is hot work—hot work"), had been defeated at White Plains, and followed Washington in his retreat through New Jersey, that retreat which, by the ingenuity of its commander, was somehow robbed of despair.

Henry W. Dwight, son of Abigail and the Brigadier, was clerk to General Fellowes. When not commenting upon American achievement he would note in his diary, "Nothing remarkable." Mark Hopkins was taken sick on the field at White Plains and carried to safety by his erstwhile pupil, Theodore Sedgwick. Perhaps he and Elnathan Curtis met at the time, unconscious of their common grandson, the great Mark Hopkins, yet unborn.

The war had been going on for over a year and except for the conquest of Ticonderoga and the evacuation of Boston, the Americans could point to little military success. Yet there was plenty more action for Berkshire regiments. Some of them followed Washington across the Delaware and were with him when he surprised Lord Howe at Trenton on Christmas morning; some of them were with him at Valley Forge. Later on, Samuel Brewer led a company against Ticonderoga, and Gates at Saratoga had his assignment as well.

Meanwhile things at home had not stood still. Since the very beginning of the war, the Indian note had sounded. The friendship between Indians and whites, founded upon John Sergeant's experiment, blossomed again, forced in the hothouse of emergency. In 1774, the Indians under Jehoiakin Metoxin had enlisted as minutemen. The Provincial Congress, quickly realizing the asset of Indian sympathy, had notified them, at a good deal of pains to make themselves clear, that the Americans had been forced to arm in self-defense, with the object of protecting their rights and privileges, which had been invaded, and their property which had been confiscated. At the same time a blanket and some ribbons had been voted for each Indian as a present—not to say a bribe.

After a council of two days, Solomon Uhhaunhauwaumut, chief sachem, answered, summing up the position of his tribe: "Brothers, you remember when you first came over the great water I was great and you was little, very small. I then took you in for a friend and kept you in my arms so no one would injure you. Since then we have been friends. There has never been any quarrel between us, but now our conditions are changed. You have become great and tall, you reach to the clouds and you are seeing all around the world, and I am very small, very little, I am not so high as your heel. Now you take care of me and I look to you for protection." Was there a hint of irony behind these touching words?

Solomon went on to say that they really had never understood the nature of the quarrel between America and England, but they were perfectly willing to do anything they could to help. He was personally inclined to think that he could accomplish more by "taking a run to the westward and feel the mind of my Indian brethren, the Six Nations and know how they stand, whether they are on your side or for your enemies." The Indians were quite sure the Mohawks would listen to them, as they had in the past, and they thought consulting them wiser than "marching off immediately for Boston," which, however, they did not absolutely refuse to do.

The Provincial Congress in reply undertook to explain the political situation in words of one syllable. "We have now made our hatchets and all our instruments of war sharp and bright. All the chief councillors who live on this side of the big water are sitting in the grand council house at Philadelphia." It advised the Indians to do whatever seemed best to them, at the same time insidiously suggesting that if "some of your young men should have a mind to see what we are . . . doing here, let them come down and tarry among our warriors."

Indian scruples were of no more avail during the Revolution than at any other time, and it is not surprising to learn that early in the war a full company, made up of all the fighting men of the tribe, had enlisted under Abraham Nimham. Another story goes that Captain Goodrich and Charles DeBell asked permission to form two companies of Indians who, however, enlisted with one stipulation—that if they were to fight they must do it in their own Indian way.

They brought their bows and arrows, their wives and children with them, and added their wigwams to the armed ring encircling Governor Gage. Some even went with Arnold to Canada and some to New Jersey with Washington. They were known to fight well, if savagely, and the Commissioners of Indian affairs considered them good military allies, although the Continental Congress demurred for some time before using them. However, as time went on and the war proved harder to win than was at first expected, Washington wrote to Timothy Edwards that Congress had changed its mind and was anxious to have Indian help as soon as possible.

Early in the struggle, it was apparent, even to Indian intelligence, that the old sin of drunkenness was encouraged by wartime conditions. In a petition to the Provincial Congress the Stockbridges admitted that they were improvident and asked that some measure be devised which would prevent their getting too much "strong drink." They wanted Timothy Edwards and Jahleel Woodbridge to dole out their wages as the most hopeful means of insuring sobriety.

The part the Indians took in the Revolution bears a horrid similarity to their part everywhere else. Abraham Nimham's company was hacked to pieces at White Plains, and a little later he was killed and his body devoured by dogs. A pathetic petition to John Sergeant from thirty-two Indians at this time asked for blankets, coats, and money which were owed them. Loyal and brave the savages had been, fighting perhaps too well. At one time George Washington thought they might be used as scouts but they were eventually discharged because they were so hard to keep in order. Direct primitive methods burst so easily through the thin veneer of white men's fighting civilities.

Stockbridge had other things besides the Indians to think about. By March 17, 1775, its patriotism had been well established, for in voting measures of national autonomy, the votes were forty-two *for*, one *against*. Town meetings were kept busy steadily voting men, money and supplies. The system of enlistments for three months, six months, and three years meant the continual outflow of men—299 in all. Those whose enlistments had expired came home and doffed the glory of war to return again to their fields. Not all came back, however, and extra work fell upon the women who stepped into their husbands' shoes, getting in the crops, cutting the firewood, and even taking the plough. In addition, they learned to make wartime substitutes, to use the juice of the cornstalks and pumpkins, instead of molasses, and to weave cloth for their men's uniforms. For the eight years of war they welcomed the veterans home and sent recruits out again, as if they were only another kind of crop.

For Stockbridge as for Berkshire, however, the immediate source of excitement lay not so much in the battles of the war as in the unrest at home. The county was in a ferment. When the call came for every fifth man to go to Ticonderoga, there was general reluctance to obey "until the Tories are taken care of as they are something insolent." New forces had been let loose. The old, closely-knit social and political system was cracking under the weight of the popular thrust. Conservative Berkshire had become radical.

In 1775, the ballroom of the Red Lion Inn opened its doors to another convention—a convention which voiced the growing popular resistance to the Provincial Congress. Parson Allen stumped the length and breadth of the county, preaching against the new charter it had proposed, a charter which he felt put altogether too much power in the hands of the governing body. Their only security lay in demanding a constitution chosen by the people, in whose hands all power ought ultimately to rest.

Before the days of Hamilton and Jefferson, the local struggle foreshadowed the future national one. A paper signed by

John Ashley, Samuel Brown, Mark Hopkins, Theodore Sedgwick, Jahleel Woodbridge and others, denied all traffic with the recent convention, contending that it savored of anarchy, and testified their allegiance to the existing government.

Times were hard for the conservatives. Hysteria, not unlike the witch hysteria in Salem, seized upon the community. Timothy Edwards's patriotism was beyond question. He had exchanged his good money for £1,000 of worthless Continental currency to provide the American army with some hard cash and had parted, too, with much of his good flour in the same way. Yet even he was set upon while riding back from Lanesboro—whither he had gone to answer the summons of "two very respectable gentlemen" in an effort to curb the rampant radicalism there—and severely beaten by five men who called him a Tory. Theodore Sedgwick, who served as aide to General Thomas, preferred the discomforts of a military life to the tender mercies of a "Berkshire mob." Early in the war, Henry Van Schaack had written that Berkshire patriotism was insatiable and, in Pittsfield, Israel Stoddard, among other misdemeanors, had been heard to say that he thanked God he was not a Whig, and had had to run away afterwards. A royalist was strung up in Lenox and barely escaped death, while the one man in Stockbridge who had voted against national autonomy had been chased into the mountains, where his family fed him until the worst of the excitement had died down. "Our Tories," wrote Thomas Allen, "are the worst in the province . . . They are mute and pensive and secretly wish for more prosperous days to Toryism." In Egremont, Whigs and Tories volleyed shots at each other in a miniature war of their own.

It is not surprising that Elijah Williams should have come under the ban. During the war he was always in trouble. Called into court to face a charge of treachery at one time, he was held to be sent to General Gates for trial. At another, he was sentenced to be put into jail "till he give and full and sufficient satisfaction . . . that he would join his country-men in their opposition to the present measures of administration." Elijah must somehow have satisfied his accusers, for upon the back of the paper arraigning him are the following words: "We the subscribers have at the request of . . . Colonel Williams heard his declaration and being satisfied therewith respecting his political sentiments are of opinion that he ought to be released from his present confinement and . . . restored to the charge of all good people." Although Elijah carried this paper around with him until the end of the war, he was again accused of treachery and ordered to be sent to the jail at Northampton as the one in Berkshire County was "too weak and insecure." A big man, his just wrath might have shaken out the iron bars! Again, quite without warning, he was clapped into the "common gaol at Boston." Used to the comforts of life, to homespuns from England, and gold vellum lace, Elijah considered the whole affair an outrage—"the apartment to which I am confined being very loathsome and uncomfortable." What is more, his saddlebags had been taken away, by which means he was "deprived of necessaries to keep himself decent and comfortable." Elijah maintained that he could not imagine what the whole thing was about. He asked the Committee of Inspection in Stockbridge for a hearing, demanding that his detractors appear before him in public. He announced that he was about to be tried by the Superior Court and asked that evidence be produced against him. Again his blustering innocence must have carried the day, for he was acquitted, and returned, perfectly furious, to West Stockbridge.

There was no gainsaying the fact that the liberal party was growing stronger every day. The upshot of Thomas Allen's policy was to be that for six years Berkshire allowed no interference in its internal affairs. It contributed men and military supplies, paid its taxes, sent a representative to the General Court and conformed as part of Massachusetts in its relations to the outside world, yet it permitted no interference within its borders. No courts were held until a new state constitution had been adopted.

Though this course characterized the county, Stockbridge itself was fairly conservative. When, in 1778, a general vote was cast as to whether or not the courts should be held, Stockbridge voted twenty-six *for* and thirty-six *against*. Great Barrington came out definitely *for,* but Pittsfield, under Allen's dominion, carried the day with a sweeping negative majority of fifty to twelve.

Meanwhile the current of national changes was sweeping smaller eddies out into its broad stream. In 1776, the town, in voting for a representative, stated that "it is the mind of this meeting that should the great and important question of the independency of the United Colonies of Great Britain be discussed in the great and general court and assembly that he give his vote in the affirmative."

The state, also, was not idle. Orders were passed to raise clothes, blankets, and shoes, to be paid for in the paper money so fast depreciating in value. Sometimes the committees of correspondence would go into each house, count how many articles there were, and pay for them. Even the blankets were stripped off the beds in order to meet the state order to collect 4,000. Unnecessary traveling was frowned upon and such was the fear of disloyalty that watchful committees had to vouch for new citizens. Thus an old Stockbridge paper endorses the respectability of yet another Williams:

> "these Lines may Certify to houme they may concern that Capt. Daniel Williams of this town is a Good inhabbitant and has ben a towns man for a number of years &

a Capt. of the Melishey & a Deacon of a Church and (and a true Sun of libbity) now is about to move this famerly to the town of Stockbrigg in the Massachusetts bay and I hope all persons Will Sho Him (& his family) Respek as Cristins frinds and he and I Was Born and Broght up Ny Nabers.

aTest   William Morgan Justice of ye Peace
and a Commity of in Spection"

Lesser aggravations rubbed daily life the wrong way. There was an embargo on tea and, the story goes, a local divine craved a forbidden cup before leaving for the wilds of New York State, where he was missionary to the Oneida Indians. He invited his friend Dr. West to share it with him. The blinds were carefully drawn and the two, sitting opposite each other, stirring their spoons, felt terribly wicked—but how pleasant it was to relax occasionally in this matter of patriotism! A knock was heard at the door. In sudden terror Dr. Kirkland jumped up, caught the urn in his sleeve and spilled the boiling water over his lap. Afterwards he could never explain to the waiting Oneidas just why he had been so delayed in reaching them.

Events at last were shaping to a conclusion in which Stockbridge, as well as the rest of Berkshire, was to be involved. The British plan for cutting New England off from the other colonies was now in full force. Burgoyne, coming down from Canada, planned to lay siege to Ticonderoga—that strategic point whence hostile armies could descend upon Berkshire, and proceed down the Hudson to Albany—while Sir William Howe, from New York, was to sail up the river to meet him. The war was dragging and General Philip Schuyler complained that he had to let his men go back to their fields for harvest, or they would leave of their own accord. He wrote to Stockbridge saying that the enemy was advancing on Ticonderoga and that it was very important to call out the militia, "each man being provided with as much arms and ammunition as possible." It must have been hard for Philip Schuyler to send out this request. Disciplined soldier that he was, the nonchalant and ungoverned ways of the Berkshire men exasperated him. They were always either complaining that they did not see enough action or else begging to be sent home. His dislike was cordially returned. His dignified old-school formality rubbed frontier democracy the wrong way. Berkshire rang with rumors of his treachery. He was said to be in league with Howe, and his friendship with Benedict Arnold, whose scurvy treatment of John Brown was now well known, counted heavily against him. In spite of prejudice, however, Stockbridge responded instantly to his request. "The militia of this county are on their march," announced Erastus Sergeant and Asa Bement and, a little patronizingly, advised the towns of Hampshire to follow suit.

By now the military focus had changed from east to west. Many of the men who had first volunteered were ready, after a season at home with their crops, to start out again. Jahleel Woodbridge was commander of the band. Patriotism even stirred in the breast of Agrippa Hull, the negro servant whom formal Stockbridge employed to serve at banquets. He volunteered under Kosciusko, the noble Polish adventurer, upon whose fall Freedom had "shrieked aloud."

With a shift in locale the struggle had taken on a different meaning. No longer was Stockbridge being merely requisitioned by a Provincial Congress in the eastern part of the state; no longer was it voting to support a government in far-away Philadelphia. It was, quite simply, defending its own homes.

About eight o'clock of a Sunday morning the village was wakened by a cry "To arms!" Jahleel Woodbridge and Deacon Nash appeared at the corner beside Timothy Edwards's store and each solemnly fired a gun. The Sabbath peace was shattered. People rushed to their windows to see what was going on, and the square filled with soldiers. Dr. West, called upon to officiate in military matters, climbed the porch steps of Timothy's house, prayed and counseled, and blessed the young farmers who were going to war.

The booming of distant cannon, coming over the hills from Bennington fifty miles away, brought the seriousness of the situation home to everyone. Burgoyne's march was no longer merely a thing to read about in the papers, like Trenton and Brandywine. His recent recapture of Ticonderoga struck at the very heart of Berkshire's safety as well as its pride. For had not Berkshire men rallied to its defense? From Pittsfield, the now thoroughly patriotic William Williams had sent off an indignant letter to the General Court, exclaiming against the disgrace of its surrender. As soon as General John Stark, sulking under the weight of his grievances against Congress, heard of the march upon Bennington, he offered to serve, solely under the sovereignty, however, of New Hampshire—insubordination which history has canonized. His countrymen rallied around him.

Thomas Allen was among the volunteers. "We, the people of Berkshire," he told John Stark, "have been frequently called upon to fight, but have never been led against the enemy. We have now resolved, if you do not let us fight, never to turn out again." "Do you wish to march when it is dark and rainy?" asked the General. "Not just this minute," was the answer. "Then if the Lord should once more give us sunshine, and I do not give you fighting enough, I will never ask you to come again."

A little later, "There's Parson Allen; let's pop him," said a Tory on the English side, and the Battle of Bennington had begun.

Stark was as good as his word, but the Stockbridge men again arrived too late. Elnathan Curtis, however, who had

THE REVOLUTION 147

left his wife shortly before childbirth, was there, and Dr. Partridge is said to have dressed the wounds of the German Colonel Baum. As for Thomas Allen, after vigorous fighting, he tended the wounded and then went home, changed his clothes and preached a sermon.

The American victory at Bennington was complete. Fear of invasion was permanently lifted off village shoulders. Stockbridge kept on conscientiously voting supplies for the army. £80 was voted to the families of soldiers who had served in the war. In 1780, £4,500 was assessed to buy horses and £50 raised to pay volunteers for the militia for three months, over and above the state wages. £3,000 was voted for the clothing of the army and, in October of 1780, £7,000 was granted to purchase beef, and Thomas Sedgwick, back from military service, was appointed commissioner for procuring it. A little later £18,000 was again assessed for the purchase of beef, this amount being payable in money or in rye at $54, corn at $45 or oats at $27 per bushel.

Only once more was Berkshire to have a taste of war. Bennington had been but the beginning of Burgoyne's final debacle. He had proceeded down the Hudson and made his way with difficulty through the woods and over the bad roads, but his meeting with Lord Howe had been unaccountably delayed. At Saratoga he met Gates's army, and after two fierce battles surrendered, or, as he preferred to say, "signed a convention." His men stacked their arms and were ordered to march to Boston and to set sail for England without fighting again. Their dreary way led them through Claverack, Hillsdale (Nobletown), and Egremont, and at Great Barrington they stopped to get supplies. Here little children amused themselves by putting their heads into the cannon which had been surrendered at Saratoga. Burgoyne himself, feeling ill and discouraged, took refuge at Elijah

Dwight's. The many wigs, the various pairs of military boots and the spinnet he carried in his train were of little use to him now. For once these reminders of the sophisticated life he had left behind had lost their comfort, and turned daggers on him instead, presaging his home-coming and the storm of criticism which awaited him.

But Burgoyne could not dawdle, and presently his army left Great Barrington, and took the road across the mountains to Tyringham and Westfield. Tradition has it that they passed through a cleft of Bear Mountain immediately to the southeast of Stockbridge, between the mountain's main ridges and the peak known as Laura's Tower. This trail is still called Burgoyne's Pass, but it is difficult to understand just why the General should have gone out of his way to try a rough hill-path when the regular road was the shortest route, nor has any definite evidence beyond hearsay been advanced in favor of the idea.

In spite of the barrels of liquor offered them at Sandisfield and the ox roasted at East Otis, the Hessian soldiers in Burgoyne's army did not like the countryside. "A rougher and more spiteful people I never saw," wrote one of them. "Our patience was often stretched to its highest tension . . . Most of our officers were not allowed to cross their thresholds, but . . . had to take up their quarters in filthy stables and barns . . . At first we swore at the abominable roads, but ceased when we found they became worse, as cursing would not do them justice." The weather was so terrible that two men died on the way.

Several customs of the inhabitants troubled the Germans a great deal. They were shocked, as foreigners are today, by the domination of American women over their men, who would work out their lifeblood buying their wives articles of personal adornment. Nevertheless, the girls had a way of frizzing their hair, and gathering it up in a puff at the front, which was very attractive and, despite their strictures, some of the Hessians were so beguiled as to forget their grievances and marry and settle down, which accounts for the number of German names throughout the county.

The war ended on the old, appropriately sentimental note. In recognition of the services of the Stockbridge Indians, Washington ordered an ox and rations of whisky to be given them for a barbecue, which was held on Laurel Hill, with John Sergeant presiding. An effigy of Benedict Arnold was shot, scalped and burned, and a war hatchet was buried.

The Revolution was over. Along the Tyringham road from the east, up the Great Barrington road from the south, slowly the village veterans dribbled back, returning to sow and reap unmolested in their own fields.

Chapter VII

SHAYS' REBELLION

THE glow of the Indian barbecue on Laurel Hill, symbolizing the triumph of the war, died down in the cold dawn of peace. America, the infant Hercules, was wobbly on its new-found legs. The next difficult years were to teach it to walk alone.

Stockbridge was no longer an outpost of empire but part of the new State of Massachusetts, which in its turn had become part of the Union, held loosely together by the Articles of Confederation. In 1780, the state had been accorded the new Constitution and Bill of Rights, which Berkshire had been so vociferous in claiming, but its government was as yet untried. Berkshire County was growing and if, during the controversy over the courts, Pittsfield's voice had been louder and more insistent, Stockbridge as a community was still upon its upward curve.

For one thing, the Plain was becoming fashionable. Square, amply proportioned houses gave a sense of stability and tradition to the village street. Henry W. Dwight, back from the war, was county treasurer and tax collector, and had built Old Place at the western end, overlooking wide meadows and the curving river beyond. In the middle of the Plain, Theodore Sedgwick had built himself a large square house of the simple colonial type. His law practice had prospered in Sheffield and he had married Pamela Dwight and come to Stockbridge to live. Right under Laurel

Hill, Senator Jahleel Woodbridge, Judge of Probate and the Court of Common Pleas, ruled over his farm and household with the just benevolence of a patriarch. Only Abigail Dwight maintained the old tradition. After General Dwight's death, she moved back to the Hill, to the same house she had lived in as John Sergeant's young wife.

During the post-war period industrial possibilities also were being realized. Elnathan Curtis had been quick to avail himself of the water power in the northwestern part of the town and by 1782 the outlets of the Stockbridge Bowl were punctuated by saw and grist mills. The Curtises became captains of industry and prospered in the settlement known as Curtis Mills and later on as Curtisville. Others followed in their wake, the Dressers, the Fairchilds, and the Churchills. In 1813, a woolen mill with an annual output of 40,000 yards, employed eighteen men. It was soon rivaled by another which turned out 14,000 yards of satinet a year. A trip-hammer shop and a clothier's works did thriving business, while the Churchills embarked on a chair factory large enough by 1813 to employ thirty men and manufacture 8,000 chairs annually. By 1828, one cotton mill alone employed forty-two hands and had twenty-four power looms turning out 150,000 yards of cotton sheeting. In the section of the Stockbridge township known as Mill Hollow, and later on as Glendale, a woolen factory was opened in 1813, which ran for a time under the direction of Lester Avery, while the Stockbridge Cotten and Woollen Company and the Stockbridge Cotton Manufacturing Company were both incorporated in 1815.

With all this prosperity people could afford to be charitable, and care of the town poor became a frequent item among the selectmen's duties. In one year the town appropriated $233.67 for "boarding, nursing, clothing and doctoring" a pathetic list of names ending with Miss Carswell.

She had evidently seen better days, since hers was the only name to which *Miss* was attached, and she was cared for to her death, "including funeral expence." Not only civic responsibility but private philanthropy played a part in the lives of such shrewd business people as Abigail Dwight and her son, Elijah, for more than once they contributed the sum of six shillings and eight pence to the Humane Society.

Although Stockbridge might preen itself upon its civic growth, there was one respect in which it was outdistanced by its northern neighbor. After 1780, when Berkshire once more allowed the courts to function within its borders, the question arose as to where they should be held. The Supreme Judicial Court (formerly the Superior Court of Judicature), which had tried Berkshire cases in Springfield until 1783, was to meet in the county itself. Until now the lower courts had been held in Great Barrington, but in 1782 some gentlemen from Berkshire, disliking this arrangement, petitioned the Legislature to decide upon the future county seat.

It may have been at the Red Lion Inn, then owned by the Widow Bingham, that the urbane committee from Boston, prepared to listen to countless grievances, met the representatives of twenty Berkshire towns. After great deliberation, they decided in favor of Lenox, which was in the center of the county and most easily reached from every side. It was one thing, however, for an impartial committee to decide such a matter upon grounds of geographical justice and another to carry out its plans. Numerous petitions voiced numerous protests. For instance, it was obvious that the county could not afford the new buildings which would be required. Besides, why should Lenox, so small and so new, be favored? Couldn't the Court of Common Pleas be held alternately at Stockbridge and Pittsfield? Finally—an ambitious question—couldn't the Supreme Court be held at Stockbridge?

Perhaps Boston had had too much of Berkshire obstinacy. Perhaps it had not forgotten the long years when no courts had been held there at all, and wished to avoid possible future controversy. At any rate, in 1787, an order was issued that the Court of Common Pleas and the Supreme Court were both to be held in Lenox in February, and there was no gainsaying its authority. Yet even then, although Lenox functioned as the county seat, the matter could not rest in peace, and the disturbing question remained at simmering point for many years to come.

When the judicial controversy was not to the fore other matters pressed upon village attention. For one thing, the practice of medicine was sadly antiquated. Doctor Sergeant's pupils, whom he taught at home as Dr. West taught theology and Theodore Sedgwick law, had hitherto learned their profession merely by holding their master's basins, grinding his powders, making up his pills, and running errands for him upon the Plain. In order to remedy this state of affairs, to stimulate interest in medical matters and "encourage a spirit of union and make the faculty more respectable," the Massachusetts Medical Society appointed a committee consisting of Dr. Sergeant and Dr. Partridge to form the Berkshire Medical Association. In 1787, it met at the Widow Bingham's for the first time, and drew up a set of rules which could upon occasion be severe. Any doctor who refused to belong to this association was to be treated "with entire neglect." Medical education was fixed at three years and no man could become a pupil until he had a good knowledge of mathematics and could construe and parse the Latin language accurately.

Hardly had the association been formed and medical students started on their more arduous studies than its meetings were interrupted by that climax of political events to which the discontent of post-war years had been leading.

The peace and prosperity which veterans had promised themselves on their return from the war had been a pipe dream. To the soldiers who had come home and the families who greeted them, the snapping of the wartime tension had been only a temporary relief. Taking stock, they found themselves poor. The soldiers had been paid in Continental currency which by now had shrunk to almost nothing, so that a night's lodging cost $40 and $400 was paid for a mug of flip.

Debt hung like a black cloud over the horizon. The state debt alone had jumped from £100,000 before the war to £1,300,000 afterwards. Taxes were unevenly distributed and Berkshire, for its part, felt that its assessments were much too high. Public debt was as nothing to the private liabilities. The courts were clogged with lawsuits, so that it sometimes seemed as if the lawyers were the only prosperous men in the county, and they were hated in consequence. Many people were evicted from their houses, and the Great Barrington jail, which had been too weak for Elijah, was quite strong enough for the host of half-starved wretches which now filled it. Country people blamed the city people. Jahleel Woodbridge and Timothy Edwards shook their heads over the way the market was flooded with foreign luxuries so that all the money was leaving the country. "The articles of rum and tea alone," wrote Porcupine, the savage Federalist journalist, "would pay all taxes, but when we add sugar, coffee, gauzes, silks, feathers and a list of baubles and trinkets, what an enormous expense."

The grievances of the poor were far greater. Now that the war was over they thought that heavy taxation ought to be over likewise. Surely the country had not resisted King George's encroachments only to struggle under a more rigorous form of self-imposed tyranny.

In Hatfield, a convention of the delegates from fifty towns, whose proceedings were especially printed for Berkshire's benefit, listed eighteen sources of prevalent discontent. It favored the emission of paper money, subject to depreciation—a plausible and popular idea at this time—based upon the theory that the more paper you printed, the more money you had.

Not long after this convention the court-stopping which had been so effective during the Revolution was adopted once more. A mob of 800 men prevented the sitting of a court in Great Barrington, broke open the jail, and released the prisoners. Three of the judges were forced to sign a paper agreeing not to act upon their commissions until the people's grievances had been redressed.

Stockbridge, itself still quiet, waited eagerly for news. The conservative rose under a new name, Friends of Government, smelled as sweet. Theodore Sedgwick had been representative to the Legislature for several years and made no bones of his opposition to the popular side. Gradually he was becoming one of the leaders of the new Federalist party in the western part of the state, throwing all the weight of his overbearing personality on the side of constitutional law and order without understanding the just grievances of "the popular mob." Jahleel Woodbridge, Timothy Edwards and Henry W. Dwight all agreed with him. During the Revolution resistance to England had been, except for the Tories, a common political denominator. Now the popular party had lost all leadership from the conservative class. Throughout the rebellion that was to follow it showed a timidity and lack of initiative characteristic of men who have been used to being led. This accounts for "that want of enterprise in the insurgents for which their obstinacy and perseverance was an inadequate substitute" and "that entire lack of moral power" which the historians, Minot and Holland, so priggishly deplore.

By 1786, resistance to the established government was in full force. Petitions, conventions and court-stoppings had become the order of the day. Daniel Shays, a handsome, plausible fellow, had become the leader of the insurgents, who numbered one third of the entire population of the state. At this critical juncture, Governor Bowdoin acted with firmness, and called out 4,400 men under the command of General Lincoln. Shays had marched to Springfield intending to seize the arsenal there, but Lincoln arrived before this was accomplished and the rebels beat a retreat for Petersham where nearly all of them surrendered.

For Stockbridge all these events were but the prelude to its own drama. The village was convinced that Shays would now take his stand in the Green Mountains, where other followers would join him, and whence he could raid the western counties of Massachusetts to his heart's content. What virtually amounted to a threat of civil war hovered over the community. In the silence of the smaller farmers, the mechanics, and of the very servants in their houses, Jahleel Woodbridge and Josiah Jones read sympathy with Shays. Timothy Edwards taught his son, William, to stand at an attic window and point his gun so expertly that in case the Shays men attacked the village, he could shoot down two of them at the same time. Green hemlock branches worn in the hat meant a Shays man; a white cockade, loyalty to the government. In Pittsfield, Van Schaack prudently decided that he could serve his state better if he didn't wear any badge; his Tory banishment was still fresh in his mind. At Curtis Mills, Abel Curtis, turned an eighteenth century New Dealer, sympathized openly with the rebels, and shocked his conservative entourage. The tension grew rapidly worse. Muddy Brook Road became so infested with rebels, that a company of Sheffield militia did not dare go to Great Barrington until that town had sent another company to guard its way. To cap the climax, eight sleighs slowly and mysteriously drove out of Stockbridge, carrying supplies to the rebels.

Clearly something had to be done. The government asked the several communities to defend themselves without calling on the state militia. Accordingly 500 men, among them Timothy Edwards's son, William, organized themselves as an independent force and made Stockbridge their headquarters. Men on guard stopped citizens going to their homes and asked for the password. Soldiers sat in church of a Sunday. Theodore Sedgwick's life was threatened and when he went away from home he thought it prudent to leave his papers at Dr. West's for safe-keeping.

All this military preparation was not wasted for in West Stockbridge Paul Hubbard, one of the Shays men, had succeeded in collecting about 200 followers, and threatened daily to become more powerful. From over the mountain an oncoming tide of sedition, gathering recruits on its way, became more than a possibility.

To meet this contingency three companies were formed in Stockbridge. The central one took the road through Larrywaug, while the others were to converge upon West Stockbridge from the north and south respectively. An advance party of the central division reached the village first, only to find, at the junction where the three roads met, a considerable force lined up against them. The Shays sentries fired and their company was ordered to follow suit. They greatly outnumbered the small body of loyalists, only thirty-seven infantry and seven cavalry in all, who confronted them. Perhaps the sight of the familiar faces of their townspeople, the friends they had drunk with at the Widow Bingham's, the men with whom they had made roads and repaired bridges, gave the rebels a minute's pause. At any rate they did not fire immediately and in that moment a solitary figure emerged, riding toward them. As he drew near, they recognized him.

In their hesitation, Theodore Sedgwick seized his opportunity. "Lay down your arms," he commanded in that voice which always seemed to his children like the Thunder of Jove. Their new-found freedom and their courage flickered out. Their ranks broke, vague firing started somewhere; some ran away, others surrendered without further struggle. The supporting loyalist divisions now came up. Two rebels only were wounded but eighty-four of them were captured and summarily marched off to Stockbridge. For the most part these men took advantage of the Governor's offer of pardon to all who would lay down their arms. And so ended on an ignominious note the boasted glory of their military career.

The affair at West Stockbridge, damaging as it must have been to the insurgents' morale, did not mean that the rebellion was at an end. On February 5, 1787, General Patterson of Lenox—the same Patterson who had commanded the Berkshire militia in the Revolutionary War—found it necessary to ask General Lincoln to bring his state troops into Berkshire. It was a relief to the loyalists when Lincoln answered that he would immediately "throw a very sufficient force into your county." Before he could arrive, however, 250 rebels had gathered at Lee to prevent the sitting of the court. The militia was called out to meet them and a story goes that a yarn beam, which the insurgents rigged up to look like a cannon, was effective in securing them easier terms in their inevitable surrender.

The rebellion, hitherto marked by no loss of life and practically no bloodshed, was nearing its close. The insults heaped upon the insurgents by contemporary historians are hard to balance with the mildness contained in Shays' petitions, the comparative restraint of the silent court-stoppings and the righteous complaints behind the popular conventions. "Their boastings and their threatenings, their insolence and malice, their outrages and their robberies" seems strong language in which to describe the quiet and, at many times submissive, course they pursued. The twentieth century is remote from the fear of governmental paralysis, however, which was a daily consideration in the minds of men at that time, and which accounts in part for the severity with which the dumbly resisting farmers of Shays' Rebellion were treated by their chroniclers.

It remained for Berkshire and particularly Stockbridge to witness a final flare-up of hostilities, which came nearer than any other event to placing the rebels in the violent rôle assigned them. From Lebanon, Eli Parsons, a rebel leader who was known to have 400 men at his command, proclaimed: "Friends and Fellow-sufferers—Will you now tamely suffer your arms to be taken from you, your estates to be confiscated, and even swear to support a constitution . . . which common sense and your consciences declare to be iniquitous and cruel? And can you bear to see . . . the yeomanry of this commonwealth being cut to pieces by the cruel and merciless tools of tyrannical power, and not resent it unto even relentless bloodshed?"

Parsons's plan was a simple one. He proposed first to capture General Shepard's army, then to enter the county of Berkshire to "carry our point, if fire, blood and carnage will effect it."

The words carried horror to the Stockbridge community— horror which still echoes through the pages of its muffling histories. Horror did not strike home to one of its peaceful householders, however, who, shortly after Parsons's edict overheard a passing horseman say to his companion, "Now is our time to come in." To her the stranger was innocent of menace, and his words seemed merely irrelevant. She did not guess that he referred to the fact that Stockbridge was doubly exposed, partly because the volunteer army had been disbanded at the approach of Lincoln's regular one, and partly because a company of militia from Sheffield had been marched to Pittsfield where reinforcements were in urgent demand.

In the dark, early hours of February 27, 1787, young Timothy Woodbridge, sleeping with his father, Jahleel, was to remember afterwards how he woke to find the room filled with soldiers, their arms gleaming in the candlelight, and waving green hemlock boughs over his bed. His father had time only to push the little boy into his older sister's arms before being taken prisoner. A party of Shays men, under young Perez Hamlin, had entered the village from Larrywaug and had made for the Widow Bingham's, where they divided themselves into three companies and set off in separate directions to seize what prisoners and property they could. It has been suggested that their motive was deep-dyed and that, knowing their cause to be on the wane, they counted upon procuring prisoners valuable enough to secure them better terms of surrender, but it is difficult from their actions to believe them capable of thinking out any such concerted plan.

After plundering Jahleel Woodbridge's farmhouse, they drove that gentleman out into the snow, where his habitual benevolence towards mankind no doubt temporarily deserted him. They made for Deacon Ingersoll's, where they found the good deacon at his prayers. His wife, more quick-witted than pious, bethought herself of a bottle of brandy which she gave her visitors so that they promptly forgot what they had come for and departed in high spirits. Down on the Great Barrington road, Ira Seymour barely escaped capture by running barefoot out into the snow. On the Hill, the house of Captain Jones was entered. Here the rebels availed themselves of military supplies and drove the Captain, his two sons, a negro servant and a houseboy out into the cold.

Next door, at Dr. Sergeant's, Miss Mercy Scott, the village seamstress, who happened to be staying there, had her silver shoe buckles stolen. The doctor, two medical students and Moses Lynch, son of Lawrence, were captured. The latter was asked, "Why do you wear that white cockade?" When he retaliated appropriately enough, "Why do you wear that green bough?" he narrowly escaped being pinned to the wall by the thrust of a bayonet.

This was the rebels' heyday. The world had turned topsy-turvy for a while and it was theirs—theirs to drink and to take, to threaten and to bully. Did they realize this could not last? For all Eli Parsons's bravado, their leader, Shays, was lurking at Petersham, a defeated man, and young Hamlin must surely have known his cause a lost one.

Yet it is possible that, even in that delirious moment, old ties had not entirely snapped. Perhaps it was timeworn respect that made them spare the house of Dr. West, or merely the fact that it was now time to get back to the village.

On Plain Street, at the office of Theodore Sedgwick, two young law students were led away. The appurtenances of gentility—"ruffled shirts and parlor costumes"—were tossed out of the window. At his house, bayonets were thrust under beds in the hope that the owner might be lurking there, though it is difficult to think of so much autocracy in so undignified a position. Instead of their hoped-for victim the rebels were confronted by the Negro woman, Mumbet.

Mumbet had barely had time to hide the silver in a trunk in her own room and arm herself with a heavy fire shovel, before the house was filled with men searching the closets and drawers and loudly demanding to taste the wine that gentlemen drank. In the cellar they broke the top off a demijohn of porter but Mumbet threatened them with a blow of her fire shovel if they tried to break anything else. With elaborate sarcasm she offered to serve them, like gentlemen, with proper glasses. The porter, however, was sour to their taste and, muttering that the "gentlemen who drank such stuff were welcome to it," they returned to their search. When at last Mumbet's room was reached, she tried sarcasm again. "You'd open a poor nigger's trunk, would you, you who consider yourselves so fine." Upon thinking it over, the proposition seemed a little beneath their dignity. After all, it was very unlikely that the room contained anything valuable. "You call me a poor nigger, yet you'd stoop to robbing me," her voice went on, like a gadfly stinging them, until they were glad to leave the house. And the family silver was saved.

Meanwhile the prisoners were being paraded up and down on the green in front of the graveyard. They hadn't had time to dress properly and the cold was intense. They now numbered forty-one in all, and Hamlin was anxious to get them out of Stockbridge. Timothy Edwards's store had been raided for liquor so successfully that by this time several of the rebels had sublimated their efforts into a state of blissful unconsciousness. The expeditious Widow Bingham took advantage of the general confusion to hide Captain Jones in the capacious chimney closet at the Red Lion Inn so that no one missed him when the party finally marched away.

As Perez Hamlin guided his bizarre company, some of them drunken and some of them undressed, along the Great Barrington road, his heart may have misgiven him, but his men's spirits were high. They did not know that the alarm had gone out, nor that Dr. West had told Captain Stoddard of the volunteer corps, that the Plain was full of Shays men and that the Captain had instantly rallied his band for the pursuit. One citizen was so anxious to alarm the neighbors that he is said to have stood up in his sleigh, worn out his whip, and then used his ramrod on his horse all the way to Great Barrington to get there in time to spread the news.

When the rebels reached that town, the mood of conquest was still upon them. Their appetites whetted, they wished to taste more of the joys of liberation. They wanted more to drink and they wanted to see the jail which, conveniently enough, was in the same building as the tavern. They wished to be sure it was strong enough to hold their prisoners when the time came to put them there. They set the debtors at liberty and, in the general rejoicing, the *double entente* of Mrs. Bement—wife of the jailer and sister-in-law to Asa Bement in Stockbridge—was lost upon their simple minds. As she opened the cells for their inspection, she chanted the hymn, *Ye living men come view the ground, Where you must shortly lie.*

As Great Barrington had by now been thoroughly alarmed, and the rebels knew it would be difficult to obtain any more plunder, their motley crew turned off to Egremont, hoping to get to New York State as quickly as possible. But their hourglass was running low and the triumph of their drunken voices was shortly to be stilled. By the middle of the day, Colonel Ashley of Sheffield, joined by Captain Dwight and Captain Ingersoll of Great Barrington, marched out in pursuit.

It was on the road from South Egremont to Sheffield, where now uncomprehending automobilists pass an awkward stone marker commemorating the last battle of Shays' Rebellion, that the two forces met and the affair of West Stockbridge repeated itself on a larger scale. The rebels formed a line across the road while the government troops converged upon them through the woods and along the open ground, firing as they came. Everything happened so quickly that the Shays men hardly had time to hide behind their prisoners to load their muskets before the whole affair was over. The fire of eight or ten government men was sufficient to scatter the entire rebel force. Fifty or sixty prisoners were taken, two were killed, and about thirty, wounded. Among the wounded was young Perez Hamlin, whose heart must have sunk within him at the ease with which his comrades surrendered their cause.

Two of the government men were killed. One of them was Solomon Glezen, a Stockbridge schoolmaster who, finding himself before the enemy's fire, suggested quite practically to one of the Joneses who was beside him, that they run away. In so doing, Glezen was shot in the chin, thereby gaining an immortality which otherwise would have been denied him, since he was thoroughly unpopular both at school and at home. There is a tilted stone in the Stockbridge graveyard, dutifully stamped with a funeral urn and inscribed with verses which brought a touch of poetry to the unlettered back country and turned the overshadowing pine trees into a classic grove.

> Solomon Glezen
> Made prisoner by the Insurgents,
> Fell in the battle of Sheffield
> February 27, 1786
>
> "Oh for a lodge in some vast wilderness
> Some boundless contiguity of shade,
> Where rumor of oppression and deceit,
> Of unsuccessful or successful war,
> Might never reach me more."

So ended the fiercest battle of Shays' Rebellion. From now on the spirit of the insurgents was completely broken, and Governor Bowdoin grasped the reins of government more tightly in his hands. The Shays men were clapped into jail at Great Barrington, where so shortly before they had once hoped to put prisoners of their own. "He who laughs last laughs best," thought young Stockbridge blades, as they picked up the accoutrements the rebels left behind and joined the line of sleighs filled with the remaining prisoners. This line was so long that, when the head of the procession passed by the Hill church in Stockbridge on its way to Lenox, its tail had not yet turned the cemetery corner. How amused Mumbet must have been, as she watched it pass up the street. Old neighbors, their late division ended, talked to each other, compared notes, and even joked. The Stockbridge raid and the Sheffield encounter had taken place on the same day. Suspense and tragedy in the morning were followed by comic opera in the afternoon.

Although the rebellion was virtually over, government troops were not disbanded until the following September. The precaution seemed hardly necessary since the last rumblings shortly died down. Most of the insurgents were promptly pardoned, but fourteen men—six of them from Berkshire—were sentenced to death. These, too, in time were released, with the exception of one Berkshire man whose sentence was commuted to hard labor for seven years. Theodore Sedgwick acted as one of the defense attorneys for the accused. His letters to the General Court, recommending clemency, showed the side of his nature that his children loved, instead of the harsher angle he often turned upon the world. He was by no means alone in his leniency. The mild course pursued by the government at this time reflects the widespread and popular sympathy with the rebels, which expressed itself even after their defeat.

Chapter VIII

THE FEDERALIST PERIOD

IN the quiet that followed the tumult of the rebellion, the patine of civilization smoothed rough frontier edges. When Madam Dwight drove out to call upon her son and daughter, Stockbridge for the first time acquired a past. Although she inspired youth with her "true virtue and piety," she still loved the things of this world. She carried a watch—a badge of authority—and dressed in rich silk, personifying dignity and tradition.

She hardly recognized the village she had known as a girl. New stores had opened along the Plain. A white one near the Red Lion Inn belonged to Daniel Pepoon, while Phineas Ashmun advertised "Twilled Lambskins, Casimers and Satinets—at the new store a few yards west of Hon. Theodore Sedgwick's." In return, he would pay cash for "Old Pewter and Brass, Old Silver, Beeswax, clean cotton and linen rags." Mark Hopkins's brother, John, had gone into trade and undertaken to nourish both man's body and soul. Together with "Jamaica Spirits, good French brandy, Malaga and Teneriffe wines, hyson, skins, and Bohea tea," he offered his customers "the Testaments, psalms and hymns." Under the heading "Comfortable Things," Josiah Dwight offered "French Brandy, St. Croix Rum, and old Jamaica Spirits for ready pay only."

More people were moving into town, some from the eastern part of the state, many from Connecticut. By 1792,

THE FEDERALIST PERIOD

Jeremiah Buck was settled at the northern end of the Stockbridge Bowl. By 1800, Jesse Stafford owned a large farm on Goodrich Street, and up on East Street, near the little school, the Carters had become fixtures. A voting list for 1815 contains many names familiar to the town today: Bidwell, Buck, Byington, Carter, Jones, Lynch, Lincoln, Plumb, Pomeroy, Palmer, Seymour, and Smith follow like beads on a string throughout the nineteenth century and into the twentieth.

The farming village was becoming more urbane. In 1788, the first newspaper in the county, *The Western Star*, was published by Loring Andrews, who was recommended as "a sober and ingenious man and a Federalist," and Theodore Sedgwick suggested that a post be established between Stockbridge and Kinderhook, so that the paper could be sent there. In 1792, the first post office in the county was opened on Plain Street, in a simple white wooden house a little to the east of Timothy Edwards's store. Andrews was postmaster as well as editor and listed in his pages the mail not promptly called for. There, too, could be found detailed accounts of what was happening in Congress, and local items, useful and nondescript. "Whereas my wife Anna," complained Lemuel Hill of Alford, "hath of late behaved herself in an unbecoming manner, all persons are hereby forbid entertaining or trusting her on my account, as I will not pay any debts of her contracting after this date." Luxuries were advertised to tempt the village palate: "Oysters for sale at the dock . . . of Kinderhook landing." One of the Woodbridges took the opportunity to announce that he wanted to buy some good chestnut rails, while Mr. Pomeroy Noble quite baldly stated, "That elegant stud horse Flag of Truce . . . will stand two days in each week . . . three dollars for a single leap, six dollars to warrant a foal." Mr. Noble, a man of few words, believed that "encomiums were fulsome."

When John Bacon's top chaise or Elijah Brown's two-wheeled carriage, or Theodore Sedgwick's brand-new phaeton, drew up at Loring Andrews's for the weekly paper, they carried back news of foreign affairs. Europe was in a ferment. "The first army under Bournonville; and that under General Moreau, and the Archduke Charles was advancing by the Rhine towards Swabia." Catherine of Russia was taking arms against Mahomet Khan. And one day the village received an astonishing piece of information. Napoleon, whose advancing autocracy was a horror to all republican hearts, was pronounced upon good authority to be a fraud. "A gentleman of respectability" in Paris had written to New York: "Dear Friend, The likeness of General Bonaparte having just come out a singular discovery has been made concerning the place of his origin. He happens to be a countryman of yours and even one of your friends instead of a Corsican as first reported. Bonaparte is an assumed name, his family name is Shaler, from Middletown, Connecticut. You will no doubt be able to judge of the truth directly and not fail to ascertain the fact in case the people of America have any doubt about it."

Although Andrews was deep in local politics, his columns covered subjects ranging from farmers' grievances to ironic comments upon Doctor West's religious beliefs. Even before 1800 liberalism had begun its insidious work. Literature of every kind was available at the printing press. Andrews did not allow his political allegiance to interfere with bookselling and on a list of literary wares the Tory Governor Hutchinson's *History of Massachusetts* rubbed shoulders with the works of the radical Tom Paine. For serious reading Seneca's *Morals* and Paley's *View of the Evidences of Christianity* were but two out of a list of more than forty books, while *The Sentimental Journey, The Arabian Nights, Don Quixote, Sandford and Merton, Robinson Crusoe,* and

The Mysteries of Udolpho took the place of the fiction shelf in the bookstores of today.

Buying books, then as now, was an expensive business and beyond the reach of many respectable citizens. Twenty-five of these, believing that "attainments of the mind are very important and advancement in knowledge and literature a very laudable pursuit," subscribed a share apiece towards the Berkshire Republican Library organized in 1789. As children's books were few and far between, about 1812 the little girls of the village decided to form a lending library of their own, and its rules suggest little girls as well-behaved as even Maria Edgeworth could wish. "Fine for turning down a leaf—turning over a leaf with wet, greasy or dirty fingers—a drop of tallow, or a blot of ink, not less than sixpence—for tearing a leaf—bruising or cracking a cover, not less than one shilling, and as much more, in each case, as the Librarian shall adjudge. . ."

In 1806, a number of young men formed a debating society. Jared Curtis, who later carried his talents into schoolteaching with marked success, was chosen the first president. The club met at different members' houses and, in order to maintain a cool impartiality, no discussion of party politics was allowed. Questions, of a mildly exciting pitch, were followed by lengthy discussions: "Are dancing schools on the whole beneficial?"; "Are theatres beneficial to the public?" In one debate, however, there was no discussion at all: "Are the original intellectual capacities of women equal to those of men?" was quickly and finally negatived by Sedgwick and Curtis. "Is the present degree of luxury in the United States compared to what it will be in the future too great?"; "Is the marriage state more happy than celibacy?" and "Is virtue its own reward in this life?" were decided in the affirmative. With correct village loyalty the suggestion

"Is a town life preferable to a residence in the country for a man of education?" was definitely denied.

Frontier simplicity was becoming a thing of the past. Young gentlemen wore frilled shirts; young ladies, whose parents could afford it, went to finishing school. In the last decade of the eighteenth century, prosperity had indeed rounded the corner. Barnabas Bidwell, son of the Tyringham minister, had moved to Stockbridge to practice law and could say with justice in his Fourth of July oration: "Agriculture is converting our country into a vast garden of fruit and flowers . . . Manufactures are springing up among us . . . works of enterprise and utility are bound to succeed beyond the most sanguine expectations." There was more time for leisure. Stockbridge could afford to be gay.

The services of Agrippa Hull were constantly in demand to help with parties. He would leave off cracking jokes or telling the village children stories—of how he had once dressed in his master Kosciusko's clothes, and of how that master had discovered and punished him—to get the tables ready for a feast. His wife, Peggy, was also a village institution, ready to make a wedding cake at anyone's request. A bill for a ball held in 1799 is the measure of contemporary sophistication:

To 4 candles @ 1-	4d
2¼ Gall. Port wine @ 9.6	1.3.9
1 Gall. Sherry wine @ 9.6	9.6
½ Gall. Brandy 11-6	5.9
½ Gall. Spirits 8-	4.
6 lb. Lump Sugar 2-	12.
2 gross Biscuit 6-	12.
Room (paid Capt. Pepoon)	15.
	£4.6.4
Musick	2.8

THE FEDERALIST PERIOD

Agrippa	16.
Taylor	9.
1 pt Shrub	4.9
6 lbs. Cheese	3.6
5 oz. Candles	.4
	8.7.7
2 packs cards	3.
Paid B. Rossiter for Printing	6.
	£8.16.7

Upon similar occasions invitations were appropriately formal. A faded card marked *Ball* briefly sums up past tremors and anticipations. "The company of Miss Lucy Pierson is requested at the Stockbridge Assembly Room on Thursday . . . at six o'clock." Henry W. Dwight and A. Byington were to be managers.

Nevertheless, there were dreary stretches of monotony during the winter months. So at least thought the two Sedgwick girls, Theodore's eldest daughters. "They think Stockbridge the most intolerable place in the world and would prefer Greenland to staying here," wrote their mother. "We live without much company and know very little of what goes on in our neighborhood. The girls generally find amusement in conversing upon and scanning the characters of their male acquaintance. They have very few parties and but two balls this winter." They had to content themselves with going to a dance in the scanty, windswept village of Lenox, even though they "had no Gallant."

During the years that followed the Revolution, politics crowded religion off the front page of people's minds. Politics gathered men into corners and set the children to quarreling at school. Everyone had a personal stake in the formation of the new country and, although every village was a microcosm of national events, Stockbridge could boast two actors on the national stage. The Federalist party, which demanded a strong centralized government, had received new impetus from the scare of Shays' Rebellion. Theodore Sedgwick, its Berkshire protagonist, was a member of the Continental Congress from 1785 to 1788, and after that served in the House and Senate off and on until 1801. He might be taken as a composite photograph of the ideals and prejudices of his party. In his single mind, right and religion allied themselves to property in an unshakable combination. He did not analyze his friend Hamilton's political theory or stop to examine its underlying cynicism. The abstract belief that self-interest is the ruling passion of man, and must be enlisted on the side of government, was for Sedgwick invested with the weight of a religious sanction. No disturbing half tones muddied the primary colors of his canvas. "I declare I consider Jefferson the greatest rascal and traitor in the United States," he wrote. "They say ——— is a Federalist, but he is a fool, so he must be a Democrat."

During his congressional career, ancient enemies of revolutionary and rebellion days confronted him. The Republicans, like their colonial forefathers, scented tyranny in every breeze and stood for the sovereignty of the States, and liberty for the forgotten man. Thomas Allen was still alive and maintained that "the great majority of moral and religious characters in Berkshire are firm friends of our Republican government and resolve never to give it into the hands of the Federalists." The county was no pocket borough for Federalism like the seacoast towns where commerce predominated. Sedgwick's majorities at times were pitifully small, and right on the Plain he had a formidable rival.

Barnabas Bidwell was appointed County Treasurer in 1791 and served as State Senator from 1801 to 1805 when he was elected to Congress. In 1807, Massachusetts appointed him Attorney General. Being of versatile interests he had produced *The Mercenary Match,* a distinguished example of early American drama, while still an undergraduate at Yale. Bidwell played Jefferson to Sedgwick's Hamilton on the county stage. They were a good contrast—the one adroit and cool, the other direct and vehement. A local wag summed them up in a piece of doggerel which he pinned on the Lenox courthouse: "Duke Ego the bully and long winded Barni."

The Federalists looked to England as their political ideal. To them Republicans and Jacobins were synonomous. "I came forward in a torrent of invective against the Jacobins," wrote Sedgwick, "as the authors of all the evils I had felt or feared. I trust in the valor and resources of Great Britain as the last protection of civilized society against the assault of Jacobinism in the war it has waged of men against property, of atheism against religion and morality." Even his wife's letters, when not taken up with the schooling of the little boys, and the condition of the roads, reflect an orthodox and respectable fear of the "terrible republic."

The light which beat upon Sedgwick and Bidwell did not reach their wives who went about the prosaic business of ordering their households and bringing up their children in a country town. Mary Gray, the Stockbridge girl who married Barnabas, was summed up in her funeral oration:

> "Her husband, dumb and bathed in tears,
> Her children next behind the hearse,
> Her parent bowed with weight of years,
> Are not the subject of my verse.
>
> "She's dead, the friend that used to please
> To sweeten joy and soften grief;
> Forgetting her own health and care,
> In granting others kind relief."

When her husband was at home Pamela Sedgwick kept open house. Henry Van Schaack, the erstwhile Tory, would come over from Pittsfield with a new kind of wine for

Sedgwick to taste, or William Lawton Smith, the southern Federalist, called and complimented him upon having the finest house in town. The young law students at the office had to mind their *p*'s and *q*'s and he did not let them slump in his absence. "You will endeavor to make the young men in the office industrious," wrote Sedgwick to one of the young Williamses who took charge of the law business and collected money for the family when he was away. "It was with pain I saw their idleness and inattention. For their welfare and for my honor and the reputation of the office let me entreat you will be kind enough to assume upon yourself the necessary task of improving their conduct."

Between bursts of glory, life was at once difficult and simple. Fences were breaking down, animals invading the property, wood had to be brought in from the swamp, and hay procured from Timothy Edwards for the cattle. Sheep supplied enough wool for clothes, which must be cut and sewed by village women, and when Pamela wanted luxuries she had to send away for them. Decanters and wineglasses were shipped from New York, and when she went into mourning for her half sister, Electa—who had rashly undertaken a perilous journey to Clinton, New York, to see her son Sewall—she had to write to New York for some black silk and the newest pattern for making gowns.

Then there were children to educate. The oldest boy, Theodore, "seemed to be impressed with the importance of a constant attention to his studies." "I am much pleased," wrote his father, "because I find you begin to love your book. Now, now, my sweet child is the time. Do you not observe how much men who have improved their time well are respected? It will make you feel very ugly to reflect that you might grow up and have people say of you that you would never improve your time, that you was a lazy idle foolish fellow and although your papa gave you great opportunities how to do good you had neglected them all. No, No, my son will never permit this to be said."

Sedgwick was kept in touch with home not only by his wife's constant letters but by his faithful henchman, Loring Andrews, who retailed political affairs. When a delegation of Republicans arrived in the village, Federalists were on their stiffest behavior. Sniffing like hostile dogs and treading cautiously, they declined a dinner invitation from the Republican candidate but afterwards condescended so far as to take a glass of wine with him. Judge John Bacon in his comfortable farmhouse on the Hill might have learned by now to keep his political opinions to himself, but evidently he did not for Andrews considered him "as damned a Jacobin as ever met in any conclave of sedition within the limits of America."

Even Dr. West was called into the controversy. Most gentlemen of the cloth, except for that nuisance, Thomas Allen, had rallied to the Federalist cause and the Stockbridge minister found himself forced to admonish "those who murmured against government." "You should have seen," wrote Andrews upon this occasion, "the champion of democracy among us drumming his fingers upon the pew and staring at the floor."

It was a bitter moment for Sedgwick when, in 1800, as Speaker of the House, he announced the election of Thomas Jefferson. He retired the following year and accepted a judgeship on the Supreme Court of Massachusetts, where he devoted a large part of his time to fostering a higher standard of manners on the Bench, at that time far less polished than the Bar. The disappointment of his life occurred in 1806 when he lost the Chief Justiceship of his state. Characteristically, he was furious. "My friends try in vain to soothe me," he wrote. "They say I am reconciled . . . they lie like hell." He was a die-hard Federalist, cut and measured to order some time since, and Massachusetts wanted a new style. In young Theophilus Parsons of Newburyport, they found their man.

Meanwhile through Jefferson's triumphant years, Barnabas was becoming more and more adroit. His chief depended upon him to put difficult measures through the House and he was instrumental in bringing about the Louisiana Purchase. Yet, finally, a gleam of triumph lighted Sedgwick's latter years for by 1811 Bidwell had gone beyond himself. How Jefferson, by now in retirement at Monticello, must have sighed at the weakness of human nature, for Barnabas, despite his clerical father and impeccable family, had helped himself to $12,855.59 of the town's funds. The Federalist press fairly screamed its triumph. In an article entitled "The Defalcations of Barnabas Bidwell," the *Columbian Sentinel* pointed out that the Democrats raised a loud cry over the salaries of Supreme Court Justices "but are profoundly silent in regard to the substantial sum of money embezzled by one of their chiefs." Bidwell departed for Canada where he spent the rest of his life.

Bidwell had left the stage, Sedgwick was growing old, yet the era they represented was in fullest bloom. Even the impartial debating club admitted the question: "Was it better for England to make peace with France at the present time?" Bonaparte was a world menace, disturbing even young Archibald Hopkins, son of Electa Sergeant and of Mark, who had died in the Revolutionary War. Archibald was a conscientious young farmer who, Atlas-like, bore the burden of his whole family. He took care of his mother and sister, and saw that his brothers received the liberal education of which he had been deprived. He had married the witty Mary Curtis, daughter of Isaac Curtis, old Elnathan's son, and the young couple lived in Hopkins's farmhouse, Cherry Cottage, which had once belonged to King Ben.

Archibald had been commissioned lieutenant of a company in a squadron of cavalry. In 1810, he received an order to see that his company was provided "with a sufficiency of cartridges without Ball." He had to leave off cutting the corn to read this order aloud to the troops on the village green. It pointed out that "the whole of the eastern world is convulsed to its centre, and the nations of the earth are dashing against one another . . . Ours is the only republic on the globe which is left amid the wreck . . . Let it then be the ambition of every man to be so equipped . . . as to be ready . . . to face, in the field of battle, the enemies of his country."

With these considerations in mind, it seemed too bad that so many of the militia turned up without uniforms. Archibald, with his brother-in-law, Jared Curtis, who had added military to debating fame and had become a brigade major, saw to it that their company was properly equipped, and performed a weekly drill.

After all this practice the target for it was destined to change, for when conflict came, it was with England, not with France. Not many years elapsed before England's policy of impressing American seamen and plundering American property drove Madison into the war of 1812.

Instead of uniting the village as the Revolution had done, the new war only caused a deeper rift. The manufacturing interests in Curtisville were delighted with the embargo upon British goods, and relatives writing home from the West expressed their satisfaction in a war which would free the United States of all disputes about the Canadian border. However, the President's action was too much for the Federalists to bear. They did not even pretend to back the war, and some of them talked of secession and a separate peace. John Hopkins's store was ruined because the Republicans, by a series of machinations, took away his trade. One

Federalist went so far as to build his house upon the Plain with no doors or windows on one side, so that he would not be beholden to his Republican neighbor for light and air. The Association of Churches proclaimed a day of fasting and prayer in view of the distracted state of the nation, and other towns observed it with appropriate and public sedateness but, in Stockbridge, the Republicans were so angry at the idea of invoking God to interfere with their war that the proceeding had to be abandoned and Federalists were forced to pray in secret for the speedy ending of this national disgrace.

The cost of living soared. Flour went to $15 a barrel and the best tea cost $18 a pound, but it was not until 1814 that more than pocketbooks were touched. Now once again shades of Bennington passed fleetingly across men's minds. The British had planned to cut off the New England States and their victories upon the Great Lakes and the taking of Plattsburg pointed toward the successful outcome of such a scheme. Once more Stockbridge was called to the defense of Boston. Dr. West, marveling at how history repeats itself, led in prayer, and blessed the men assembled on the village green. Once more, when the troops reached their journey's end, the emergency which had summoned them was over. They had a pleasant change of scene for six weeks and then, like the King of France in the nursery rhyme, "They marched right home again."

News of the Treaty of Peace did not reach America until February 11, 1815. Great exultation followed. Stockbridge was illuminated and the conchshell, inevitably produced for the occasion, blew its loudest and most triumphant note. Although the war was virtually a stalemate, America's European cord had been cut. As one nation she had dealt with another and held her own. Henceforth she was treated with respect abroad and at home a period of contention was at an end. The Federalists had scolded themselves into the

THE FEDERALIST PERIOD

Hartford convention: the Republicans were left in possession of the field, a generation which had grown up since the United States was a nation was coming to the fore, and the Era of Good Feeling made its opening bow.

During the War of 1812, the West, that wilderness beyond the Hudson River had found a national voice. Difficult economic conditions caused by the war stimulated the emigration westward which had already been going on for some time. Berkshire land was wearing thin, the frequent wheat crops were beginning to deplete the soil so that glowing tales of the richness of New York and Ohio fell upon willing ears. Besides, debating clubs, libraries, stores, and two-wheel top carriages were tame to men who loved a fringe of pine trees to cut down. *The Western Star* advertised as Wanted to Hire: "a number of able stout hearty young men . . . such as are good axe men . . . fifteen or twenty such may meet with good encouragement to go to the westward for the purpose of cutting a road from the river Paliwa to the Cayuga lakes . . . which will give them opportunity to explore that fertile country."

In the course of settling a boundary dispute between Massachusetts and New York State at the close of the Revolutionary War, two townships lying between the Chenango and the Susquehanna rivers had been ceded to Massachusetts. The General Court granted a tract of land between the rivers Owego and Chenango to Samuel Brown and his associates, who included most of Stockbridge's solid citizens. So many not content with merely owning the land moved out there, that Dr. West plaintively declared that if any more went he would go too.

Not long after this the Genesee speculation sent fortunes skyrocketing up and down the Plain. One citizen went so far as to say he could never spend the interest of his income, only to find himself destitute. A note was pinned up on a public house suggesting a subject for discussion in town meeting: "To see if the town will move to New York and enter the business of speculation." It was in land there that Timothy Edwards recouped the fortune that he had lost during the Revolution.

In 1819, Henry Brown, son of Samuel, left his comfortable house on the village street and bought a tract of land which he called Brownhelm, in Northern Ohio. It was a part of the northwest township of the Connecticut Western Reserve, on the southern shore of Lake Erie. Hither he brought nineteen people from Stockbridge, among them Grandison Fairchild and his two-year-old son, James Harris Fairchild, who was later to be the first president of Oberlin College. At Oberlin, too, Hiram H. Pease of Curtisville cut the first tree and built the first log cabin.

Meanwhile, Alva Curtis, one of Elnathan's sons, sold out his share of a family paper mill, receiving one fifth in cash and the rest at $3.50 an acre in "New Connecticut" land. He dragged his wife and his two little girls, Calista and Pamela, the long terrible journey through the wilderness to the neighborhood of what is now Cleveland. Part of the time they had to walk, wading through the mud and camping in whatever shelter they could find. Calista sickened and died of exposure on the way. When they reached their destination Pamela used to beguile her solitude by watching the thousands of pigeons that flew by. "I am sure they are not as lonesome as I am. I have no little girl to visit nearer than two miles." Still, there were some things that happened everywhere. Pamela heard that her cousin William Hopkins had been drowned in safe, civilized Stockbridge. "So we see that little children die in Stockbridge as well as in Ohio," she wrote.

To these emigrants Stockbridge had now become what Boston had been to the earlier pioneers. A shoeless little boy in Brownhelm exclaimed to his mother, "Look they are rich!" when some neighbors received a box of provisions from the village. Had Dr. West been alive to visit these colonies he would have felt quite at home. The icy winds would have poured into the chinks of his cabin at night, as it had in the Stockbridge John Sergeant had first known. The church would be as like the first Indian church as homesickness and axes and hand-wrought nails could make it, and the school like the Indian school. Even the land would be somewhat similar, for pioneers always picked soil which in their experience was known to be the richest, and looked for places resembling those they had left behind. So Stockbridge was no longer merely a destination—but a point of departure. It had become a link in the vast chain of western migration which was taking place over New England, whereby the descendants of the Puritans carried their civilization with them, intact and rounded, as the snail its shell.

Chapter IX

GOING OUT INTO THE WORLD

AT the beginning of the nineteenth century, Stockbridge's early youth had passed. The self-conscious age had not yet arrived. Up to this time distinguished visitors had merely commented rather prosaically upon the pleasant scenery. "The lands are good and well cultivated and the plain well covered with settlements," wrote William Laughton Smith. Madam Dwight showed surprise when her young guest, Eliza Quincy, went into raptures over the view from her window. She had been too busy rearing children and wresting an uncomfortable living out of the wilderness to notice things like that.

For the main part, life was still lived simply in the patriarchal style. Yet, insidiously, the outer world was creeping in. It had taken fourteen days for Theodore Sedgwick's letters from Philadelphia to reach the Berkshires and when the roads were bad he was ten days getting home. In 1807, the Stockbridge Turnpike was completed and a stage ran through the village, at first three times a week and then every day, stopping for a rest and change of horses at the Red Lion Inn. An advertisement in *The Pittsfield Sun* appeared in the form of a dialogue:

"How much is the stage fare from Lee, Lenox, or Stockbridge on to Hudson?"

"$1.75 from either place."

"How often do you run?"

"Every day except Sunday."

"Where do you dine?"

"At Hicks' in Stockbridge coming up and at Hillsdale going down."

Though communication with the world beyond the hills was easier, it had little adulterating effect upon the solid village core. Stockbridge even then was self-derivative, expressing a definite personality of its own. Entrenched in its seniority, it could look down its nose at Pittsfield, whose rapid industrial growth seemed only a sign of vulgar prosperity, and it considered Lenox a dreary little upstart of a town.

The younger generation of the early 1800's who attended the Elm Street school, wove the village into a loose network of relationships and, as the nineteenth century wore on, their lives blended into the life and growth of the village, so that the two patterns are inextricably intertwined.

In the two-room schoolhouse, the older scholars studied upstairs while the lower room was kept for younger children. In 1828, the upper school was incorporated into Stockbridge Academy, with Jared Curtis in charge; and in 1833 a new schoolhouse was put up where the present one now stands. In early spring, pools of water surrounded the building and children had to wade to their lessons as best they could. Nevertheless, this was the most important educational center in the town. The East Street school up on the hill in the northeastern district, remained its unsophisticated country neighbor. In the northwestern district, even the little red schoolhouse, where John Bacon and Stephen West had had their controversies, had to play second fiddle. Though the East Street school, opposite Oak Lawn, boasted only one room, it kept a very careful record of its doings. Pupils outside the Stockbridge line were admitted on the payment of a dollar fee. Wood for the fireplace, supplied by the lowest bidder, was cut and split on the first day of July of each year, and piled neatly in the woodhouse by the first of October. Parents paid Prentiss Bliss the sum of one dollar annually for fixing the fires. Teachers' salaries varied, according to their sex. Maria Brown was paid $5.10 a month, while John O'Brien at $11.50 did considerably better. Measures to keep up their morale were not wanting, and the most elaborate of progressive schools could hardly be more tactful: "The prosperity of this school depends very much upon the course pursued by the friends and parents of the children at home and . . . the utmost caution should be observed to do or say nothing in a manner likely to come to the ears of such children as to injure the reputation of their teacher."

Interest in schools was keen enough to create a society for their improvement. Committees of three persons in each district were appointed to visit and report upon the progress of the pupils, the condition of the schoolhouse, the interest of the parents in the school, and whether expenses were to be defrayed by private subscription or public appropriation. In 1832, $800 was appropriated for schools; in 1840, $1,000, and in 1860, $1,200.

Education was but part of the duty life held for children, only a part of the serious pattern of their lives. To Archibald and Mary Hopkins's sons it was an interlude between ploughing and mowing. The Sedgwick boys had to drive the cows to pasture before they went to their lessons. Theodore had definite responsibilities. "You will see that the lambs are taken care of and tell the men they must go to plowing as soon as possible," wrote his father.

What did they learn, these serious children? A pamphlet, entitled *The Literary Repository*, and published for the use of schools, gives a list of dates that were considered essential, solidifying the universe into an orthodox mold:

Creation, 4004 B. C.
The Deluge, 2348 B. C.
Babel built, 2347 B. C.
Moses born, 1671 B. C.
Destruction of Troy and Rape of Helen, 1184 B. C.

"Our minds were not weakened by too much study," wrote Catherine Sedgwick. "Reading, spelling, and Dwight's Geography were the only paths of knowledge into which we were led . . . I did go in a slovenly way through the first four rules of arithmetic, and learned the names of the several parts of speech, and could parse glibly."

Schooling may have been elementary; reading at home was not. Literature had no middlemen in those days and the classics or nothing fed an earnest youth. Even Catherine Sedgwick, who escaped much of contemporary sternness, sat up all the evening, at the age of eight, to hear her father read *Don Quixote* or *Hudibras*.

Throughout the century, Stockbridge's significant men and women fall into three groups: those who attained distinction after they had gone out into the world; those who acquired it while remaining at home; and those who arrived already garlanded. The Fields and the Hopkinses are bracketed in the first category. More than their destiny, a natural affinity links them; plain living, high thinking and a plenitude of ability, set in relief by scarcity of cash. In a fluid society still to be molded by vigorous hands, the American tradition of success could flourish. Ability inevitably rose to the top.

It was with almost a melancholy acceptance of responsibility that young Mark Hopkins early realized his own mental powers and wanted a college education. His mother had bequeathed to him the character and capacity of the Curtises; he had inherited the Hopkins mind. He took life so hard that his mother was afraid he would never be entirely happy about anything. When he was thirteen years old, his Uncle Sewall asked him to come to Clinton, New York, to help on his farm, where he received board and schooling in return for the labor of his hands.

Life was not all work, however, to Mark's younger brother Albert at the age of nine. "On my coat I have thirty or forty buttons," he wrote, "which make a most brilliant appearance, so that I am daily strutting about in fine style."

Harry, the youngest, inherited the gaiety which life was crushing out of his mother. He was eleven years old and had already attended the school on Elm Street when he wrote to Mark: "Your absence renders it necessary that much of the management of business should fall to the agency of one particularly capable, and although my health has been much impaired yet I rejoice that my uncommon abilities quite makes up the deficiency of health as far as regards business."

Harry's letters are like a sudden streak of sunlight across the bleak New England scene. It was Harry who always knew where the pickerel were to be found, who nearly split his sides laughing when his grandfather fell over a fence, who knew the village gossip, and who liked to dance. "There has been a continual noise and buzying amongst the younger inhabitants for . . . the dancing master has again come to town and advertises that he will positively commence his dancing school at Mr. Hicks' . . . at two o'clock in the afternoon for ladies and at six in the evening for gentlemen. His terms are . . . 15 dollars for a family," wrote Mary Hopkins.

Seriousness gained gradually upon Albert, who considered dancing a trifling business and would be quite "in a fit" whenever it interfered with his studies, and wish he had never attended the "dumb dancing school." He liked better the evenings when, after tea, the books were brought out. A table, with candle and spectacles on it, stood before the fire. Seated around it Archibald would pore over the encyclopedia until nine o'clock, Harry, the lightweight, would read Plutarch, and Albert, *The History of the American Revolution*. Albert was sorry that he couldn't spend his evenings working at his Latin and wanted to have a little bag made in which to bring home his books at night. It was difficult to keep up with his brother Mark, however, for Mark could write letters in the Latin tongue.

In those days Williams College was the lodestar for all ambitious young men in western Massachusetts, but its situation was considered remote and at one time there was actually a chance of its being transferred to Stockbridge, which Dr. West's School of Prophets had already established as an intellectual center. Various Berkshire villages bid for the privilege of having it and Stockbridge subscribed the amount of $13,000 while Archibald, though he could ill afford it, gave $100, for he figured it would save him more than that to keep his sons at home while they pursued the higher branches of learning. Finally, however, the authorities decided to keep the university where it was and hopes of Williams for the Hopkins boys had to be temporarily abandoned, for their Uncle John, whose store had been ruined by the Republicans, died, leaving three orphan girls, and without an instant's hesitation, Archibald decided to adopt them. His usual fate had overtaken him. It was a long time before he could bear to tell his son Mark this news—Mark, who had never disappointed him in any way. "You must continue to be a good boy and I hope you will make a great man," he had written. Even then there was something unusual about Mark. A visiting cousin, Edwin Welles Dwight, on his way through New York State stopped at the Sewall Hopkins farm, and had been struck by his mental ability.

When, at last, in a semi-illiterate hand, Archibald wrote his son what had happened, the boy showed a disappointment, the maturity of which is seldom encountered at seventeen today: "I had rather have a liberal education and nothing else than to have considerable more money than to carry me through, but if you want my help I know that I owe a very great debt and am willing to pay what I can."

There was no way out of the difficulty and Mark had to come home. He soon found, however, that he could teach at a school near by, study for college in his spare time, and pay a hired man to take his place at home. He worked all through vacations along with the other farmers' sons who mingled theology with sawing wood and Latin verbs with milking cows.

Meanwhile, in the village, it was fearful to contemplate the laxness which might overtake Stockbridge if for a moment standards were let down. The heavy teams driving through the village in the War of 1812 had desecrated the Sabbath, and who could tell where such disregard of the Lord's Day would lead? In consequence the Society for the Preservation of Christian Morals was formed. Its constitution reads: "Believing that vice and immorality tend to bring down the judgments of a Righteous Providence . . . we the subscribers, for the more effectual suppression of vice and promotion of good morals . . . agree to bind ourselves by the following:

". . . The Members of the Society shall by their conversation and example encourage all virtuous conduct, and shall discountenance vice generally; and principally, the vice of Sabbath breaking, intemperance in the use of spirituous liquors and profaneness . . .

"It shall be the duty of each member to furnish the poor, as far as in his power, with the means of employment, that indolence may not betray them into vice . . .

"Any person of a fair moral character may become a member of this Society . . ."

Unfortunately, the society was on too high a plane for human nature. It was abolished because some people considered that it interfered with the province of the law. Other societies sprang up eagerly in its place, however, all of an aspiring nature. An auxiliary branch of the American Temperance Society was formed in 1826. The County Educational Society, the Berkshire Bible Society, the Sewing Society, tract societies, and societies for the education of young clergymen, trod close upon one another's heels. Various juvenile societies pushed in, too.

The Missionary Society was a favorite one, and it remained for Edwin Welles Dwight, the son of Henry W. Dwight, to introduce a variation on an old Stockbridge theme which went straight to the heart of New England. Before Dr. West's death, Edwin brought Henry Obookiah to call. Edwin was a pious young man and very much the son of his mother, upon whose tombstone were engraved the words:

> She brought up children.
> She lodged strangers.
> She washed the saints' feet.
> She relieved the afflicted.
> She diligently followed every good work.

Inclined to priggishness, he considered the discipline at Williams College lax, so he transferred himself to Yale where he studied for the ministry and showed a desire to enlighten the "waste places" of the state. It was in New Haven that he encountered a dark-skinned Hawaiian boy, dull of countenance and dressed in sailor's clothes, crying upon the steps of one of the college buildings. The lad explained that he was crying because all the knowledge within was denied him. This extraordinary statement intrigued Edwin, who took the boy home, saw that he was properly cared for and taught him English. From then on Henry Obookiah's tale of stark horror—he had seen his parents and brother killed before his eyes in the far-away island of "Owyhee"—elicited kindness, care, and education from New England ministers. His desire to learn seemed to them almost too good to be true. Along with English and mathematics, they dosed him with piety, which he readily absorbed. While tilling the fields in return for his board and lodging, he wrestled with his soul's wickedness in such real agony that, had he permitted such an ungrateful thought to cross his mind, he must have questioned the kindness of substituting the enduring terrors of eternal damnation for the more fleeting ones of the easy pagan world.

In due course Obookiah was converted and the good ministers' perfect work was done. He was chosen to preach the gospel to his people and his undeniable virtue was a constant reassurance that great work lay ahead in heathen lands. Dressed in a white frilled shirt and an overcoat, and looking rather like an organ-grinder's monkey, his appearance at missionary meetings brought in more money than any other appeal. But monkeys are delicate and Obookiah disappointed his benefactors in one respect: he died. Yet even then he was helpful. Edwin Dwight published his memoirs, which went through seventeen editions and was translated into several languages, including Choctaw.

Stockbridge contributed to the Berkshire Missionary Society and even boasted a missionary of its own. Before entering the ministry, Cyrus Byington had studied law with Jahleel Woodbridge. When he first heard of Indian Missions, he declared that his heart caught fire. In 1821, a large baggage wagon, with a basket hung between the seats in which to lay a baby, creaked its way through the village. A company of missionaries were on their way from settled New England to a Georgia wilderness, and Cyrus joined them with the pious books his mother and sister had given him under his arm. Eventually he joined the Choctaw Indians among whom he conducted a mission, which he wistfully called after

Stockbridge. He translated the Bible into Choctaw for his flock, and they also had their copy of Obookiah's memoirs. Thus Stockbridge was fulfilling the destiny laid down by John Sergeant. Now that everything was becoming civilized, tales of the conquest of heathen souls supplied the element of adventure which was fast being muffled at home.

In 1819, two years before Cyrus Byington started out to take care of his Choctaws, another young minister, who had given up a Connecticut parish to tend the souls of the emigrants on Lake Ontario, obligingly preached several times for the aging Dr. West. The now rickety meeting-house on the Hill seemed almost luxurious to him for he had been riding through the wilderness of New York State preaching in log houses. This young man, David Dudley Field, was so thoroughly orthodox that even the congregation which had been indoctrinated by Dr. West, could find no liberal loophole in his theology, and gave him a formal call.

Not since the War of 1812 had Stockbridge seen such heavily loaded wagons as those that made the journey from Haddam, Connecticut, bringing the new minister's belongings. It took them a week to come and return. They were piled high with beds, tables and bureaus and heavy boxes full of books, a wife and six children. On the way in from Great Barrington, the procession turned left at the corner by the Inn, continued down the Plain past the Dwights' house and across the river, past where the Indian boarding school had been, until it unloaded upon a hill where, in a later generation, Charles E. Butler was to build a summer house.

Out of the caravan stepped Submit Dickinson Field, whose youthful figure is hard to detach from the loving bromides her son Henry has placed like funeral wreaths about her. He has awarded her every quality admirable in womankind, yet out of his picture, as out of the lacework of an old-fashioned valentine, comes a very pretty girl, who went gaily about the task of taking care of her husband and final family of nine children on $700 a year. There was no New England holier-than-thou attitude about her devotion. One day she told her son Cyrus, "The doctor says I am very ill, but I shall be up tomorrow." It was this spirit rather than the host of virtues heaped gratefully upon her that lay behind the strength of will which enabled her sons to reform American laws and lay the Atlantic cable.

Only two or three months after their arrival, a new Field came into the world. He was tactfully named after two village figures: Cyrus, for Cyrus Williams, one of the new family of Williamses who had come to town, and West for his father's predecessor.

After two or three years, the Fields moved right into the village, just west of Jonathan Edwards's house on the north side of the street, and here the children settled themselves to the business of growing up. To the original quota—David Dudley, Emilia Ann, Timothy Beals, Matthew Dickinson, Jonathan Edwards, Stephen Johnson—were added Cyrus West, Henry Martyn and Mary Elizabeth.

The Fields began each day with prayers. They sat around the fire, their Bibles in their hands, and each took turns reading a piece a day until they got from Genesis to Revelations, then started all over again. After this the children who were old enough trouped down to the village school. It was here that Dudley first saw Mark Hopkins. Although the two were somewhat divergent, their backgrounds and their futures met. They were to be friends for life.

The new Stockbridge minister had a loud, ringing voice and an Old-Testament kind of face which his son Cyrus inherited. In his narrow, illumined mind every word of the Bible was directly inspired by God. It was he who established the Sunrise Meeting, a service held early upon New Year's morning, which became a village institution for over a hundred years. Mark Hopkins was tremendously moved by his sermons but there were people who complained that he was old-fashioned and preached *at* his parishioners. Some of the criticism was perhaps not worth taking seriously, however, since it emanated from that English family, the Ashburners, who had just settled in the town and were inclined to fancy themselves, and from the Pomeroys, who, everyone knew, were Unitarians.

When Dr. Field was not standing at his desk writing his sermons, he was engaged upon preparing *A History of the County of Berkshire,* a work which goes exhaustively into the geology, flora and fauna as well as the historical achievements of the county. Sometimes a gleam of humor relieved the minister's austerity. When his house burned down and he saw his sermons go up in flames, he remarked, "They give more light to the world than if I had preached them."

Several years after his arrival a crisis arose in the church. A new meetinghouse on the village green was suggested to take the place of the old church, which had never really pleased anyone and now was becoming dilapidated. The Curtisville members of the congregation protested. The extra stretch up Church Street, after the long drive over the meadows, put too great a strain upon even Curtis energy. They wanted a church of their own and Dr. Field was told that a society had been formed which felt it "necessary to be dismissed from the church under your watch and care." The Stockbridge members, on the other hand, did not consider it in the interest of the Redeemer's kingdom to have a church in Curtisville at all. A good deal of bickering went on until a meeting of the clergy of the surrounding towns met to hear both sides of the question.

Not since the days of Lavinia Fisk had the assuaging balm of a council been more needed. This one performed its functions admirably. On the one hand it lamented the fact that the Stockbridge members had insisted upon placing the church where their neighbors did not wish it, and on the other hand reproved the members from Curtisville for so abrupt a withdrawal. In the end it was forced, with some reluctance, to let the "aggrieved brethren" have their way.

The council's recommendation was enthusiastically accepted, and sixty-two members of the former Stockbridge church were thereupon incorporated into the North Congregational Church at Stockbridge. Money and materials were pledged for a meetinghouse and the seating was arranged along worldly, rather than spiritual, lines. The Curtises and Daniel Fairchild led off with $100—and the best pews. Herman Whittlesey offered two of his finest pines and Lyman Churchill twenty pairs of thick shoes or the equivalent value in boots or shoes of any kind.

After more bickering, a site was chosen and the Reverend Nathan Shaw installed. Sometimes the minister from Stockbridge would drive over the meadows to preach to the rebellious portion of his flock. He usually took two of his boys up into the pulpit with him, and at the last long prayer would put a hand on each of their sandy heads, "to be sure they were there."

The new Stockbridge church, a fine, red-brick building, unusual enough to catch the eye of the passing young Frenchman, Beaumont, who made a sketch of it, was dedicated in 1825. It stood only a few rods from the spot where John Sergeant's meetinghouse had been. Later on, it was painted white and the Ladies' Sewing Society hovered over it, putting in blinds and carpets and chairs and even a "sofa" for the pulpit. Soon after the new church had settled into the landscape, a wave of revivals swept the village. All those anxious for their souls were asked to stand up in their pews. There was such a poor response that the minister decided a feud in the village prevented a more abundant stirring of the spirit.

Up at Cherry Cottage, Harry Hopkins cast a skeptical modern eye upon the revivals. In vain his brothers begged him to become converted. Albert was sure he stood a chance of having his soul burned in the very center of hell. Mark, too, was troubled. They had both pursued their own chosen careers while Harry had stayed at home to look after the farm. Yet his radiantly unselfish nature was to them no guarantee of salvation, and saving one's soul for the next world remained the most important concern of this.

Gradually, however, Mark worked out of his earlier religious narrowness and came to a compromise with the more tolerant conceptions of the nineteenth century. He established a halfway station between Jonathan Edwards and Channing, where men and women could nourish a reasonable hope of salvation, beside a passionate belief in a personal God.

Before going to college, Mark taught school for a while in the South, where he met and conversed with one of those "monsters called atheists." After his graduation he became a doctor and had started to practice in New York when he was called to be Professor of Moral Philosophy and Rhetoric at Williams College, of which he later became the head. Here his rigid integrity, intellectual breadth, and the nobility of his character, placed him securely among the greatest college presidents in the country.

Albert, who achieved distinction second only to Mark, was appointed Professor of Mathematics and Natural Philosophy at Williams. Later he was Professor of Astronomy as well. His religion always remained of the darker tinge, so that Harry once exclaimed, "If I am forgotten in consequence of his religion then let all the world go, I care not if I die . . . If he is so altered that he will never be Albert to me again, I declare to you that I believe that religion to be false and desire never to know it."

One day Harry discovered he could draw animals with charcoal on the marble slab in front of the fireplace; also the view from his window at Cherry Cottage. So he decided to become a painter and went to New York, where Robert and Harry Sedgwick, by that time distinguished lawyers, befriended him. Unfortunately he embarked with them upon a business venture for making bricks out of soft coal, which Mark mistrusted as impractical and so did Catherine Sedgwick. They were right, and Harry came back to Stockbridge, where, in spite of Mark's offer to send him through college, he remained for some time writing delightful letters to his brothers about the quantity of marriageable girls in the village.

Meanwhile David Dudley Field had left Williams and was ready to start out in the world. Upon the occasion of his leaving home, his father behaved with classic simplicity. He gave his eldest son a Bible and $10, and taking him into his study, commended him to the protection of Almighty God. Dudley studied law in Albany and afterwards entered the law office of Harry and Robert Sedgwick in New York.

He did not suffer the pangs of homesickness which afflicted his brother, Cyrus, when, in his turn, he went out to seek his fortune. Despite his father's encouraging words, "I am sure you will succeed, for your playmates never could get you to play until all the work for which you were responsible was done," the fifteen-year-old Cyrus spent many lonely evenings watching the boats go up the Hudson, and thinking of home. He remembered how only a month or two before he had taken a part in *She Stoops to Conquer,* given by the students at the Stockbridge Academy, and wondered what his schoolmates, Henry Dwight and Edward Carter, were doing. He was so miserable that his mother, who did not have time for unnecessary emotions, told one of his brothers that if Cyrus was still so unhappy he had better come home. Mark

THE FIELD BROTHERS
DAVID DUDLEY, HENRY MARTYN, CYRUS WEST, STEPHEN JOHNSON

Hopkins, who chanced to run across the boy one day at his brother Dudley's, was very consoling. "I would not give much for a boy if he were not homesick upon leaving home," he said.

In those days, the business world, still unexploited, was a fat oyster to a capable young man. Cyrus's business career reads like a Horatio Alger story. Upon his arrival in New York, he entered the great dry-goods store of A. T. Stewart, as errand boy. His first year's salary was $50; his board cost him $2 a week. Just as Mark Hopkins had stood ready to help Harry, so Dudley lent Cyrus the money necessary to eke out his earnings. Families stood together, solid clans against the onslaughts of the world. Cyrus kept careful accounts of all his expenditures and sent them home to his father: "From Stockbridge to New York, $2.00 . . . To one vial of spirits of turpentine (used to get spots out of coat) 6¼ cents."

After working at A. T. Stewart's for three years, Cyrus left to go into the paper business. He prospered until, through no fault of his own, the firm failed. Characteristically he assumed, and eventually paid, his partner's debts. He married Mary Stone and went to live in Gramercy Park, next to his brother Dudley. A door was cut between the two houses so that the family solution would not be diluted.

The Field brothers anticipated the modern conception of the "tired business man," with the difference that they never seemed to be tired. For many years Cyrus's children saw him only occasionally, for he ate his breakfast by lamplight and had his dinner and supper downtown.

As for Dudley, who shortly became a distinguished lawyer, his day was hardly less crowded. After an early ride in Central Park, he worked steadily until just before dinner after which he took a short nap and then was ready to work on his hobby, the recodification of the laws of New York, until late into the night. His evenings, he considered, were merely a "healthy diversion after the strain of the day."

Dudley was fond of saying that the only men who made a lasting impression upon the world were fighters, and his life bore out this idea. Tall, straight and handsome, he had the look of a sulky mastiff who could take up his enemies one by one, shake them, and throw them off. He was brilliant, arbitrary, and ruthless. The cases he argued before the Supreme Court have passed into history. Yet, accused of illegally arranging an election for his shady clients, Jay Gould and Jim Fisk, in the Erie Railroad litigation, his conduct was questioned by the bar of New York. No vote was ever taken, however, on the report of the investigating committee. Acting upon the principle that every man has a right to be defended, Field incurred further criticism when he served as chief counsel for the notorious Boss Tweed.

Law reform, however, remained his chief interest. After years of struggle he succeeded in getting the legislature of New York to appoint a commission to "reduce into a written and systematic form the whole body of the law of this State." Dudley did most of the commissioners' work, and although his Penal Code was not adopted by New York until 1880, his Civil and Criminal Codes were accepted in many other states, and he drafted an outline of an international code and helped to form the Association for the Reform and Codification of the Law of Nations.

Meanwhile, in Stockbridge, the family continued to grow up. The beautiful Emilia Ann was married to Josiah Brewer from Tyringham. Josiah had previously been sent by the American Board of Missions to look into the condition of the Jews in Turkey and perhaps it was due to his influence that Stockbridge became sufficiently aroused to the plight of the Jewish race to found a society for "meliorating their condition." How much was accomplished on this ambitious program no one can say, but Josiah decided to shift his interest to the Greeks, and came home only long enough to carry off Emilia Ann. They went to live in Smyrna, where he opened the first Greek school for girls. In 1837, Cyrus could write that The Ladies' Greek Association of Stockbridge held their fair on the Fourth of July on Little (Laurel) Hill and raised all of $127. Perhaps they had the Brewer school in mind.

The Brewers' oldest son, David Jonathan, was later to become a member of the United States Supreme Court. There he was welcomed by another member of his family, his uncle, Stephen Johnson Field. As a young man, Stephen had gone out to California in the gold rush. He early displayed the family business capacity by selling chamois skin he had bought in New York for gold-dust bags at an excellent profit. He became the leading lawyer in the boom town of Yubaville, and in 1864 was elected Chief Justice of California and finally Justice of the Supreme Court, where he served for fifty-four years.

Henry Martyn, the youngest of the "four famous Field Brothers," was smaller and more delicate than the rest. Perhaps because of his relatively small size, he put on a pompous front and would walk into a room, stiff-legged, rubbing his hands together in self-congratulatory appreciation of a pleasant world. After all, even he had gone to college at twelve years of age, and had delivered an address on temperance in Tyringham at the age of fourteen.

Henry, like his father, became a minister, but of the broader, nineteenth century brand. He had European aspirations, and his brother Dudley, always ready to help his family, offered him money that he might study in Germany, an offer negatived by the elder David Dudley because of the dangerous rationalistic tendencies there. New Haven was considered a safer substitute.

Henry managed to get to Europe, however. He went to Paris and observed the Revolution of 1848. He went to Rome, observed Roman Catholicism and lamented it. Anxious to burst New England swaddling bands, he was delighted that his first parish was in St. Louis, where he was pastor of the Presbyterian Church. Later he became editor and owner of *The Evangelist,* an important Presbyterian periodical. He was also the family biographer and from his Victorian pen the massive Dudley, the inexorable Cyrus, emerge like Titans resting on pink clouds.

There was one respect in which the little Henry outtopped his brothers. Field wives heretofore had fitted into the Field picture, in no way disturbing the masculine preponderance of its composition. Dudley had had three of them, the first, a Stockbridge girl, Lucinda Hopkins, one of the Hopkins cousins raised under Archibald's roof. But Henry's wife stuck right out of her setting. Little Stockbridge children used to call her "the French Mrs. Field."

While observing the Revolution of 1848, Henry had met a young woman who had been implicated in one of the country's most famous murder trials. Henriette Desportes had been a governess in the family of the Duc de Praslin. He and his wife were unhappily married and, when the duchess was found murdered, Henriette was accused of instigating the crime. The trial had far-reaching political implications, and did much to shake Louis Philippe's already tottering throne. Henriette was acquitted, however, and sailed for America, where she again met the young American who had been so kind to her during the harrowing period of her imprisonment. They were married in 1851, an act which took courage on Henry's part, for it could not have been easy to bring a French wife with such an equivocal background into the solid phalanx of the Fields. She was undoubtedly charming, with soft brown hair framing a serious, intellectual face, and her knowledge of the world, of books and of painting far exceeded that of most well-turned-out American young ladies. In New York everyone went to her parties. She would never allow Henry to be overshadowed by his more famous brothers.

"Where is dear Henry?" asked Mrs. Cyrus one day.

"Dear Henry is upstairs," was the quick reply, "writing dear Cyrus's speeches."

The story of the Field brothers was running its usual, well-regulated course when in 1854 came its most dramatic and unpredictable chapter. Cyrus, at the age of thirty-four, had succeeded in paying back all his debts and considered retiring on the comfortable fortune he had accumulated. Life was hanging slack on his hands when his brother Matthew introduced him to a man named Gisborne, who had conceived the idea of running a telegraph line between St. John's, Nova Scotia, and the mainland of America. When Cyrus heard about it, another idea, more romantic, more impossible, lodged in his shrewd Yankee brain and was held there immovably for thirteen years.

Few adventure stories equal that of the laying of the Atlantic cable. Even Henry's gentle flow of words is powerless to clog the excitement of its action. Gisborne was first bought out and a company of solid millionaires were placed in charge, shepherded by the guardian brother, Dudley. After two and a half years spent, among other things, in cutting down the primeval forest and in putting a road through the wilderness of Newfoundland, the optimistic promoters considered that now only the actual laying of the cable remained.

Such an event, like big-game hunting later on, promised plenty of excitement. The latest of modern wonders was to be shown. Consequently the arrival of the ship from London carrying the first portion of the cable, which was to stretch from St. John's to the mainland, was a great social event.

One of the most modern steamships, the *James Adger*, flags flying, set out from New York for Newfoundland with a crowd aboard. There was Peter Cooper, one of the millionaires; there was Professor Morse, and several gentlemen of the press. There were a great number of ladies, "whose presence gave life and animation to the party." There was the ubiquitous Henry, flying hither and thither with words of wonder and of praise. There, too, was a white-haired old gentleman, with burning eyes, who had come down from Stockbridge to see how this wild scheme of his son Cyrus would turn out.

It was some time before the big steamer discovered the little cable ship, which was hidden among the rocks, but when it did, the two started across the Gulf of St. Lawrence, the cable ship in tow. Halfway across a storm came up and the cable had to be cut.

A second attempt at laying a cable from Newfoundland was successful and Cyrus went to work to organize a company in England, to which it became fashionable to subscribe. Finally, in 1857, two ships set out from England with the first Atlantic cable. Several hundred miles out at sea it broke and half a million dollars were literally at the bottom of the ocean. Three times more the experiment was repeated; each time a different method was used and each time it failed. Many people now wanted to call the whole thing off. It was so obviously a harebrained scheme and Cyrus was either a knave or a fool. After a fourth attempt, however, he was able to send his father the laconic message: "Cable successfully laid. All well." Cyrus's mother broke the news to his wife simply and to the point, after the Field manner: "Mary, the cable is laid"; and then, "Thomas, believest thou this?"

The bells were rung and guns were fired. Children let out of school shouted, "The cable is laid! The cable is laid!" And the rest of the country echoed Stockbridge's wild joy.

GOING OUT INTO THE WORLD

A special celebration was planned by the village for the receipt of the first cable message: "Europe and America are united by telegraphy. Glory to God in the highest; on earth peace, good will toward men." This was sent by the directors of the company in England to those in America, and was followed by a long message of congratulation from Queen Victoria to President Buchanan. In order that the New York papers might have a detailed account of the Stockbridge celebration, a telegraph line was put through from Pittsfield to Jonathan Edwards Field's law office, the little white building next to Mr. Treadway's present house, in order that the New York papers might have an account of the proceedings, and the story goes that young Stephen Field, Cyrus's nephew, took the message when it came. For Stockbridge the cable was still a family affair.

In New York a huge parade was followed by a magnificent banquet. Churches were covered with flags, placards posted in store windows, modestly stating, "Our Field is the Field of the World." The festivities were hardly over when news arrived that the cable had ceased to work.

The world swung into reverse. The adventure was discredited and before long the Civil War occupied everyone's attention. Cyrus Field's business was in a state of collapse. His New York office and warehouse were burned. During these years his face became more and more like that of a Hebrew prophet and a sweetness softened its fine, unyielding lines. Those who worked with him never heard him grumble. Undaunted he formed another company. Again he chartered a steamship, this time the *Great Eastern,* the largest in the world, again obtained a cable, better insulated than its predecessors, and again put to sea. Not only once, but two and three times more, was his work in vain. It was not until 1866 that the first Atlantic cable was finally successfully laid.

Despite their individual achievements, the Fields, remain primarily a family, and as a family they reached their apotheosis in 1853, when the Field parents celebrated their golden anniversary. Thirty-five members of the clan met in Stockbridge and a room called the Golden Wedding Room was added to the Rectory for the occasion. There were Dudley and his wife and three children. There were Emilia Ann and Josiah Brewer home from Smyrna with six of their seven children. There was Matthew, who had made a name for himself building suspension bridges, with his wife and six children. There was Jonathan Edwards, with his wife and two of his five children. Jonathan Edwards had come back from Ann Arbor, where he had practiced law, to live in Stockbridge and go into politics. Although a Democrat, he was so popular that the Republicans elected him President of the Senate three times. In 1862, he took the lead in putting the first water system into the town.

Cyrus, with four of his seven children, Henry with his charming Henriette, and Mary Elizabeth, the youngest of the family, were there also. Only Stephen Johnson, who had not been able to get back from California, and Timothy Beals, reputed the most brilliant of them all, who as a young man had enlisted in the navy and disappeared at sea, were missing links in the chain. The same strongly marked features, the blue eyes, high brows, and sandy hair could be found in different sizes all up and down the line. A blurred daguerreotype recalls them, and in the midst of the group Submit Dickinson's face shines with the quiet radiance of fulfillment. Her children were together as in the old days, and as in the old days her husband rose and commended them to the God of Isaac and the God of Jacob.

Chapter X

THE VILLAGE BECOMES LITERARY

IN the 1820's, just as Stockbridge had become sophisticated to the pioneers of the Western Reserve, it underwent the inspection of visitors from the East who put it in its place. Cultivated Europeans, wishing to study the habits of the strange New World, got out their field glasses and recorded their observations, which were apt to be unfavorable.

William Ashburner was the first to arrive but he, surprisingly, did not have to be coaxed into liking America. He had brought his family over from England with the avowed purpose of leaving the decadent Old World behind and putting his agricultural theories into practice in the new. His daughter Anne did not share either his theories or his enthusiasm. When their forlorn little party stopped at the Red Lion Inn, the red-faced owner, Mr. Hicks, and his fat, good-natured wife seemed the "essence of vulgarity and just the persons to keep such an inn." Anne could not bring herself to do anything but curtsy until her father told her to shake hands, and it was in her new country that she learned her first lesson in democracy—to be ready for "general cordiality without distinction of person."

The Ashburners took lodgings with the Widow Jones, in an ugly, unpainted house where the front door led without ceremony into the parlor. Here the talk seemed to Anne dull, consisting mostly of questions and answers and she would be nonplused by a shrill "What say?" to her attempts at making conversation.

She saw nothing pretty about the village street and much to criticize. The irregularly planted maple trees gave an occasional patchy shade to the ragged footpaths that ran along their base. Some people didn't even bother to clear away the garbage from the front of their houses, and the cemetery was an open eyesore, unfenced and sprawling. There were other drawbacks as well. Mrs. Jones had no flowers, only vegetables, in her garden. Anne's little sisters were given altogether too much pie. In winter the large Franklin stove in the parlor hardly served to counteract the cold air which poured in at the doors and windows of the boarding house. During school vacations, great oafs of farmers' sons filled the kitchen, and Anne felt left out of the discussions concerning new churches, missionary meetings, and lectures. Her polite inquiry, "Have you been for a walk this fine day?" met with no response in a community where leisure for such idleness was unknown.

After a year or so, William Ashburner built a house just outside the village under Bear Mountain, which brought Stockbridge a step nearer European sophistication. Built upon an English plan and designed by an architect in India, it was called Bombay Hill and bore no possible relation to Berkshire requirements. There was a long hall leading from the kitchen so that cooking smells, all too prevalent in America, could not penetrate into the dining room. The house required more servants than the family could afford to employ and by the time Captain Basil Hall of the King's Royal Navy and his wife came to visit them from England the Ashburners had fallen partially into low American ways. They breakfasted between five and six. Mrs. Hall, however, showed so plainly that "to get up at that hour was an effort beyond her nature," that the meal was postponed until eight.

THE VILLAGE BECOMES LITERARY

During Basil Hall's sojourn in this country, he formed definite opinions upon the moderate intelligence of its people, their limited information, and their incapacity for self-government. His American friends, anxious to shine in English eyes, had begged him to go to their villages and talk to their farmers, where, they were sure, he would find the high-minded and intelligent citizens of the country, and the Captain, willing, if not anxious, to give the devil his due, consented to try this broad-minded experiment in Stockbridge.

During his visit, he was taken to the meeting of the Agricultural Society, an affair of great local importance. Here farmers brought their oxen and sheep, their peaches and apples, to be exhibited. William Ashburner wanted to show his fancy Mangel Wurzel and Rutabaga grown in specially drained fields, and importations never seen here before. Harry Hopkins came down from Cherry Cottage to compare notes about farming implements and to get new ideas on planting. His nature responded to the flutes and drums, the flags, and the bright muskets of the militia which added a note of gaiety to the occasion and he didn't mind, as Basil Hall did, even when it rained.

When the ploughing match, the chief feature of the fair, was over, the men repaired to the tavern and the women went home. Basil Hall felt there should be more mingling and gaiety between the sexes. "The Americans," he remarked, "are a very grave people . . . they appear woefully ignorant of the difficult art of being gracefully idle." The smell of tobacco smoke and whisky was so unpleasant at the tavern that, although treated with gratifying courtesy, he found the meal, like many others in America, "a mere business to be got over, not a rational pleasure to be enjoyed." Afterwards, a long procession filed into the church and listened to a sermon pointing out the fact that a proportion of more than two-and-a-half gallons of liquor to every man, woman, and child was consumed annually in the village. The Captain was not in the least surprised. He considered America the only place he had ever traveled where the use of ardent spirits was not confined exclusively to the vulgar.

Altogether the Captain left in full possession of his original ideas. Unlike Anne, he conceded that the village was a pretty one, and the houses gave entirely the impression of belonging to gentlemen. He admitted, too, that he had come in contact with "instances of that character for which New Englanders are so deservingly distinguished," but at the same time he had not seen anything so peculiarly remarkable in the people as they themselves were continually leading him to expect.

The Captain was followed by Lord Morpeth. A kindly, solid, squarely-built man, he wore a bright red waistcoat and exuded the beef and port of Old England. When he asked to see a typical American, Theodore Sedgwick took him to call on Captain Roswell Palmer, who lived upon the Hill where John Bacon's house had stood. Two old soldiers, Lord Morpeth and the Captain compared notes about the Revolutionary War, and Morpeth carried away so high an opinion of American sturdiness and independence that he won a grateful place in hearts peculiarly sensitive to English criticism.

At about the time of Lord Morpeth's visit, two elegant Frenchmen, Conte Alexis de Tocqueville and Gustave de Beaumont, arrived. Their curiosity had been so piqued by the rumor that a real authoress lived in this American wilderness that they had put themselves out considerably to call upon her. Even Basil Hall would have shared their interest. Stockbridge had more lures than cattle shows, and he had pronounced himself "gratified to a very high degree by making acquaintance with the accomplished author of several admirable works of fancy."

They were not more surprised than Catherine Sedgwick herself when, in 1822, *A New England Tale* turned out to be a best seller, and she found herself hailed as one of the coming fiction writers in America. *Redwood, Hope Leslie, Clarence,* and *The Linwoods* followed. Their success was immediate. "Her works were admired," said Bryant, "and added to our household libraries, without asking, as had often been the case in regard to other American authors, permission from the citizens of Great Britain." Judge Theodore's careless, extravagant little girl, eating nuts and sausages between the sessions of morning and afternoon school, feeding her passionate love of reading upon Rollin's *Ancient History,* had gone away to boarding school, seen Boston and New York, had even traveled as far as Montreal, and come back to write about Stockbridge. The backwoods of America had found a voice, and New England characters like Debby Lenox and Crazy Bet were promoted from life into literature.

Catherine was one of the buffer generation who stood between the rigidities of her father's world and the full sweep of nineteenth-century thought. Bryant speaks of her works as showing "the old Puritan spirit, tempered somewhat by the gentler medium through which it has passed." Like himself, Catherine belonged to the first blooming of American literature and, like him, her petals turned towards the sun of New York, rather than the bleak dawn of Boston. There Washington Irving had already achieved the position of gentleman-of-letters and James Fenimore Cooper was hailed as the American Scott.

Catherine resented it when Basil Hall undertook to tell her how to write, for a new confidence had been bred of America's independence. Yet she could not fail to be pleased by the accolade of British praise. "She is the most popular writer, we believe, in the United States. Her works have warmed the national heart," said *The Westminster Review.*

Europeans, who looked at "the prosaic types of the founders of the Republic and considered them the only types that America would ever produce," welcomed this "first utterance of a national mind." An American woman whose education sufficed to give her something in common with Europeans was writing about her own country in language they could understand.

It is difficult for us in the twentieth century to separate what those early reviewers considered the fresh and lively treatment of scenes in actual life from the stock-in-trade of romanticism, daggers, hairbreadth escapes and spotless virtue, which Catherine had at her command. Stuffed now away into attics, crowded on top shelves, is her sentimentality, redolent of pinks and lavender. Vanished is the elevating moral tone through which her heroines walked their sinless way. The scene in *Hope Leslie,* laid upon Laurel Hill, where the Indian maid, Magawisca, shields her lover from a violent death, no longer moves us to tears as so many of her scenes did the hardened Mr. Wesley Harper, one of the original brothers of the publishing firm.

> "Mononotto (the wicked Indian) . . . brandished his hatchet over Everell's head, and cried exultingly . . . 'I will pour out this English boy's blood to the last drop, and give his flesh and bones to the dogs and wolves' . . .
>
> "Everell sunk calmly on his knees, not to supplicate life, but to commend his soul to God . . . The chief raised the deadly weapon, when Magawisca, springing from the precipitous side of the rock, screamed 'Forbear!' and interposed her arm. It was too late. The blow was levelled—force and direction given; the stroke, aimed at Everell's neck, severed his defender's arm, and left him unharmed. The lopped, quivering member dropped over the precipice. Mononotto staggered and fell senseless, and all the savages, uttering horrible yells, rushed toward the fatal spot.
>
> "'Stand back!' cried Magawisca. 'I have bought his life with my own. Fly, Everell—nay, speak not, but fly—thither—to the east!' she cried, more vehemently.

"Everell's faculties were paralyzed by a rapid succession of violent emotions. He was conscious only of a feeling of mingled gratitude and admiration for his preserver. He stood motionless, gazing on her. 'I die in vain, then?' she cried, in an accent of such despair that he was roused. He threw his arms around her, and pressed her to his heart as he would a sister that had redeemed his life with her own, and then, tearing himself from her, he disappeared."

Naturally Magawisca did not die, and recovered only to be more noble, while Everell was appropriately grateful.

At Catherine's zenith she was ranked close to Cooper, but even in her lifetime her vogue began to pass and by 1880 she was "more respected than read." As life went on ethical angles claimed more and more of her attention. She wrote little essays on the value of women learning how to cook, the undesirability of gossip, and the importance of manners. "Illiterate and vulgar language is an obvious sign of ill-breeding. Profane and indelicate terms are rather violations of morality. Cant phrases, and what is called slang, which school girls as well as college boys are addicted to, is ill-bred." Her friends rejoiced that her power over the human heart was given over to the highest and noblest ends, and good Doctor Bellows rated her as among the most efficient missionaries in the Lord's vineyard.

Like others of her generation Catherine had revolted from a Calvinistic upbringing and found spiritual liberation in William Ellery Channing's conception of a benevolent God. *A New England Tale*, criticizing the older religion, "miffed the Calvinists," yet although her religion lapsed often into moralizing, it was still intensely vital and maintained, like that of Mark Hopkins, a personal urgency, minus the ancient curse.

Catherine's personality had little to do with her books. Only in her journals and letters does it come out refreshingly alive. "My author existence has always seemed something accidental, and independent of my inner self," she wrote. Her portraits vary from that of a middle-aged, hook-nosed schoolmarm to that of a handsome young woman, synthesizing piety and romance, wrapped in a Byronic cloak, appropriate to her literary calling. Neither is recognizable in Anne Ashburner's description: "There was an absence of all stiffness about her—the long, natural curls of an unstudied headdress, the bonnet untied and as often in the hand." She had a natural independence of thought and did as she pleased, leading skating parties of boys and girls upon the meadows where the river had overflowed and letting herself be pulled about on a sled in a manner which some of the village considered most unsuitable.

Catherine moved, like the sun, within her family orbit, staying first with one brother and then another. Although she never married, the legend of forty-eight suitors amply supported her feminine charm. She demanded affection and gave it in return. "God only knows how I have loved my brothers," she wrote, "the union of principle, of taste, and of affection, I have had with them." In the midst of nieces and nephews, her life had a rounded fullness usually associated with marriage and children. One never thought of her as an old maid.

With Catherine, Stockbridge had taken another step on its career. Other literary figures heard about the lovely village where the authoress lived, and wanted to taste its charms. That was the time, too, when women were becoming emancipated and could indulge in friendships with other women, based upon more than the comparison of patterns, recipes, and children.

So it was that in the autumn of 1835 a handsome young creature, worn down with unhappy domesticity and bursting with intellectual eagerness, was deposited with Catherine for a visit by a tired and exasperated husband. After this,

Catherine Sedgwick

THE VILLAGE BECOMES LITERARY 213

Fanny Kemble Butler came often to Berkshire. "It is a region entirely inhabited by Sedgwicks and their belongings," she wrote, and made friends with all the family. Mrs. Basil Hall had found Catherine passable but thought her brothers awkward, country bumpkins, who took turns staring in admiration at her husband. To Fanny, however, they were refreshing after the monotony of her days at Butler Place. Later, when her marriage had ended in divorce, she bought a house in Lenox. Here, by her dramatic genius and the amplitude of her personality, she triumphed over the separation from her children which was the tragedy of her life.

The informality of Berkshire enchanted her. Characteristically she flung herself into elaborate descriptions of the countryside, which were becoming the fashion. "I look at it [a sketch of the Stockbridge Bowl] very often with yearning . . . for the splendid, rosy sunsets over the dark blue mountain tops, and for the clear and lovely expanse of the waters reflecting both, above all for the wild white-faced streams that come leaping down the steep stairways of the hills." In Italy, she thought with longing of Berkshire solitudes, where she could ride for hours without seeing anyone. Man, however, was still untutored. "The ugly, mean, matter-of-fact farm houses or white-washed, stiff, staring villages" could not compare with the picturesque houses of the Italian peasants.

Fanny invested daily life with theatrical overtones. One day, getting out of her carriage, she turned to the man who was driving and announced in her most dramatic manner: "You have been driving with Fanny Kemble." "Madam," was the quick Yankee answer, "you have rid with John Smith." Her outspoken frankness shocked many people. When she gave a Shakespeare reading in Stockbridge, shades of the Society for the Preservation of Christian Morals stalked abroad. Word got about that she was going to read *The Merry Wives of Windsor*. Not since Mr. Fisk had propriety been so offended. Something of his spirit, too, underwent a reincarnation in Fanny's words as she came forward without waiting to be introduced and began: "Ladies and gentlemen, I have been met in my robing room by a committee of your town and they have requested me not to read The Merry Wives of Windsor. Ladies and gentlemen, I have been met in my robing room by the clergymen of your town and they have requested me not to read The Merry Wives of Windsor. Ladies and gentlemen, I have been met in my robing room by the school teachers of your town and they have requested me not to read The Merry Wives of Windsor. Ladies and gentlemen, I now take pleasure in reading to you—The Merry Wives of Windsor."

Shortly after Fanny's first visit, another celebrated English woman came up to see Catherine. Ear trumpet in hand, Miss Harriet Martineau arrived to take notes on the New England scene. Stockbridge rose to the occasion and "Lafayetted" her, putting that jaundiced but intrepid devotee of causes into a lenient frame of mind, so that when her turn came to be taken to the Agricultural Fair she shared American amusement over the supercilious Basil. When offered a "piece" of pie, for instance, he had answered that "bit" was the correct expression.

Never before had Miss Martineau been the cause of such a jubilee. She liked being given roses by the village children. In fact, she liked Stockbridge so much that she came to visit once more, boarding on the top of the Hill for the sum of two dollars a week. From her window, she watched the people going to the red-brick church on the village green below. Black specks would gather from every side, disappear and, at a given moment, emerge again like ants. Houses and trees were planted on a carpet of green, which stretched from the bottom of the Hill to her very doorstep.

Miss Martineau breakfasted every morning at half-past seven upon "excellent" bread, potatoes, hung beef, eggs, and strong tea; but in the matter of the bread, her good humor must have run away with her for we have Fanny Kemble's authority that there was no good bread in Berkshire county. Fanny maintained that both Catherine and her brother Charles were martyrs to dyspepsia on this account, and Fanny sent a recipe for making "effervescing bread" to Catherine.

Harriet loved to walk, and found, like Anne Ashburner, that Americans did not. She rambled about, hunted up marsh flowers, and even tramped to Lenox. Arm in arm with her friend Catherine she walked beside the "sweet Housatonic." Although bluestockings, they were also women and must have discussed their friends. Catherine was all enthusiasm about Fanny Kemble, whom she considered "a captivating creature, steeped to the very lips in genius." Harriet could not agree: "There was a green-room cast of mind about all the Kembles." Catherine thought Pierce Butler rigid and exacting while in Harriet's opinion, Fanny had "sported so perversely with other people's peace that her notorious misfortunes were self-inflicted."

As the two friends continued their walk, there was always literature to be discussed, if they kept safely to the subject of Harriet's works, *Devotional Exercises and Addresses* and *Illustrations of Political Economy,* since Harriet thought the less said about Catherine's novels the better. There was the great question of slavery, too, which occupied everyone's mind. Catherine and her family were extremely timid about expressing their feelings on this subject, her friend reproached her, adding that it was an American trait. She herself did not mind being socially ostracized for openly espousing the Abolitionist cause. Now it was Catherine's turn to disagree. Why, one of her own novels had been banned in the South for the mere mention of slavery. With so many states hypersensitive upon the subject, the Abolitionists were simply making trouble and secession might be the result.

The intransigeant Harriet was nothing if not obstinate. "A human decree which contravenes the laws of nature must give way," she declaimed, "when the two are brought into conflict." The probable outcome of the matter, as she saw it, would be the dissolution of the Union. The friends became more and more edgy as they walked by the river bank for Harriet had not reckoned upon the patriotism of Daniel Webster's generation. "The dissolution of the Union!" cried the gentle Catherine, turning suddenly fierce and snatching her arm away. "The Union is sacred and must be preserved at all costs."

They were an ill-assorted pair, the angular English woman and the softer American, and their friendship did not long survive. Harriet considered Catherine addicted to flattery, like others of her race, and did not hesitate to tell her so, pointing out that when she opened her letters she found only praise of herself, instead of what she really wanted to hear. Catherine's feelings were hurt and she considered her literary lioness inclined to be "rash and rough." Now, a few English violets on the bank beside the Sedgwick house, a present to Catherine, are all that is left in Stockbridge of Miss Harriet Martineau.

But other feminine friendships sprang up in her place. Mrs. Anna Jameson, the well-known art critic, fitted into the picture admirably. Like Harriet, she was serious; like Fanny, unhappily married. Then came Frederika Bremer, the Swedish novelist and believer in women's rights; Lucy Stone, the Abolitionist, who spoke in Stockbridge; and Sara Parton, alias Fanny Fern, who visited there. Fanny was popular as the author of several works, among them *Fern-leaves from Fanny's Portfolio* and *Little Ferns for Fanny's Little Friends*. So, too, came her brother, N. P. Willis, handsome and foppishly dressed, author of *Pencillings by the Way* and *Loiterings of Travel*, of whom Oliver Wendell Holmes had said that he was "the remembrance of the Conte D'Orsay and the anticipation of Oscar Wilde."

Now literature had come to the village it was complicating the daily routine of life. Young Theodore Sedgwick had inherited his father's house and his tradition of hospitality. His wife, Susan Ridley, followed in Pamela's footsteps and superintended the curing of hams, the making of soap and training of servants, and was also the author of a brace of uplifting volumes for the young. Her abilities were more social than literary, however, and she boasted the only parlor bell in the village. "I went by invitation to a party at Mrs. Susan's," wrote Harry Hopkins, "who presided with the dignity and the grace of a duchess,—it makes a fellow feel elegant to be where she is." Of a Sunday evening, sweet meats and cream, apples, almonds, and wine would be passed around and Anne Ashburner, when she came to call, always wondered whom she would find.

In the first place there were likely to be a good many of the family about, giving rise to the complaint of the young New York society man, Mr. Devereux Barker: "For the first ten days I was here I was out all the time at evening parties, picnics, expeditions to the ice glen, and all sorts of things. I was charmed for a while, but at last, when I was driving home of an evening, it came to seem to me that the Katydids and the frogs and the tree-toads had but one song and that was "Sedg-wick, Sedg-wick, Sedg-wick!" Since then I have kept to the house, and the most seductive invitations failed to lure me from it."

The Judge had left his family comfortably off, and under the shelter provided by his broad shoulders, they had been reared in an atmosphere as nearly resembling leisure as could be found in that part of the country. When they grew up, they displayed a propensity either to come back to Stockbridge if they went away or else never to go away at all. Theodore had given up his law practice in Albany on account of poor health and led the life of a country gentleman. Harry and Robert came home for summer vacations. Charles, the youngest, who never thought himself as clever as his brothers, stayed in Lenox and was busy doing everything that no one else had time for. When nothing practical offered, letters, displaying a lambent quality of charm and humor, expressed his overflowing family love. His wife kept a boarding school for young ladies in Lenox and found time to write advice to the young on the side, as well as novels—diluted editions of Catherine's.

The talk which Anne Ashburner heard on a Sunday evening, voiced the liberalism in politics corresponding to the unitarianism in religion which flourished in spirits freed from the narrow tenets of an earlier day. The extravagant lack of national confidence displayed by the Federalists had given way to an almost complacent satisfaction in the United States. Theodore had become an ardent Democrat, edited *A Collection of the Political Writings of William Leggett,* the radical journalist, and supported the movement for liberal education sponsored by Horace Mann. Americans, proud of their own institutions, were anxious to help other democracies whenever they could. Harry and Robert supported the Greek government in its case against two New York companies; their cousin, Senator Henry Dwight, in Washington defended Greek rights in the matter of neutral shipping while young Timothy Field went out to fight for the Greek cause.

THE VILLAGE BECOMES LITERARY 219

Anne never felt as homesick at the Sedgwicks as she did everywhere else; nor did their world seem so different from that she had left behind. She could talk over the latest Waverley with Catherine, or an article in *The Westminster Review*. Here, too, she would find familiar town figures: Judge Byington, a well-rounded gentleman, who enjoyed a distinguished reputation on the bench yet could discuss with her father peaches and apple trees as well as books; or William Pitt Palmer, the young poet, who made the little red schoolhouse famous by *The Smack in School,* and who used to tell of how as a boy he had walked all the way to Albany to see General Lafayette. There, too, would be other village characters, the storekeeper, the tailor; and in 1837, like birds of bright if battered plumage, a group of Italian patriots, among them Castillia, Confalonieri, Foresti and Albinola, who had been released from the horrors of an Austrian dungeon. The historian, Sismondi, had given them letters to Catherine and, her warm heart touched by their sad faces, she had bustled about and asked her friends to take Italian lessons. The foreigners were so gentle and unassuming that it was easy to be nice to them and later on Albinola, who had prospered in New York, gave Stockbridge a fountain, in memory of the peace and hospitality he had found there.

Anne might also have seen the poet William Cullen Bryant, who was Harry's particular friend. Bryant also had revolted from a narrow Federalist upbringing and as a journalist in New York his liberal opinions were gaining substantial recognition. Yet, despite the luster of his prose career, he would always remain the country poet whom Berkshire hills and streams had fashioned for their own. Like others of his generation, Bryant made the nineteenth-century transition between the old religious autocracy of Jonathan Edwards and the modern uplift note. At the time that Albert Hopkins was still troubled about the probable burning of his brother Harry's soul, little children were absorbing the new and kindly optimism of the lines:

> "He who from zone to zone,
>   Guides through the boundless sky thy certain flight,
> In the long way that I must tread alone,
>   Will lead my steps aright."

Bryant had long been established as a well-known journalist in New York when, in 1850, Nathaniel Hawthorne decided to come to Stockbridge "for a cheap, pleasant, and healthy residence." This he found in a small red house with a picket fence in front of it, at the northern end of the Stockbridge Bowl. In the enthusiasm of arrival, he said he could not write with that view of the lake and mountains under his window.

Hawthorne had just written *The Scarlet Letter* and was on the threshold of his great fame, so that although, as usual, he longed for solitude, it was harder than ever to avoid callers. His wife thought they saw more people than they had in Salem. Fanny Kemble in particular must have been a nuisance. Dressed in queer clothes, she would invade his privacy and carry off his little Julian on a big black horse to return him again with a dramatic flourish, "Take your son, Julian the apostate!" With Catherine, Hawthorne had little in common. She belonged to an earlier generation, and the new literary effulgence in Concord, and the Brook Farm experiment, affected her as little as Berkshire affected him. Yet they would have agreed about what Catherine called the "fog" in which the Transcendentalists lived and moved, had he cared to get behind the barrage of word games, breakfast parties and children's festivals with which she surrounded her declining years.

As always, Hawthorne arranged his life to his own liking. He took a daily walk to the Lenox post office; and although

THE VILLAGE BECOMES LITERARY 221

he worked every morning, he found hours in which to lie on his back and look at Monument Mountain, "the headless sphinx wrapped in a Persian shawl," or tell his children stories of Greek heroes until the children and the stories mingled with the countryside to be later transmuted into *The Wonder-Book* and *Tanglewood Tales*. After the fluffy sentimentality of most contemporary descriptions of the landscape, Hawthorne's meticulous observations have all the reassurance of fact. Yet he disposed of his Berkshire interlude by a few descriptions recording, as in a dry-point etching, the effect of tumbling brooks, leafless trees and clouds. During his stay, he wrote *The House of the Seven Gables,* a novel brewed in Salem, the sinister, crabbed New England wherein he had been formed. The open hills and lakes of Berkshire had come too late; they could afford him neither the inspiration they had to Bryant, nor the release they had to Fanny Kemble.

Hawthorne sent the manuscript of his novel to G. P. R. James, the English author of more than one hundred historical novels, who had recently come to Stockbridge and taken William Ashburner's house. James was delighted and found it difficult to take his attention off *The House of the Seven Gables* and concentrate upon "a packet of seventy gabbles," the themes of Mrs. Charles Sedgwick's girls, which she had sent him to review.

James was as flamboyant as Hawthorne was saturnine. Thackeray's parody of his style hardly exaggerates it. "It was upon one of those balmy evenings of November, which are known only in the valleys of Languedoc and among the mountains of Alsace, that two cavaliers might have been perceived by the naked eye threading one of the rocky and romantic gorges that skirt the mountain land between the Marne and the Garonne. The rosy tints of the declining luminary were gilding the peaks and crags."

An adequate nineteenth-century E. Phillips Oppenheim, Mr. James brought a smoothness to Stockbridge which suggested London drawing rooms. He had met Campbell, Southey, and Byron and was known to be a friend of Walter Scott's. Urbanely used to success, he took his talent with sophisticated ease and never worked after eleven in the morning. The first draft of his manuscript, which he rarely changed, was dictated to his secretary, an invaluable catchall of a person who was his master's valet, the brother of an Irish baronet, and the master of several different languages as well. James went in mildly for gentleman farming and declared, somewhat as if he were writing one of his novels, that although he knew "many localities where individual features constituting landscape pageantry were vastly more imposing, nowhere had he seen the most desirable all grouped together in a combination so charming and complete."

James's man-of-the-world exterior prevented any more than superficial cordiality on the unsocial Hawthorne's part. At first the American novelist found himself equally tongue-tied by the fantastic Melville, with the bushy hair and full, square beard, who came down from Pittsfield to call. It was only after a walk upon Monument Mountain when it rained, and they waited in the shelter of a cave, that the two men discovered each other. After that Melville came more and more often and Hawthorne would celebrate the occasion by mixing a wonderful drink of champagne and beaten egg; or the two men would lie in the barn and take sun baths and talk philosophy.

Oliver Wendell Holmes and Longfellow were not far away in Pittsfield; Holmes on his grandfather's farm and Longfellow with his wife's family, the Appletons. Nathan Appleton, his father-in-law, had bought some property in Stockbridge—later owned by Mr. Southmayd—and gave it to

Longfellow, who intended to build. But the plan was given up and only a weathered letter from the poet to Thomas Wells about repairing fences remains to take the place of all the literary reminiscences that might have been.

In 1853, Henry Ward Beecher rented a house upon the Lenox road, where he spent several summers. He had first looked at Dr. West's old house and decided against it—fortunately for all the religious proprieties. The ghost of the little doctor would surely have haunted this huge sensual man, with his broad beaver hat and lionesque head, who held congregations spellbound by his particular blend of religious emotionalism. Several of his *Star Papers,* written during his stay, expressed his delight in the country. He rolled in it like a great St. Bernard dog. He put God into nature and exulted in the synthesis, discovering the spiritual value of mountains and of clouds.

From Lenox George William Curtis drove over to Stockbridge to call, and even Thoreau, that inner god of the New England shrine, conferred at least one anecdote upon Berkshire, an anecdote of characteristically charmless touch. He spent the night in the old observatory on Greylock while mice nibbled his toes and he nibbled scraps of country newspapers which littered the floor, as the only intellectual nourishment he could find.

So the literary reel went on, two steps forward, bow and back again to your place. The Berkshires were lovely for a holiday. Only Hawthorne wouldn't keep in step. "My soul gets troublous with too much peace and rest. I need to smell sea breezes and dock mud and to tread pavements." And again, "This is a horrible, horrible, most horrible, climate—I detest it!—I hate Berkshire with my whole soul and would joyfully see its mountains laid flat." Hawthorne was the exception who proved the rule, however, and Fanny Kemble's enthusiasm kept everybody going. She would read *Romeo and Juliet* upon Greylock or give a picnic party on the lake. Literary excursions were organized upon Monument Mountain and Melville declared that if Longfellow were indeed at the Oxbow, "The winged horse would neigh at sight of him." Pitt Palmer at Mark Hopkins's instigation, continued to publish his poems. Mrs. Theodore and Mrs. Charles collaborated upon writing a hymn for their darling William Ellery Channing who pronounced them the most docile of authoresses. Mark Hopkins came down from Williamstown to give the young gentlemen and ladies of Stockbridge a course on anatomy, and Oliver Wendell Holmes read a poem entitled *The New Eden* at the Horticultural Fair.

Berkshire had bred no new school of thought, established no literary precedent. Nature alone was capitalized and written up so that rustic innocence fled forever before cultivated pens. Stockbridge began to learn that like the dairy maid its face was its fortune. So the distinguished visitors came, wrote their descriptions and went away again. Literature, before the era of wealth or fashion, found time for self-renewal within the rim of hills.

Chapter XI

THE VILLAGE EXPANDS

REGARDLESS of the opinion of visiting celebrities, the village went on its way, meeting new needs as they arose. By 1824, the revolt against the Calvinism of Edwards and West had grown so strong that a new church was in demand. The Methodists had held meetings since the year 1837, but so far their sect had not gained much ground. Long before this, in 1770, the first service of the Episcopal Church had been held in Stockbridge and the first child baptized in that faith. By 1834 five families were Episcopalian, and Dr. Caleb Hyde, a sound churchman and a public-spirited man, considered "that now is the time to build up the Church in Stockbridge, the whole community are in a state of excitement, a new order must take place and we believe the peaceful and . . . regular system of our church will embrace the most respectable and enlightened part of our people." At his instigation St. Paul's Episcopal Society was formed in Laurel Cottage. Judge Byington, always interested in village affairs, presided at the meeting and a few months afterwards young Dr. Samuel P. Parker conducted services in the shabby old Academy on Elm Street. Though the windows were small and dirty and there were no cushions on the benches, the English-born Anne Ashburner opened her heart in unspeakable relief at the prayers and litany "so pleadingly read in a sweet earnest voice by our teacher."

In 1844, the first Episcopal church was built upon the site of the present one. Made of wood, it had a square, perpendicular gothic tower and carried on "the sweet tradition set by Anglican churches in Kent and Sussex." At first the parish could not afford an organ, so ministering ladies paid Henry Carter $5 a month for playing his tuning fork. Not long after Dr. Parker came Mr. Allen, who gave a Stockbridge boy his first impression of the Church of England: "Mr. Allen was the embodiment of austere ecclesiastical tradition in look and manner, erect, clean-shaven. He walked through the street, as a man set apart from other men, a Levite, an incarnation of the awe-inspiring respectability of the English Church. Archbishop Laud must have looked like Mr. Allen, especially when Mr. Allen mounted the pulpit; stole, surplice, immaculately starched, as in Heaven's laundry, gown caught up with a proud reverence in his left hand, his sermon, of moderate, dignified brevity in his right, the embodiment of God-originated, Holy Church perpetuated, impeccable ecclesiasticism. Seeing him, I learned the history of all those proud men—Hildebrand, Thomas à Becket, Wolsey, Richelieu—who attained by their interpretation of Holy Writ the right to a high place of command in the church militant. All he lacked was a tonsure; and I think he must have put his hand up now and again to feel if he had it or not."

No sooner had the Episcopal Church been established than the Unitarians of the village, numbering at that time only one family, of Sedgwick affiliations, invited Dr. Charles Follen to preach to them. Catherine, and Eliza Pomeroy were delighted, especially Eliza, who could hardly force herself to hear Dr. Field, even the meager twice a year that her father thought decent.

During Dr. Parker's ministry his interest had not been primarily in his church, but in the school he kept for boys.

His anxiety for their entertainment brought a new and exciting suggestion to his mind. It was in the summer of 1841 that he led a small band, armed with lighted flares, up the slope of Bear Mountain and into the northern end of the rocky gorge known as the Ice Glen. The lights went out and the boys had a hard time scrambling through, but it was worth trying again and soon became an annual affair.

The custom was still young when Sophia Hawthorne, who had come over with her husband and children to stop at the Dudley Fields', wrote, "We went to a bridge where we could see the torchlight party come out of the Ice Glen and it looked as if a host of stars had fallen out of the sky and broken into pieces." Afterwards she watched the girls from Mrs. Charles Sedgwick's school at Lenox get into an "endless omnibus," Mrs. Charles in the midst of them. The girls looked like a bouquet of bright flowers as they waved good-by and the boys waved and shouted in return.

In later years the parade became more elaborate. A procession formed at the Red Lion Inn—at that time known as the Stockbridge House—and marched down the street to the foot of Laurel Hill, where a huge bonfire shot into flame, lighting up fantastic costumes. Everyone held hands and danced around it, singing songs, then lighted kerosene-soaked torches and started for the Glen. Red, blue and white Bengal lights had been placed on the highest rocks along the way. As the procession, still singing, worked its way through the narrow passage to an open field at the other end, it might have been some fantastic scene from a romantic novel.

The Ice Glen parade expressed the emphasis upon scenery brought to the fore by visitors, but in the first half of the nineteenth century Stockbridge still had its roots essentially in the soil of agricultural and economic necessity. It had to find an outlet for its agricultural products, and for its manufactures. Now a new one was available.

As early as 1826, Theodore Sedgwick, together with some other citizens, raised enough money to survey a possible railroad route through Stockbridge to the Connecticut River. Young Albert Hopkins assisted in the undertaking. He began the survey at West Stockbridge and worked his way east, through Stockbridge, Lee, Becket, Otis, and Blandford; but the project was never completed and Albert went back to work on his father's farm.

The following year Sedgwick presented a bill to the Massachusetts Legislature providing for the construction of the Boston and Albany Railroad. Horses instead of steam power would have to be used in getting over the high grades, and the cars could not be expected to go more than ten miles an hour. The report of the Directors of Internal Improvement was conservative. It suggested two ways of approaching the problem: first, constructing a railroad without "stationary powers"—which meant the use of twenty-two horses to pull the cars between Boston and Albany, and would cost $21 for twenty passengers—or a railroad with "stationary powers" for which only sixteen horses were needed and which would cost $16.50. It would be difficult to estimate the increase of traveling from so "easy, safe and rapid a conveyance." Such proposals seemed to Basil Hall "loaded with anticipated magnificence." "What would you carry on your railroad, if you had it?" he asked Theodore. In the Captain's opinion the country was not in the least suited to such an undertaking and several navigable rivers afforded better means of commerce than any railroad could provide.

Nevertheless the idea persisted. Several possible routes were proposed, one going right through the village; but the first railroad actually built was the West Stockbridge and Hudson and Berkshire which opened for travel in 1838. The Stockbridge and Pittsfield Railroad was chartered in 1847 and on January 1, 1850, the first train ran through to Stockbridge.

THE VILLAGE EXPANDS

Despite the railroads, had Elijah Williams come to life again in the years before the Civil War, he would not have been greatly confused. He would have easily understood selectmen's bills, for instance, one of which included:

To half a day disposing of town poor	$ .50
To half a day viewing bridge by factory	$ .50
For two coffins and a hearse	$17.50
Dig child's grave and vaccinate	$ 2.00
To abate nuisance—viz dead horse from river	$10.00

Farmers still brought their butter and eggs to trade at Cyrus Williams's store, the largest in the county, just as they had to Timothy Edwards's. The same products had merely increased in amount. In Stockbridge alone 43,035 pounds of butter were churned, 28,625 pounds of cheese made, and 14,780 bushels of oats, 2,242 bushels of rye, 11,228 bushels of fruit were grown in the course of a year. Although manufactures had become more complicated, they were the great oaks grown from the acorns of Elijah's day. The woolen mill in Glendale now used 208,000 pounds of wool annually and produced 275,000 yards of satinet. The lumber mills on Yale Hill were busy cutting 50,000 feet of lumber. There were two establishments for the making of wagons and sleighs, one chair and cabinet manufactory, while two tanneries, one of them right below the Ashburners, turned out 800 pairs of boots and 1,000 pairs of shoes annually. In 1833, the combined water power and plants of Curtisville were sold for the large sum of $30,000 to the Curtisville Manufacturing Company, and in 1849, Rewey & Evans built the first paper mill in the district.

What wonder that the village felt in mellow mood. The years had been fruitful; it now stood ready to receive the congratulations which it felt were due. Accordingly it took its part in the first Boost-the-Berkshires movement, known as the Berkshire Jubilee. It was time to welcome home the distinguished sons and daughters which the county had sent forth. It was time also to show them what had been happening at home: how although the old fishing holes were what they used to be, the old oaken bucket intact and the squirrel and partridge still to be hunted in the same old hills, nevertheless the great Western Railroad had come in, and the "uplifted hand of labor, honest, thriftful labor could be descried in the quarries and lime furnaces, and the grist and saw mills which sprang up on almost every stream . . . We are willing to set our Berkshire villages, whether in education, in refinement or in wealth, in contrast with any commercial metropolis in the country . . . Come from the pent up atmosphere of the city and breathe the fresh mountain air of New England! Come and see our beautiful lakes, our green fields and our famous trout brooks, leaping along in the bright sunshine."

The occasion proved a triumphant one. A wooden stand, with seats enough to hold more than 5,000 people, was set up on a hill just outside Pittsfield. As the exercises began a heavy rain interrupted the speakers, accompanied by the rushing sound of the opening of umbrellas. But the weather had cleared by the time Mark Hopkins stepped upon the platform. His sermon was a high-water mark of deep religious emotion, yet as he stood there he need not have said a word. His mere presence was the reason and the answer to the Berkshire Jubilee: he typified the best the county had produced.

Afterwards a round of hymns, poems, odes, speeches, and toasts followed close upon each other's heels hardly interrupted by a magnificent banquet held upon the grounds of The Young Ladies Institute the next day. Dr. Allen put on his tortoise-shell pince-nez and read a very long poem. Julius Rockwell followed with two pieces by William Pitt Palmer, *The Mother Land's Home Call* and *The Reponse of the*

Home Comers. Sentiment had a luxurious blooming in Mr. Palmer's loyal heart:

> "Return, and boyhood's faded spring
>   Shall bloom round manhood's homeward track;
> And memory's refluent sunshine fling
>   The shadow from life's dial back!"

Edward Carter then read a blushingly feminine poem by Mrs. Sigourney, entitled *The Stockbridge Bowl:*

> "The Stockbridge Bowl!—Hast ever seen
>   How sweetly pure and bright,
> Its foot of stone, and rim of green
>   Attract the traveller's sight?—"

Charles Sedgwick read an ode by Fanny Kemble, and Oliver Wendell Holmes supplied a needed touch of comic relief:

> "Then come from all parties, and parts, to our feast
> Though not at the 'Astor,' we'll give at least
> A bite at an apple, a seat on the grass,
> And the best of cold—water—at nothing a glass."

The great actor, Macready, made a short speech. Theodore Sedgwick proposed a toast summing up the self-confidence of his generation: "The stock of New England . . . the stock of old England, their virtue, their intelligence with equality added." The Reverend David Dudley Field said a prayer, and his son Dudley oracularly offered the sentiment, "The Children of Berkshire. They have only to be steadfast to the principles into which they were born." By this time nearly everyone was in tears.

Almost while everyone was talking, "the Mother Land" was changing. The emigration westward which had been going on through the years, had drawn away many of the original smaller farmers and tradesmen. Their places were gradually filled by Irishmen who, like the New Englanders in the West, brought their own institutions with them. Much had happened since Deacon Ingersoll's widow had exclaimed, "The shop turned into a Cathedral! No, I would rather burn it!" at the suggestion that Mass be celebrated in the small hat shop she had rented to one of the town's first Irishmen. Some years afterwards, Mass was said on the grounds of the present golf club and the story went that one woman walked seven miles to take part. It remained for Jane Sedgwick, a niece of Catherine's, who had swung to the opposite pole from William Ellery Channing, to build St. Joseph's, the Catholic Church. "We have had a great occasion in our dear valley," wrote her aunt in the year 1866, "the laying of the corner stone of the Catholic church in a beautiful spot just under Laurel Hill. Think of my being able to see a procession of Irish Catholics from one end of the Village to the other."

Changes were coming slowly, shaping Stockbridge along its modern lines. In 1825, the Housatonic National Bank had opened with a capital of $100,000. In 1839, the Town Hall had been built. In 1842, the name Stockbridge Academy was changed to Williams Academy, in honor of Cyrus Williams, who bequeathed it a fund of $3,000. In 1866, the old school districts were abolished, and several years later separate schools were built in Curtisville and Glendale, and a new building put up in Stockbridge under the double title of Williams Academy and Stockbridge High School. Academy funds were appropriated for the building of the high school even though the population did not require it by statute law.

One of the first principals of the Academy was E. W. B. Canning, a cultivated, kindly gentleman who wrote upon historical subjects, and whose pupils always remembered how the scene before Bennington jumped right out of the pages when he taught it, and how they could almost hear the prayers of Dr. West. Miss Lucy Bliss had charge of several generations of Stockbridge's ABC's who tagged behind her on the way to school, struggling to see who could hold her hand. Not until 1914 did the school building change its old

THE VILLAGE EXPANDS

gray wooden front for the brick colonial building of the present time.

At the mid-century mark, Henry J. Carter kept a boarding school for boys on the spot where Jonathan Edwards's house had stood, and about 1854 he sold it to Ferdinand Hoffman who had come to the village due to a mistake. For the past few years the sufferings of Hungarian exiles had succeeded those of Italians in warm Stockbridge hearts. A fair was given for Kossuth whose portrait hung, garlanded with laurel leaves, at the Academy. Six ladies clubbed together to take lessons in any or all of the languages Hungarians had at their fingertips. When, through the kind offices of an absent-minded friend, Ferdinand Hoffman, who could speak only German, turned up instead, everyone, including the young German, was equally confused. In 1855, he opened the Edwards Place School. His prospectus pointed out that "the situation of the school could present no incitement to wrong, while the taste must be cultivated by the beauty of the surrounding scenery." Parents were assured that the preceptors did not lose sight of the fact "that boyhood is naturally an imperfect state." Imperfect is a mild word indeed judging from the relentless records which were kept of the pupils' behavior, for Mr. Hoffman had transplanted to the New World some of the rigorous methods he had learned at the Prussian government school at Pforte. For seventeen years he trained and pruned these sturdy New England saplings, many of which later grew into trees of magnitude and grandeur.

Years had gone by since Harriet Martineau and Catherine had walked by the river bank, and during this time opposition to slavery had become more and more outspoken. In 1842, shortly before his death, William Ellery Channing preached a sermon in Lenox upon the emancipation of slaves in the West Indies. His congregation was deeply moved at his words: "Among these vast works of God the soul naturally goes forth and cannot endure the thought of a chain." When the Reverend George Uhler, preaching at Curtisville in 1857, boldly declared, "Ministers must preach against slavery. Christians must pray and labor and vote for its overthrow," David Curtis, Daniel Fairchild, and others insisted upon having the sermon published. A note of more practical cooperation showed itself in two underground railways, one to the south and the other to the northwest of the village.

Yet, although sympathy with the negro had become more vocal, there was still a strong desire to avert war, and in January, 1853, forty-five citizens signed a Petition of Peace addressed to the Honorable Senate and House of Representatives of the United States:

> "The undersigned citizens of the town of Stockbridge in the State of Massachusetts, deploring the great and manifold evils of war, and believing it possible to supersede its alleged necessity, as an Arbiter of Justice among Nations, by the timely adoption of wise & feasible substitutes, respectfully petition your Honorable Bodies to take such action as you may deem best for this most desirable end, by securing in our treaties with other nations, a provision for referring to the decision of Umpires all misunderstandings that cannot be satisfactorily adjusted by an amicable negotiation."

Such pleas, however, were unavailing and the approaching storm only gathered force. When it finally broke there was no such cleavage in public opinion as had existed during the War of 1812. Harriet Martineau, back in England, could consider herself correct in the statement that "the North worshipped that parchment idol, The Act of Union," for although, when "that bullying state of South Carolina" seceded, many minds echoed the exclamation, "Let the damned little thing go," there is no record of protest when war was declared. Solid Republican majorities upon the voting lists argued no difference of opinion in regard to politics. At first slavery and even the Union were not the direct home-thrust that Bennington had been. When, in 1861, the President called for 75,000 men only forty-two enlisted from Stockbridge, although names eligible for military service in the years immediately preceding the Civil War numbered as many as 121. Later on the town voted a bounty of $125, to every man who would volunteer, and finally a draft was necessary. As the war went on, the system of sending substitutes gained ground. Charles Lynch joined the Union Army, but after a few weeks in camp he was needed back again on the farm. Someone had to take the homemade cheese to Hudson between three and four in the morning and his father was getting old.

Yet patriotism found adequate expression in the eighty townsmen who fought at The Wilderness, Petersburg, Chancellorsville, Antietam and other battles of the war. Canning was with the army of the Potomac. James Dwight wrote home from the valley of the Shenandoah. As in Revolutionary days the town voted various sums for the support of soldiers' families. "It seems hardly the fitting time to make large expenditures on our own homes. Thoughts of those fighting for us have possessed us," noted the minutes of a village society. By 1864, $39,891 had been expended, $5,416 for the soldiers' fund for families, $11,600 in individual contributions, and $22,875 in bounties.

When a company of young men went off to fight, half the village followed them to the station. Women were busy as in the Revolution, but in a different way. "Nothing pleases me better," wrote Catherine Sedgwick, "than the zeal among our young women in working for the hospitals. We hear no gossip but the most rational talk about hospital gowns, comfortable socks, and mittens. Our whole community, from

Mrs. Kemble down to some of our Irish servants, are knitting."

As time went on anxiety took the place of enthusiasm. Bull Run, Fredericksburg, and the horrors of Libby Prison, like water beating upon rock, eroded hopes of a speedy victory. Catherine's letters, tremulous now with age, echo a sense of strain, grief over a nephew killed, belief in a righteous cause. Slavery and the Union had turned into daily reality. Far removed though the village was from the scene of action, the young men who did not come home brought the war to its very doorstep.

Chapter XII

THE RESORT

IN the thirty years that followed the Civil War, Stockbridge became to the outward eye an entirely different village from the one in which Catherine Sedgwick had grown up. In 1893, she would hardly have known it, "with all the bright and sumptuous villas that have sprung up on every side." It was now a summer resort, and homespun subsistence farming and little manufactures tended to fade out as the business of summer came to be the town's livelihood. But so quietly and gradually did the change come about, that it was a long time before people realized that anything had happened. Intent upon pursuing the even tenor of its way, Stockbridge did not look up and see the new village until it, in its turn, had aged and mellowed and become the old village.

The first trains, that had heaved themselves up into the valley with such difficulty, had cut a new kind of channel of communication with the world. The stagecoach, clattering over the roads in the old days, had poured life into the manufacturing interests of the town. The railroads, linking these interests to the large industrial centers, had the effect of draining that life off. Big business sweeping over the country through these new arteries swallowed up little business, and Curtisville was sidetracked. All its fine manufactures fell into disrepair and the business depression of 1857 gave it a final push. The tanneries disappeared and Lester Avery's factories at Glendale languished and died.

The trains of the second generation were larger and sturdier than the early pioneers. Importantly gushing forth cinders and black smoke, they roared up from New York, first stopping for breath at Stamford, where the passengers might partake of a refreshing cup of coffee or a plate of oysters. They were the "summer people" and must be coddled and catered to in every way, for henceforth they were to be the essential livelihood of the Berkshires. Clark W. Bryan, an enterprising promoter employed by the railroad interests, tempted the well-to-do city dweller into the country: "When travelers have the breezy hills of Berkshire for a destination [they are] often found wishing for the wings of the wind that the desired haven of rest and recreation may be reached with a loss of the least possible fragment of time." They were assured that a treat among wild and picturesque scenery awaited them, combined with all the refinements of a city life. There they could "draw closer the silken cord of social intercourse and yet throw loose some of its galling chains." There "nature ennobles by her greatness but never chills with a frown." There was nothing extreme about the Berkshires, nothing in the least uncomfortable.

The change that the summer people brought to Stockbridge was gentler and less abrupt than the transformation of Lenox, where farm land rose from fifty to one thousand dollars an acre and Swiss Chalets, Tudor and Elizabethan castles, and even an imitation of the Petit Trianon, rose upon the astonished slopes of the hills. Money with fashion in its wake poured into Lenox and the scene in 1893 is glowingly described by Susan Teale Perry: ". . . superb roads that in the season are full of gay equestrians and dashing turnouts, handsome women holding the reins of prancing thoroughbreds who drive over the hills with the groom sitting behind with folded arms. Beautiful children drive about in village carts, gayly talking and laughing, while the barefooted boy and girl of the farmhouse look on with covetous eyes."

The pace was slower in Stockbridge, the scale smaller, and it was admittedly less fashionable. "In Lenox they *estimate* their neighbors, in Stockbridge we esteem them," the village liked to tell itself. But the people who built the villas—or cottages, as they were sometimes misleadingly called—liked a generous and expansive way of life and could pay for it. The houses they put up were of the most durable materials. They were substantial affairs of stone, brick, and ironmongery, and one can fairly feel today the solidity of the incomes on which they were built. Matthew Arnold, looking at them through his monocle in 1886, found the "villa cottages original and at the same time very pleasing, but they are pretty and coquettish, not beautiful."

This period of the villas was remarkable for the character of the men who built them. They were, for the most part, men who had achieved distinction elsewhere and come to Stockbridge to spend the summers of their maturing years. Unlike the literary group of an earlier day, they were no birds of passage, but had come with a view to settling down. Charles E. Butler had been one of the first arrivals. In 1859 he built Linwood whose unpolished-marble look of indestructibility was not destroyed by the flimsy and fashionable gingerbread of the day. It stands on a lovely site overlooking a loop of the river as it winds to Glendale. Here he settled his family of six children. He married for a second time Susan, sister of Henry Dwight Sedgwick, of the third generation of this family.

Arrogant, stern, and just—that was Mr. Butler. He was one of the most able figures of his day at the New York bar, but nevertheless is remembered as terrifying as he looked down from that awful eminence on little boys. "Well, did you bring your dinner with you? You may eat it in the coal hole!" This favorite greeting, to a nephew who came to Sunday lunch, was hard to take as a joke. He drove down to the livery stable one morning and, seeing a likely-looking lad polishing up the harness, sent word that he would employ *that* boy. Pulling his forelock, the boy hastily did as he was told and entered into Mr. Butler's service, where he remained for the next thirty years.

Mrs. Butler was the appropriate counterpart. She was gentle and loving, adored by her stepchildren and, indeed, the whole village. She often drove out in her two-seated open carriage. Isaac, the mulatto coachman, sat on the box, clearly the irreproachable family servant, his looped whip carried at just the correct angle. The horses, resplendent in shining harness and beaded wih foam, tossed their well-bred heads, and Hector, the spotted coach dog, ran underneath the carriage. It was a turnout that said to the admiring pedestrian that there were other turnouts in the stable, equally good of their kind: a high carriage and a low carriage; a rockaway and a depot wagon; and, certainly, a smart brougham. It clearly bespoke the Butlers, the plutocrats of the village.

If Stockbridge was obliged to take Mr. Butler seriously, he in return took Stockbridge seriously. He and his neighbor, Mr. Southmayd, contributed largely to the building of two iron bridges at the west end of the town, which were called at the time "models of pontic architecture." In 1883, when the first Episcopal church was taken down, he gave a fine new church to the parish in memory of his second wife, who had died several years before. Charles McKim was the architect, but Mr. Butler stood at his elbow while he drew the plans. When the church was completed he told the assembled congregation that if it did not meet every aesthetic standard it was his fault, not McKim's. "My desire was," he said, "to

THE RESORT

build a church of an extremely enduring character." So it stands today, solid and permanent as Linwood itself.

Mr. Butler, curiously enough, was a Unitarian, and the Reverend Arthur Lawrence, rector for many years, always tactfully avoided preaching the sermon on Trinity Sunday, delegating this duty to his curate. Mr. Lawrence, a man of extraordinary good looks, was respected by his congregation—even its Unitarian wing—and warmly admired by the ladies. It was his conversation that Matthew Arnold found as interesting as any in Stockbridge.

Butler generosity did not exhaust itself in one generation and Mr. Butler's daughter, Virginia, will long be remembered for her kindness. A long cape thrown about her shoulders and a tall staff in her hand, she stumped about the village, an eccentric but veritable fairy godmother. Universally kind, she had a particularly soft spot in her heart for dogs and Episcopal clergymen.

Charles F. Southmayd lived next door to the Butlers. It is said that he was in love with Mr. Butler's Junoesque daughter, Rosalie, and had therefore built himself a substantial willow cabin at her gates. There was a path that connected the two places, but Rosalie never availed herself of the opportunity it afforded and Mr. Southmayd remained a bachelor. He was a genius at the law and the very substructure of that most imposing of firms, Butler, Evarts and Southmayd. He wore black broadcloth small-clothes—buttoned with a square flap in front like a sailor's—a high, stiff, pointed collar with a stock, and looked like a Cruikshank illustration of a solicitor. He belonged to that school of thought, now vanished, that believed in living upon the income of one's income, and all his actions were marked by extreme legal caution. Although he owned an excellent pair of horses and a carriage, he rode to his office in New York in the latter part of his life in a cab. When questioned upon this point, he explained that it was because of the common-law rule of *respondeat superior.* "If I hire a cab and an accident occurs, I incur no liability. That falls upon the owner."

Joseph Hodges Choate, a younger partner of Butler, Evarts and Southmayd, built his house upon the Hill in 1887. Urbane, handsome and clever, Stockbridge adored him and his witticisms were handed about like some particularly rich and delightful kind of sugarplums. "Did you hear what Mr. Choate said about the cemetery fence?" someone would say. "When he was asked to subscribe money for it, he said he thought it hardly necessary, as no one who was in wanted to get out, and no one who was out wanted to get in."

It was a constant source of pride and pleasure to read about him in the newspapers. There was the time in 1895 when he fought the constitutionality of the graduated income-tax law before the Supreme Court. It was his greatest case, performing as it did the incredible feat of making the Supreme Court reverse its former decision. The tax demanded that the rich man should pay proportionately far more than the poor man toward the cost of government. Stockbridge took an intense interest in the case, for not only did Choate argue it, but Southmayd was roused out of his ten years of retirement to write the brief. "Most men have five senses," Mr. Choate remarked, "but Southmayd has a sixth sense, very keen and powerful—a sense of property." It was delightful later, to read accounts of him when he was sent in 1899 as Ambassador to the Court of St. James's, and to pass around cartoons of Mr. Choate and Queen Victoria, or Mr. Choate leaning against the speakers' table, cultivating friendly international relations.

Matthew Arnold spent a few months in Laurel Cottage i 1886, an Indian-summer flowering of the literary group. H\ was thirty years too late to be welcomed by Catherine

Sedgwick or to sympathize with Hawthorne about the disagreeable climate. "The heat is great in summer and in winter the cold is excessive," he wrote. However, his impression was in the main a pleasant one and he wrote back to his daughter, after his return to England: "You cannot think how often Stockbridge and its landscape come into my mind. None of the cities could attach me, not even Boston, but I could get fond of Stockbridge."

More people were coming all the time but not so fast or so many that they were not easily assimilated into the village friendliness. It was still many years before Miss Agnes Canning would return from her walk spluttering, "I don't know what Stockbridge is coming to. I saw two people in the street this morning whom I never saw before." The Lucius Tuckermans came in the '70's, buying from Mr. Thomas Wells the simple old farmhouse that stood where the Indian boarding school had been. Sprouting piazza and gable, it acquired a fancy name and became the villa, Ingleside. The Frederic Crowninshields came about the same time as the Choates. Mr. Crowninshield was the forerunner of the artistic group that was to arrive a little later. Tall and spare, paint box in hand, he could often be seen making his way on his bicycle toward a view which he would reproduce in landscapes of meticulous fidelity.

Stockbridge was now giving every attention to its appearance, that it should be furbished out to match the elegance of the villas. A newspaper commented that it was too bad the tombstones should not be painted green, they showed so white and staring from the Hill. This concern for its good looks was not of recent date. As early as 1853 Mary Hopkins, own cousin to Mark, had founded a village improvement society which had the distinction of being the first in America.

This forward-looking young lady had started out on her white horse, clad in a long black riding habit. Up hill, down dale she rode, now drawing up to argue with some citizen with a sluggish and unprogressive mind, now swooping down from the saddle to whisk up a bit of waste paper. The Laurel Hill Association was named for the knoll, behind the schoolhouse, which had been a gift to the town from the Sedgwick family in 1834, and here its annual anniversary meeting took place. In the early minutes it is stated: "Every person over 14 years of age who shall plant and protect a tree . . . or pay the sum of one dollar annually shall be a member of this Association." By 1866 so many young trees had been set out that the Laurel Hill minutes boldly predicted a day when "ye next generation [will] be able to ride through ye length & breadth of old Berkshire during ye heats of summer with all ye comfort of pedestrians beneath ye green & cool arcades of ye forest, & dust & wheels alone distinguish ye drive from ye stroll." In 1880 there was a scare from a malaria epidemic which seemed to be extending up the Connecticut and Housatonic valleys. Medical authorities in alarm argued that it was the excess of shade trees that had been planted. Of course, if this were so, the Laurel Hill Association was the first to agree that hygienic considerations must override all others and "ye axe must decimate our arborific darlings with ruthless surgery to ye point where aesthetics & safety may wed & be happy." Lawn mowers were coming into use, and Laurel Hill commented on the clipped English look the village was assuming and pointed with pride to the fact that the trees were trimmed, whose lower branches interfered with "ye head-gear of tall pedestrians & umbrellas."

There were occasional setbacks to the beauty campaign. A bill presented to the town authorities to make them responsible for the removal of the Canada thistle from the highway was killed "apparently by the pressure of other (tho scarcely less important) reforms." Cattle were recalcitrant and refused to go straight to pasture in a businesslike manner but strayed and nibbled about in the streets and private gardens to the vast annoyance of the citizens. Tidy Court was a Laurel Hill institution and sat in judgment upon the reckless litterer of waste paper, old bottles and banana peels. Streets, spruced up and planted with trees, must have names to match. The Plain called itself Main Street, imitating every other town in the country. Church Street replaced the ignominious Poverty Lane, while Pine Street climbed up the historic old Hill.

One feels the steam-roller energy of Mrs. J. Z. Goodrich, née Mary Hopkins, behind many of these refurbishings. Whether it was twenty kerosene lamps to light the street (only on moonless nights) in 1868, an awning over the speaker's head on the rostrum on Laurel Hill, the first flat-arch constructed bridge in existence, built at her own expense, or a piece of George Washington's coffin presented to the Library, nothing was too big or too little to call forth her powers. The Laurel Hill Association, her child, let not a Canada thistle grow under its feet. Perhaps she is best remembered by something still to be mentioned. Feeling it appropriate to memorialize in some way the old owners of the soil, she raised enough money in 1877 to erect a stone-shaft obelisk—shaped by nature—on the ancient burying ground of the Indians. "The Burial place of the Housatonic Indians, the Friends of our Fathers" was cut into the base of what is known today as the Indian Monument.

If it was a model village—"a mecca of refinement, literature, morality and religious," according to a flattering newspaper—the Laurel Hill Association was the embodiment of all its virtues. Once a year in the late summer, Stockbridge, in its best sprigged muslin, climbed the lovely little knoll to celebrate its Anniversary Day. This was the peak of the summer season, the climax of another year of self-improvement and everyone turned out to enjoy it. Young blades struck attitudes against trees as they bent whispering over beribboned bonnets of an appropriate age. The elderly and infirm sat in carriages on the outskirts of the crowd and the youngest children were brought to toddle uncertainly from one group to another beneath the checkered shade of the great trees. The band played, and a "literary treat" was provided to an audience which enjoyed an infinite appetite for oratory. In 1871, when Mrs. Rev. Dr. Field, "the first lady speaker upon our rostrum," had delivered a delightful address of three-quarters of an hour on "The Country Life of Woman" the afternoon had just begun. Five clergymen followed each other in not very rapid succession, "after which further exercises were discontinued in favor of some Terpsichorean practice on ye turf by ye more youthful portions of ye assembly." The burden of the distinguished speakers' song was always the same, and when one of them stated that Stockbridge was not so very different from Heaven, he found an echoing response in every heart.

Henry Dwight Sedgwick was president of the Laurel Hill Association for many years. He abandoned the law in New York in 1880 to come home and make a life of agreeable leisure his profession. This Mr. Sedgwick had gone so far afield as to marry his own first cousin. He was the most benignant of men, a gentler edition of the Judge, with all the harsh lines and uncomfortable angles smoothed out and softened down. He lacked, also, some of the Judge's practical sense. He had trusted his money to a plausible fellow in New York who had promptly made off with it, with the result that he was forced to practice a strict economy as best he could. Once, because he could get it at a bargain, he bought a large consignment of note paper with a mourning band.

The family was obliged to use it for years, loudly complaining that no one would die. He acquired also an odd assortment of gloves with no thought for the sizes, and his children were provided for years with very durable but ill-fitting gloves.

The plain old Sedgwick house was put into Victorian dress, painted dark brown on the inside with a piece of stained glass here, a piece of statuary there, and what looked to the children like a series of chocolate drops geometrically arranged on the parlor ceiling. But it retained its essential character, bursting with children as it always had, and lavish with hospitality. As in the earlier generation it was a link between the world outside and the village within its Cranford frame.

Stockbridge was set in its ways, and as late as 1880 still thought itself more or less a farming community. A pig, a side of beef, and a barrel of cider were still the staples of a Berkshire winter, with the canned delicacies of last summer's work standing in solid rows upon the cupboard shelves. Pittsfield and Great Barrington were still beyond the horizon for shopping and entertainment, and fun was home-made, except on the occasions when itinerant theatrical troupes came to Music Hall. *Uncle Tom's Cabin* was sure to be played once every two or three years, and a magician in full evening dress with suspicious black whiskers could always delight the audience by pulling silver dollars out of some farmer's hair.

One of the children who passed his boyhood in the Sedgwick house, remembers some of the familiar figures of the time:

"Mr. Hofmayer must have come from Germany, for he bore the aspect of one of those Central European inhabitants, of Bohemia or Ruthenia, who look to be not remotely descended from the Kobolds. His hair was black, his eyes were black, his beard was black, and there was a kindly look of triumphant disinclination to remove the appropriate blackness from his forehead, nose and cheeks. He was always friendly, smiling, radiating that pleasant sense of *savoir vivre* that Americans born have never learned. He was at times, as I remember, a cobbler, at times a fishmonger, with a little cart; it may have had bells, but I don't remember. There was something of the spirit of Christmas in him; he would have made an excellent Saint Nick.

"Jimmy Caffrey was an Irishman. Short, bandy-legged, I fear he suffered from rheumatism, and his occupation was that of hedger, one of the race of swanked hedgers that carry me back to the graveyards of Old England and, I suppose, of southern Ireland. He had a grand pair of clippers, albeit a little rusty, and clipped the graveyard hedge. That hedge must have been very fertile, for I can't remember seeing him cut anything else. He was always there on summer days, benevolent and a bit of an artist in his own eyes, but ready to chat. He was very short and I can't guess how he managed to clip the tops of the hedge; that must have been the problem that occupied his mind, as he stood ruminating thoughtfully, on those little bandy legs of his, and why he welcomed the distraction of a conversation with any passerby, man or boy.

"At the end of Main Street by the cemetery (where Jimmy Caffrey the hedger worked), Mr. Waters, the postmaster lived, in a little typical New England house. He had a wife, as I remember, and two daughters, the elder very pretty. When I read *The Vicar of Wakefield* this family comes to my mind; Mr. Waters was a sweet-tempered, philosophic little man, who was very obliging about letters and took life as it came. He had a little thin beard, and reddish lids to his eyes, and his ways were gentle. Next to the little post office by the Episcopal Church, a glorious great tree spread its branches over and far beyond both post office and drugstore.

The drugstore was kept by Mr. William B. Clarke. I don't know his history. He was always more prosperously dressed than Mr. Waters, and had a more competent manner, but one liked better the gentle, deferential, kindly, and a little bewildered outlook on life that the postmaster showed. I think that Mr. Clarke had a license to sell beer or liquor, or both, and there used to be serious discussions about morality and the village going to the dogs, when empty bottles, which might have come from anywhere, were found of a Sunday morning, lying alongside the street under the stately elms, of which the village was so proud.

"Beyond Mr. Clarke's nearer the Lee end of the Main Street, also marked by a noble tree, was a hideous building where Mr. Dean had a nondescript shop of dry goods and groceries on one side and on the other were offices, I think. Upstairs Sticks Rathbun, the barber, a pleasant youngish man, with a ruddy complexion and a wooden leg, always stimulated, according to the best tradition among barbers, conversation, on the weather, on local politics or local gossip, or prospective sales of houses or cows or pigs. Waiting customers sat round with friends blessed with leisure, especially on winter days, and talked and spat and were very sociable.

"Across the street next to the bank was Mr. George Seymour, the grocer, who also sold (or am I thinking of Mr. Henry Plumb's shop, next door to Mr. Seymour?) fish hooks, cat-gut, sinkers and fish poles, and candy in a glass case at the end of the counter. Mr. Seymour had healthy red cheeks, liked to smoke, was pleasant and courteous to everybody. So was Mr. Henry Plumb, who looked a good deal like Uncle Sam, but he left one with the feeling that he was a little disquieted within, that he entertained apprehensions—vague but ever-present—of poor business ahead, of diminishing customers, of sickness coming to the village. Hams, onions, ears of corn, bits of harness, and other useful things hung from the ceiling at the back of the shop. Customers used to have little books in which purchases charged were noted down and balanced at the end of the month. Between them and the Red Lion Inn (it was just The Hotel in those days) stood the bank as now, very respectable with its classic portico, and with the same respectability inside, affected by people who deal with money, as being a noble occupation. Old Mr. Daniel Williams was the benevolent first citizen of the village. It must have been his successor, who dressed very carefully, was carefully barbered, and walked with dignity to and from his house which was at the end of Main Street. At the time of midday dinner, Mr. Kimball could always be seen, proceeding with high respectability to his house and, at the end of an appropriate period, going back again. But old Mr. Williams belonged to an earlier generation, of what we like to think of as pure American, venerable, benevolent, quietly philosophic and yet with a certain canny aptitude for business.

"Mr. Gourlie and his two sisters lived in the house opposite the hotel and cater-cornered from the Episcopal Church. They were little people—the brother about five feet high, the two ladies shorter, and one shorter than the other—she was the little Miss Gourlie. A friendly family of skunks lived under the house. Mr. Gourlie gave to the village the fountain of the cat and dog fighting. He was a bookish man, and early of a June morning, I suspect on a little constitutional before breakfast, he would walk up and down the village street, one hand under his coat-tails, the other holding a stick, with which he gesticulated freely as he spouted: "That is the question, whether it is better—" or "Farewell, the tranquil mind, farewell content—" or "He was perfumed like a milliner and twixt his finger—" for he knew his Shakespeare by heart and he liked the grand passages that seemed to add a cubit to his stature, as he strode slowly along.

"Farther down towards the station Mr. J. Z. Goodrich lived. Our curiosity as to what Z stood for was never satisfied, though there is something in the theory that you learn a good deal about an American, when you know what his middle initial stands for. Mr. Goodrich had served in the Legislature. He must always have been a deliberative man, suspicious of quick minds, and inclined to spend much time in considering whether to put a comma, or a semi-colon. He was a safe, good man, very remote from the Jimmy Caffrey type—dignified, dull. Boys suspected that his house must be a gloomy place to live in. Life treated him inadequately, his understanding failed and, after forty or fifty years of married life, he insisted upon keeping up *les convenances* which he feared had been disregarded, by a second marriage ceremony with his wife. He gave the Library to the town, a most successfully ugly little building, which (at least in those days) depressed the librarian, and made people speak in unusually sad and muffled tones when they came for books.

"Around the little corner beyond the library stood the tinsmith's shop, kept by Mr. John Van Deusen. He had an aspect like El Greco's favorite model, a grave, solemn, half mystical face, with a long beard. He was very apostolic, the most striking-looking man in town, tall and gaunt, and wearing a shop coat, that must have resembled those the apostles wore on Sundays. Soldering was a most momentous matter, something like a funeral, in his eyes. You couldn't have imagined that he came from the same race as Franz Hals. Possibly his ancestors were Walloons.

"There was Mr. Root, the tax collector. He should have been a Canterbury Pilgrim, for he was quite as worthy as the Reeve of a portrait by Dan Chaucer. He was a little over medium height, but looked taller because of his lean and withered appearance, suggestive of a hop pole in November. His cheeks were wrinkled, his brow furrowed, his lips compressed—designed by the Almighty from the beginning to be a tax gatherer. His overcoat, not very new, fitted him close, and his pockets never bulged, but lay flat as if to say, "See how empty these humble receptacles of Uncle Sam's dues are." As I look back, though ignorant of our fiscal system, I think he must have collected only the town's taxes, but he gave the appearance of collecting village, town, state, federal, international taxes, as he walked down the street past the cemetery. He liked to walk past it, as if to illustrate the close bond between death and taxes—and he was the only man whom Jimmy Caffrey did not detain for a colloquy. It is likely that Jimmy's dues were small—ordinary humanity often clings to small things—but Mr. Root was inexorable. It was impossible to separate the man from his office, he seemed to have been molten and poured into it, or metamorphosed by some fiscal God into a tax collector, like Daphne into a laurel. I never knew where he lived, or if he had any human ties. He seemed like a creature of fiscal mechanism, set to a certain stride, to call on certain fixed days, to grin a sardonic smile when the taxed suggested something other than immediate payment. He always had a lonely look, but that was to be expected. Who but sextons, hangmen, unfrocked dentists, or outlaws would hobnob with a tax collector? If, by any kindly chance, he had a wife, a brother, or sister at home, I do not doubt that once within doors—his cap on one peg, his worn overcoat on another, his boots off, his feet stretched towards the fire, a glass of comforting whisky and a newspaper—he became human once again, and that Terence would have dropped in with pleasure for a chat."

Although J. Z. Goodrich gave the building, it was Nathan Jackson who set on foot the movement to have a library, when in 1863 he offered $2,000 if the town would raise half that amount. The sum was doubled. Madam Dwight, the widow of the senator, gave the land for the building, which was across the street from her house. She made the provision that the building should be set far enough back not to interfere with her clear line of vision down the Main Street. The Library opened its doors to the public in 1864. The town appropriated $300 for its expenses, a librarian was engaged at $20 a month and the trustees congratulated their fellow-citizens on the prospect of this "immediate addition to our means, of Social, Moral and Religious Happiness." By 1880 the library had branches in Curtisville and Glendale, and it was noted in the annual report that the readers in these communities generally selected works of a solid character. Were they reading the works of Jonathan Edwards and Stephen West? Religion was still at a high premium but the cut of its coat had changed in a hundred years. Dean Stanley of Westminster Abbey, on a visit to Henry Field, preached in St. Paul's Church. He relegated Edwards to the shade of nineteenth-century oblivion. "Nothing can be gleaned," he said, "from the thorny speculations with which on this spot the most famous of American divines in the previous age laboured to build up the hard system of Calvin." Dr. West would have been surprised to find the *Scripture and Doctrine of Atonement* presented to the library as having "more value as a relic than for use."

Culture meant Europe, and travelers brought back books of photographs which were put on display. Three volumes of *Picturesque Europe* were gifts of Madam Dwight. "This elegant work will remain on ye table for ye inspection of visitors and will prove an unfailing source of gratification to all who have ye opportunity of examining it."

Two years after the Library opened, the village saw the meteoric rise of the wood-pulp industry. It was the first manufacture of the raw material for making paper out of wood in this country, and was also to be the swan song of Curtisville. Albert Pagenstecher, a well set-up and enterprising German, came up from New York to visit Mr. Hoffman. While strolling through Curtisville, the same thought came to him that had occurred to Elnathan Curtis so many years before. Here was unused water power; why not try an experiment? He imported from Germany the machines that had just been invented for making wood-pulp. Frederick Wurtzbach brought them over and set them up in a new building completed for their reception. The Smith Paper Company in Lee consented to try out the new material, and it immediately proved successful. For over a year Curtisville held the monopoly on wood-pulp, but the growing demand for it necessitated more water power and more mills. Until 1883 Curtisville turned out its small share, and enjoyed a last business boom before Wurtzbach left to become manager of the larger mills in Lee. Curtisville lapsed again into obscurity until the summer people rediscovered it, admired the view, and Curtisville became Interlaken.

Here John E. Parsons of Lenox, turned the old tavern into St. Helen's Home, a vacation house for city children. David Dudley Field, by then a benign old gentleman, used to make it the object of his afternoon drives. With grandfatherly benevolence he would sit on the piazza and trot the children upon his knee. Mr. Field lived on the top-most peak of the Hill, in a fine house he had just completed, and was enjoying an old age devoted largely to good works. He gave the Ice Glen to the town and offered a Chimes Tower, with clock and bells, in memory of his grandchildren. Stockbridge, always doubtful of innovation, was alarmed. "It would be ugly and quite unnecessary and the chimes would be a daily nuisance," said the conservative faction. "But consider the generosity of Mr. Field in so handsomely remembering the old town where he was a boy," retorted the opposition. It was the sort of quarrel that the village has always loved to settle its teeth into. Bonnets passed haughtily past other bonnets—not speaking—and sharp arguments took place over the teacups. The chimes party won out and the tower was put up, a massive structure built to withstand the tests of time. In his deed of gift Field stipulated that the bells should be rung for half an hour at dusk from apple-blossom time until frost. From that day to this, where once the full-throated voices of the Indians were raised up in Dr. Watt's hymns, the chimes ring out *Old Black Joe* and *Swanee River* to mark the end of the summer afternoon.

Henry Martyn Field lived near his brother on the Hill. He had remodeled an old farmhouse for his French Henriette into a cottage that would have astonished its original owner. Gambrel and gable deeply disguised The Castle where Ephraim Williams had planned and plotted over a hundred years before. Here Field composed innumerable travel books. *Summer Pictures from Copenhagen to Venice* and *From the Lakes of Killarney to the Golden Horn* were best sellers running to twenty editions over the years.

David Dudley and Henry Martyn, secure in successful careers, made a suitable background for Stephen Field, the logical nephew of such uncles. His achievement was to mark the arrival of the modern world, although the village did not pay much attention to it. In 1879, he came back from California to settle down. He was at this time a rising young inventor and had just completed the first long-distance telephone line from San Francisco to the summit of the Sierras.

Scientific inventions failed to make a dent in Stockbridge. Even the spectacular long-distance telephone failed to impress a village that looked upon the telephone itself as a new-fangled contraption, useful perhaps in cities. Stephen was just Jonathan Field's boy, grown out of a practical-joking boyhood into a burly, genial man, measuring up to the typical Field build of over six feet tall. The neighbors were not particularly impressed with his tinkering in the barn behind his house and, when he invited them over to his back yard one August afternoon to try out a horseless trolley, they were not unduly excited. With skepticism they regarded a small object four feet high and ten feet long, equipped with seats for two, and a gigantic headlight. The tracks gleamed in the sun as they curved around Field's ample lawn, and the first man to climb in beside him winked at the crowd as he jocularly advised Field not to go too fast. Rapidly and efficiently it spun around the lawn amid the plaudits of the company. Field explained that the current was supplied by a third rail placed between the tracks, and was taken up by a shoe which fitted the bottom of the car. He went on to predict that the electric car would be the modern means of transportation. That night, as the neighbors discussed the matter over the evening meal, it was agreed that this was fantastic. It was simply an amusing toy, but certainly very clever of Stephen.

Working quietly in his laboratory for over thirty years, Stephen Field changed the daily life of Stockbridge and of the world beyond. A man takes a trolley to his office in the morning (or he did until recently). He goes upstairs in an electric elevator, glances at the stock ticker, and puts in a long-distance call. That evening he may send a night message on the way home from the theater, where he has taken the complicated machinery of stage-lighting for granted. His day, at all these points, has been touched by the genius of Field. And yet he has probably never heard of him.

While Field was still perfecting his trolley, the '90's arrived in a whirl of bicycle wheels and Gibson Girl sailor hats. If one admired the height and luxuriance of the trees planted by the Laurel Hill Association, it was deplorable that the

Housatonic River was now for the first time sullied by modern plumbing, those waters that Fanny Kemble had declared so pure they should only be used for the baptism of children. The cows that had stared for so long into their translucent depths were now deserting the pastures along the river for sequestered upland meadows. The giant willow tree on South Street, with its staircase and platform with seats for forty people, was gone. It had held the village in its arms in every mood, and flirtations and secrets and story-telling had mingled with the sibilant whispering of its leaves. Even the Stockbridge band, called "Yellow Birds" because of their gay uniforms, sometimes climbed up to surprise the native inhabitants of the old tree, with cornet and cymbal and brass. The little white post office with classic portico and pillar, that once had boasted that it was the first in the county, had gone. The elm had been young then that now looked scornfully down from its magnificent height on the new nonentity of a post office. The elm was the village engagement list.

> "You shall read of an auction, a concert, a ball,
>   Of taxes requiring attention.
> Of a strawberry cramming at Music Hall,
> Of the bank or a Laurel Hill meeting or call
>   To a caucus or temperance convention."

Any citizen having a grievance vented it in a notice pinned to its seamy side. "The gentleman who left his hat in Mr. Hoffman's melon patch last night can recover it by calling."

A very frenzy of building had seized the town a few years before, and in 1884 it was equipped with town offices of pressed brick, the interior finished in beaded pine. The building was considered to be very "neat and tasteful in architectural design." In 1883, a Methodist church had been erected on the corner of Church Street, through the generosity of Mrs. Henry D. Cone, wife of the last local business magnate. The Cones lived in a Swiss villa flanked by greenhouses at the eastern end of Main Street. He was a John Jacob Astor on the Stockbridge scale, president of the Owen and Hurlbut paper mill of South Lee and of the model factories he constructed at Housatonic. He had dreamed of making Housatonic a railroad junction between Boston and Philadelphia and had secured control of a part of the line to that end. But the big railroads paralleled his route, and disaster overtook him and his model factories in the panic of 1893. So passed the last incarnation of Elijah Williams.

The Casino, a social club, had been built in 1886, with Charles McKim as architect. The Stockbridge House, run by Mrs. Plumb, was expanded in 1884 and again, after it burned down, in 1896. This time it was built to accommodate two hundred persons and reverted to its old Revolutionary name of the Red Lion Inn. A new boarding house, the Edwards House, had taken over the Hoffman schoolhouse. It stated in an advertisment that Stockbridge was a "veritable wheelman's paradise" and boasted that any summer's day would see from two to twenty wheels stacked in the yard. The bicycle craze was on.

There was discussion between the high-spirited younger generation and their more pedestrian-minded elders about bicycles being ridden on the sidewalk. Complaints were pinned to the post-office elm of damages incurred to the dignity of elderly gentlemen. Mr. Gourlie's morning constitutional was rudely interrupted by a rapid bicyclist shouting coarsely, "Hi Johnny, get out of the way." Mr. Choate observed that Ellery Sedgwick, "that giant performer on the wheel came into collision with Professor Boyeson's back and made a large dent in the same." When one of the Choate boys descended precipitantly from the seat of his high bicycle into Mrs. Doane's baby carriage, a petition was drawn up appealing to the selectmen to prevent the riding of bicycles on the sidewalks. Alexander Sedgwick, young and very dauntless, saved the day. He persuaded his father to compose a counter-petition which he presented at every house in the village until he secured enough signatures to defeat the non-sporting element.

While all young Stockbridge was bicycling gaily if unsteadily down Main Street, Joe Choate brought home from Canada three implements of the exciting new game of golf. Tomato cans formed the first three holes, measured off with precision in the meadows along lower Church Street. On this course Joe Choate practiced the strokes which in 1898 were to win him honors in the National Championship with a record low score of 175. The game soon outgrew the tomato cans and became established on a nine-hole course below the Congregational church, in the meadows from which the last cow had now vanished. In the same summer of 1895, the Stockbridge Golf Club was formed. Here the Vardons of the day performed, and Cortlandt Van Rensselaer who, Mr. Choate said, looked as if he had swallowed first a mattress and then a poker, closely followed the play. The day that Joe Choate was defeated by a foreigner from New Haven, "Corty," importantly slapping his pocketbook, declared that he would have given it and all it contained to keep the cup at home! Matches took place between Stockbridge and Great Barrington, whose team, resplendent in red coats and long stockings, arrived in a four-in-hand brake. It was invariably and satisfactorily beaten. The golf was atrocious and wonderful.

A few years later, Rachel Field, author of tomorrow's bestsellers, was trudging dutifully up Yale Hill to attend Miss Adele Brewer's school for young ladies between the ages of four and fifteen. It was at Hillside, the house she shared with her sister, Miss Emelia Brewer, halfway up Yale Hill. They were the daughters of the Reverend Josiah Brewer and Emelia Field. Stockbridge was thoroughly familiar with

Miss Adele and Miss Emelia and Miss Alice Byington, who lived with them and helped run the school. Pupils still remember the Swiss music box tinkling out a faintly martial air to which the younger children marched in, bowing formally to Miss Brewer before they took their places. Fractions were taught with pins on Miss Emelia's bed, and line upon line, precept upon precept were learned literally at Miss Byington's knee, as she sat surrounded by poetry books. Part of the Stockbridge legend is the story of Miss Emelia Brewer and the telegraph pole. It was the first sit-down strike in history. When the telegraph company proposed to plant a pole in front of her house, she refused permission point-blank. In spite of her remonstrances the men went ahead and spent a day digging a ditch for the offending pole which they proposed to put in the next morning. Miss Emelia waited until they had left, then picked up her bed, walked right out, placed it over the hole, and lay down for the night. It was a strategic position, and when the workmen met the eye of the embattled spinster in the gray light of the early morning, they hastily abandoned the idea of placing a telegraph pole anywhere within range of Miss Emelia.

In the gay hyperbole of the '90's it was to be expected that even a burglar should be extradimensional, and the one who roamed the village in the summer of 1893 was no ordinary thief but a Gentleman Burglar, who sent delicious thrills down all the ladies' backs. They were fascinated by his low, cultivated voice and charming manners, when he made his professional calls in their bedrooms in the dead of night. Although he covered his victims with a cocked revolver and his eyes gleamed cold and inscrutable over the finely hemstitched handkerchief that covered the lower part of his face, he made the strongest appeal to their sympathies, and they declared that they would hate to see him "taken up." Mrs. Swann, a daughter of Mr. Butler, was so touched by his replacing a ring she especially prized, and selecting, at her suggestion, one far less valuable that she attempted to reason with him over the foot of the bed. "Don't you think you might choose some other employment?" she asked. She was answered by an icy stare from under the delicately-arched eyebrows. All handsome and distinguished-looking males were under suspicion, and it was even remarked as a coincidence that the Rectory and the Sedgwick house were almost the only houses unvisited by the burglar. As for Mr. Southmayd, he engaged a night watchman with a dinner-bell. At last the burglar was apprehended through his excellent taste in the matter of cigars. The paper bands of a special brand smoked by the rector of the church in Lenox were discovered in the bottom of a buggy he had stolen from William Pitt Palmer. The ladies' hearts missed a beat when he was arrested, and it was a crushing disappointment when he turned out to be a laborer who had done some of the stonework on Mr. Choate's house a number of years before.

These are some of the ghosts who walk today beneath the village elms and haunt the houses where they lived their leisurely and sober-paced lives. The Gentleman Burglar just escapes detection as one turns on an electric light in a dark passage in the Martin Inn, once Mrs. Swann's house. The rustle of Mrs. Sedgwick's book muslin is audible on summer evenings as she glides down the path from the old house to the rectory to discuss church affairs over a mild scotch and soda with Mr. Lawrence. One can almost see Miss Carrie Wells's plump, upholstered figure and corkscrew curls behind a stack of books in the old wing of the Library, and Miss Emelia Brewer and Miss Alice Byington, in very large bonnets, bowing out either side of a very small carriage driven by Tom Carey. Are Mr. Southmayd's and Mr. Butler's two top hats, bowing and talking to each other the length of the village street of a Sunday morning, completely imaginary?

There was no lavish display in the way money was spent in Stockbridge. The whole village boasted only three coachmen in livery, yet almost everyone kept a carriage. There was the leisure that comes from comfortable incomes—plenty of time for picnics, and for drives about the countryside, with a tea basket in one hand and the *Golden Treasury* in the other. There were archery parties, tennis, boating on the river, and an occasional expedition to Lebanon in the livery stable's one four-in-hand for the young leg-of-mutton sleeves and their beaux, the stiff round straw hats. Leisure was a business seriously undertaken.

Very strong was the summer people's sense of *noblesse oblige*. The villas had their solid foundations deep in Berkshire soil. Their owners had not built them lightly, in any sense of the word, for they were certain that their children, and their children's children would be there after them, leading the same tranquil, kindly lives. Noise had not been invented, nor hurry, nor disorder. Perhaps the serenity of this period is rather deceptive. People and events as we look back on them have a tendency to arrange themselves into charming daguerreotypes, posed for the camera. Unhappiness and frustration, which show their familiar faces in the old diaries and letters, were sternly repressed under the smooth front that was uniformly presented to the world.

Yet the essence of the Stockbridge these people represented was unlike that of the usual small town. It had none of the cramped, enclosed feeling of a New England village and none of the snobbishness of a resort, but was a unique blending of the two. One saw here the world in village focus and its bouquet was composed of an intense spirit of place with the spacious point of view of people of the world and a strong feeling of continuity. It was inconceivable that the economic structure of life should ever be seriously threatened. It was inconceivable that the quiet, sleepy village should not jog along forever, a succession of duties faithfully performed and innocent gaieties enjoyed.

It is to be hoped that the ghosts are sleep-walking ghosts and that as they wander through the town they are safely wrapped in the dream of the Stockbridge they knew. Two minutes of consciousness would shatter it forever. Two minutes' realization of the busy, active, modern town would utterly confound them, and their exclamations of astonishment would be lost in the roar of the trucks up Main Street.

Epilogue

STOCKBRIDGE is celebrating its two-hundredth birthday this summer, and realizes with a feeling half of regret, half of pride, that the town again has moved on. It bears no resemblance today to those New England towns that the modern world has left behind to live on a nostalgic diet of past glories and faded gentility. Stockbridge has kept pace with the century and, if it has lost the gay intimacy of the old days, it is too eager planning for tomorrow to shed more than a passing sentimental tear over yesterday. If the four walls of the Casino could speak, they could tell the story as well as anyone in town. Born modestly in 1886, as a center for tennis and billiards, it grew in the early 1900's to be the pivot around which revolved not only the social but the artistic life of the village. Then, after a period of decline in the years following the World War, when it lost its prestige, it was moved the length of Main Street to the foot of Yale Hill, had its face lifted, and blossomed forth into a professional theater, able to call itself the Broadway of the Berkshires.

It was in the early years of the century that Stockbridge became talented. Daniel Chester French was working in his studio, adjoining Chesterwood, the house he had recently built. His majestic draped figure, *The Republic,* which had dominated the World's Fair in 1893, was still within an easy span of memory. Marie Kobbé was beginning to catch on paper, likenesses of children which would remain uncannily true to character and gesture thirty years later. Her friends, Lydia Field Emmet and Susan Metcalfe, built a house near the Kobbés' on Yale Hill. Miss Emmet was just becoming nationally known as a portrait painter, while Miss Metcalfe was giving her own charming interpretation to the songs of Brahms and Schubert. Young Walter Nettleton was painting realistic snowscenes, and Robert Reid was beginning to sell his large canvases, flooded with sun and sentiment, to museums all over the country. Augustus Lukeman, a sculptor known for his imposing dramatic group, *Women of the Confederacy*, and his equestrian statue of Francis Asbury, was also at work in his studio.

Owen Johnson, the novelist, came to town at a time when fourteen-year-olders everywhere were flat on their stomachs reading *Stover at Yale* and *The Varmint*. Walter Prichard Eaton had bought a house, and Ruth Draper dropped into the village occasionally, experimenting with a talent that neither she nor anyone else took very seriously.

It was art with a small *a*. Stockbridge did not have to be laboriously educated to enjoy music and pictures and plays imported from the outside world, for it was spontaneously producing them without looking at itself in the glass to observe the effect. Talents great and small rubbed shoulders at the Casino. Everyone who could paint, and a good many who couldn't, exhibited at the annual picture shows which were inaugurated in 1909. There were song recitals by Miss Metcalfe with Professor Ulysse Buhler at the piano; Cortlandt Van Rensselaer, very formal and portentous in tails and a white vest, gave a reading on the Art of Heraldry, while Frank Crowninshield convulsed the audience by his irreverence.

Youthful high spirits boiled over into vaudeville shows which offered to the public no less than "4 Little Evas, 9 Hamlets, 4 Bloodhounds, 2 Tattoed Queens, 1 Real Snowstorm, 400 Imperial Corps de Ballet and a Boy Caruso, not to mention a Sword-swallower and the Stockbridge Armless

Wonder." On another occasion, "Miss Ruth Draper in her celebrated money-logs" was followed by "the Crownie Brothers [who] in order to keep the Hall warm will turn on a little hot air." Jokes were definitely local. Everyone knew of Miss Tuckerman's passionate aversion to the chimes and her delight when they broke down one summer. Frank Crowninshield's announcement in an intermission that, owing to her unavoidable absence in Europe, Miss Emily Tuckerman would not be able to recite *The Curfew Must Not Ring Tonight* brought down the house. Unforgettable was the performance of *Cranford*. The actors just stepped in as they were, off the village street, to take their parts. Miss Adele Brewer, Miss Agnes Canning, Miss Agnes Goodwin, Mrs. Joseph Schilling, Miss Lizzie Norton didn't have to act at all, for nature had made them letter-perfect in their parts.

On an August afternoon in 1907, the whole town repaired to the Casino to celebrate Mrs. Mary Jane Pitkin's eightieth birthday. Mrs. Pitkin was niece of the poet, William Pitt Palmer, and was a repository of Stockbridge lore. Generations of children had trudged up the Hill to the old Palmer homestead to listen to stories, or look in the ancient secretary in the parlor for the secret drawer. Sometimes they were allowed the run of the attic, and dressing up in the ancestral hoop skirts they played at the history of Stockbridge. Over 400 of her friends gathered for the birthday party. There was an orchestra from the Red Lion Inn and Mrs. Plumb presented a gigantic cake, a frosted facsimile of the Chimes Tower itself. Miss Lucy White recited a poem written in honor of Mrs. Pitkin, reminiscent of an earlier day when occasional verse had adorned every social gathering. Everyone came, everybody danced and drank pink lemonade, and the grand finale was achieved when Mrs. Pitkin, light of foot and graceful as the youngest girl, led off a Virginia reel.

It was a gay, light-hearted time, redolent of a certain innocent worldliness. The ladies with their hourglass figures and mountainous hats ornamented receptions and luncheons. Plenty of good, rich food was invariably served. Mrs. Crowninshield was a combination of great kindness and intense sociability, and loved to entertain. Every detail of her parties was carefully planned in advance; just the right choice of food, and the candles, under their red silk shades, shining discreetly on immaculate linen and silver. When she went out, she was appreciative of her hostess's sense of the well-oiled wheels on which a dinner or luncheon should run. One day she attended a lunch party where all went with desirable smoothness until the poor hostess was taken acutely ill of convulsions. Mrs. Crowninshield was all bustling, warm-hearted efficiency, administering home remedies and finally getting the poor lady off to the hospital. When she arrived home she was hot and flustered. She lay on the sofa while she volubly described the whole episode to her son, Frank. He was full of sympathy and said, "But Mamma, I never heard of anything so awful. *When* did all this happen?"

"Well, fortunately, my dear, it was after the dessert."

Alexander Sedgwick inherited his father's house, and scraped off the Victorian veneer to reveal the plain colonial lines. An Edwardian elegance was added, which was the contribution of his generation. Following close in his father's footsteps, he made Stockbridge his profession and became president of the Laurel Hill Association. On Anniversary Day he stood in the rostrum, an immaculately dressed figure with a boutonnière which perfectly expressed the exotic blooming of his personality. The audience held its breath with mingled amusement and apprehension. Where would the wit, darting about like forked lightning, strike? Would the involved sentences, so brilliantly caparisoned with metaphor and adjective, contain the necessary weight of noun and verb to bring them to earth at all? Sitting behind him on the rostrum designed by Mr. French, would be the speaker of the afternoon, flanked by the distinguished gentlemen of the village. There would be Richard Rogers Bowker, gray-bearded and earnest-eyed. He was the founder of the American Library Association and president of the Stockbridge Library. Mr. Choate would be there, benignly smiling, and perhaps Dr. Charles McBurney, the eminent surgeon from New York, who had built Cherry Hill a number of years before.

In 1904, Dennis Morrissey changed his carriage shop into a garage and bought a touring car to rent out. The first automobiles began to cavort past the Casino, heavy as poor jokes. The ladies sat erect on the back seats, muffled in dusters and dark veils in which isinglass was sewed in for the eyes. Alexander Sedgwick was usually prostrate under his White Steamer, investigating a mechanism that was to remain mysterious to him to the end, while his more conservative friends drove by with carriage and pair at a rather ostentatiously brisk pace. Jack Swann, in an effort to make his monster conform to the best equestrian tradition, attempted to leap a fence near the Tuckerman bridge and landed in a confused heap of mechanism in an adjoining meadow. But it was not until 1914 that the village realized the automobile had really come to stay, when the Fire Department adopted an automobile engine, abandoning forever the Jerrys and Toms, whose flowing black manes and clattering hoofs had heightened the excitement of local fires.

Modern improvements were making rapid inroads upon the town and electric lights appeared along the streets in 1908, in spite of Stephen Field's remonstrance that they made it look like a city. But there had been one innovation to which Stockbridge, or at least half of Stockbridge, strenuously objected. The town would never agree—as the cat-and-dog fountain was there to affirm. In 1902, The Berkshire Street Railway Company proposed to run a trolley down Main Street. This issue roused all the best fighting blood in town. The "trolleyites" claimed the trolley would carry children to school, and would bring in desirable business. The "anti-trolleyites," passionately denouncing The Berkshire Street Railway and all its works, cried that the town would be ruined. *The Berkshire Courier* headlined its article on the controversy, A Hot Time in Stockbridge. Stephen Field wrote in dismay from Europe: "I heard . . . that an outside corporation having its own interest and the town's destruction at heart had applied for the rights above-mentioned. But having implicit faith in the integrity and patriotism of the old-time families of the town, the Carters, the Palmers, Sergeants, Seymours, Sedgwicks and many others too numerous to mention, the matter gave me no great uneasiness. Imagine, therefore, my distress at finding that you are seriously considering the matter . . . Why is there but one Stockbridge? Is it not because our fathers made it so? They planted these trees, arranged these parks . . . You are now petitioned by some of the descendants of these worthy men to undo what they by years of toil helped to create, to allow the invasion of our beautiful street by a so-called trolley. Such a proceeding would at once change our town from 'the only Stockbridge' to a dull commonplace station on a second-class trolley railway." Finally, it was Alexander Sedgwick, in whose character there was a strong element of the cat-and-dog fountain, who led the "anti-trolleyites" to victory. It was he who held at bay the encroaching forces of The Berkshire Street Railway, when the track was completed right up to the Lee-Stockbridge boundary line. The town raised $18,000 to pay for the property rights and an extra bridge, and the trolley took the route along by the river.

These were the years when the men who were to be the leaders of the village of today were embarking upon their careers. Young Allen Treadway was trying his political wings. In 1900, he became Moderator of Town Meeting, an office he has held to this day. Watching him wield the gavel with parliamentary precision at the annual meeting, Stockbridge reflects with pride on the steps which led to his present position. He was elected to the Massachusetts State Legislature in 1904, and became a member of the State Senate in 1908. He served as President of the Senate in the years 1909, 1910, and 1911. The following year he was elected to Congress from the First Massachusetts district, where he has served ever since, specializing in the subjects of taxation and tariff and supporting Republican platforms and policies.

John C. Lynch was holding positions of responsibility in The American Telephone and Telegraph Company, in which he was to rise to Assistant Vice-President before his retirement in 1931. During the years before his death in 1937, Mr. Lynch was the much-loved first citizen of the modern Stockbridge. The Library, the theater, The Berkshire Symphonic Festival, the Housatonic National Bank were only a few of the interests to which he gave unsparingly of his energy and intelligence.

In 1907, Dr. Austen Fox Riggs came to live in Stockbridge. He had spent his vacations in the village since his marriage to Dr. McBurney's daughter Alice, but now ill health forced him to give up his association with a busy medical office in New York and live in the country the year around. During the years spent in the practice of general medicine, Dr. Riggs had been struck with the fact that almost three-quarters of the patients who came to his office belonged to a category that the doctors could do nothing for. They occupied a borderland between general medicine and psychiatry. There was nothing physically wrong with them, and yet clearly they were ill. The size and nature of the problem these cases presented had long interested him and he now felt he had an opportunity to study them by the trial-and-error method. People began to come to Stockbridge to consult him, driving up from the station in a horse-and-buggy and boarding around in houses in the village. Other doctors became interested and came to work with him, and as the years went by and Stockbridge came to mean Riggs to an ever increasing number of people, the methods of treatment which are used today gradually evolved. By 1914 the work was outgrowing the informal basis on which it was run, and Dr. Riggs was working on a plan to put it on a more permanent and useful basis. However, after the entry of the United States into the World War everyone's energy and money were focused across the sea and the Austen Riggs Foundation had to wait.

During 1914 and 1915, no one considered that the war was going to affect Stockbridge materially. The clash of the great powers on the other side of the Atlantic was terrible, but it was very far away and very exciting. The horrors of modern warfare had not yet divested the conflict of an aura of gold lace and glory associated with battle fought in so high a cause. Grown people did not feel so very differently from the child who wrote home from France to her parents in August, 1914: "War seems so much more here than it ever would at home. I never realized how bad it was, and always thought the part when war is first declared the boring part of a novel. Now everything you read about is coming true and as I see it all around me I almost feel as if I were in the book. I am so glad to be here, for think how exciting it is for me . . . I do not think that any war at home could possibly excite me as this does. America is so huge and so cut off from other lands and anyway the army seems a detached body of people you do not particularly care about and war

could hardly touch us in any but a small way . . ." During
the winter of 1915 the ladies rolled bandages and made
surgical dressings for the Red Cross, and the flags of the Allies
fluttered under the elms. An appeal was read out in St.
Paul's Church from the American War Relief Clearing
House in Paris, for the cure of soldiers who had developed
tuberculosis in the trenches. The sum of $132 was raised for
Victor Cortyl, "the Stockbridge soldier," as he was called. It
was a twentieth-century equivalent of the excitement over
the Italian exiles, and the Fair for Kossuth in 1857.

By 1917, however, the excitement that had been mounting
for the last two years, reached fever-pitch when the United
States joined the Allied forces. No sacrifice was too great to
win this war that was forever to end wars. Mr. Choate, now
the grand old man of New York, was appointed by the Mayor
as chairman of the Committee of Citizens to receive the
French and British Commissioners on their visit to the
United States in May, 1917. He waved aside his doctor's
advice that the round of speeches, dinners, and receptions
would prove too much for his strength, and went through the
four exhausting days with his usual dignity and grace. His
welcome to the Commissioners, his words of confidence in the
ultimate outcome of the conflict, aroused intense enthusiasm
in the crowds that listened to his speeches. The wit that the
public had come to expect gave the usual high polish to his
sincerity and gave no indication of the mortal fatigue he was
feeling. On the last night of Balfour's visit Mr. Choate
asked him and Dr. Bergson and a few others to dine with him
at his house. After dinner he said he would like to propose
a topic of conversation to his friends. Everyone thought he
was going to speak of some phase of the war, but he spoke
quietly into the expectant silence: "Gentlemen, let us discuss
the immortality of the soul." A few days later Mr. Choate
was dead.

EPILOGUE

The summer of 1917 in Stockbridge presented the same scene of concentrated war activity that was to be found in every town, large and small, the country over. Perhaps there was an added intensity that was inherent in its bones; Stockbridge always does things a little harder than other places.

The Casino was called in to do its bit, and like a good old trooper threw itself into this new part: no more jokes and amateur theatricals, but crowded meetings to raise money for the Red Cross. In an evening $8,000 was collected, while altogether $20,000 was raised during that one drive. Walter Nettleton donated a peaceful Berkshire snowscene and Marie Kobbé the proceeds from five children's portraits. There was an exhibition of food under the auspices of the Food Conservation Committee with Mr. Henry McBurney as chairman to show Stockbridge "how to put the cook on the firing line." A table in charge of Miss Marion Hague displayed delicious food-stuffs made entirely from beans raised in Berkshire County, while another exhibit, in charge of Mr. David Dudley Field and Miss Agnes Canning, showed wild vegetables and fruit that could be used for food. Brilliantly colored posters lining the walls of the Casino shouted captions such as "A fine job for Mars. A decisive Battle of History is being fought in the Vegetable Garden."

Liberty Loan subscriptions climbed from $38,800 in the first drive to $130,000 in the second, and to $203,000 in the third. One hundred and forty-nine local young men registered in the Federal draft on June 5th and the town turned out to say good-by. Allen T. Treadway gave them a farewell party the night before they left. There was a dinner at Heaton Hall after which they marched down to the Town Hall, escorted by the Stockbridge cadet band. The Red Cross provided each soldier with a comfort kit, and the Congregational Church gave wrist watches to those of their members who went. The next morning they were given breakfast at the Red Lion Inn, and drove away to Camp Devens accompanied by Mr. Treadway and the Selectmen. History repeated itself with a difference, for Main Street could remember that other early morning in 1775 when a group of farmers' sons had started on the long walk to Lexington with only the heart-felt prayers of Dr. West to bid them Godspeed.

After the war, the feeling of optimism that was prevalent throughout the country found its small reflection in Stockbridge. The same child who had written at the beginning of the war, voiced the hope of her generation: "We have won our righteous cause. The Reconstruction we will have to face! A gigantic picking up—rather like how tiresome it used to be on Christmas afternoon when we had to tidy up the general mess. But it is quite a splendid thing to think of in one way, for everyone will be trying to make the world a better place and keeping it a better place. Humanity would be very debased indeed, if we weren't all better people now, when we think of the price of the noblest young men's dying by which we enjoy our liberty and all our present victorious security. We can't possibly be as extravagant or selfish as if there had not been this war."

The "mess" was far away from rich, comfortable little Stockbridge, which could devote its energies to growing and putting on still more weight.

In 1919, Dr. Riggs put into execution a plan that was to prove mutually beneficial to the town and to his work. In 1914, a patient on leaving had given him a check for $50. "Here is a little check," she said, "for you to use, so that someone who could otherwise not afford this treatment can have it." This check was the nucleus of a fund which grew amazingly. It has never been solicited and has been the voluntary contribution of grateful patients. With this money it was possible to remodel a house on Main Street into an inn, and build a "shop" for occupational therapy. In 1929, the work had outgrown the existing inn, and the property on the corner of Main and Sergeant (formerly known as Casino) Streets was acquired. Here, where Jonathan Edwards once sat and wrote *The Last End of God in the Creation of the World*, on a series of half-moon-shaped bonnet patterns carefully sewed together, the new Foundation Inn stands. Since 1919 more than 6,000 patients have been treated, and 1,700 of these have been treated either free or at reduced rates. There are also clinics, one for children and another for adults, in Pittsfield, which are supported by the Foundation, and which serve not only Pittsfield but Stockbridge and the rest of the county.

The Foundation obviously brings prosperity to the village, a prosperity that is irrespective of seasons. Apart from the number of people actually employed by the inns, the "shop" and the doctors' families, the patients themselves patronize the local stores, their relatives stay at the hotels, and they sometimes even become so enamoured of Stockbridge that they buy or rent property. They are a familiar sight, as they circulate briskly about the countryside with the unmistakable look of "an hour's walk" in their eyes that spells Riggs to the initiated. If they are sometimes loath to come in the first place, they are sometimes sorry to leave when the time comes. Tom Carey, who drives the only horse-and-buggy in the village, once was driving a patient to the station. She dissolved in tears at the thought of her departure. Tom Carey has seen many patients come and go. "Cheer up, lady," he said. "You'll be back soon." On another occasion, a lady patient, whom he had driven out for dinner, instructed him to call for her at ten. "Half-past nine in Stockbridge," he corrected firmly. Tom knows his Foundation.

At the time when the first Foundation Inn was being built, the old Casino was definitely out of the running. Stockbridge could now take all of Berkshire for its playground, and if the golf links and comfortable clubhouse did not suit, there were Lenox, Lee, Pittsfield, and Great Barrington, all similarly equipped, or one could easily motor south into Connecticut.

The Casino's tennis courts were not as good as those at the Golf Club, and people who had once taken an active part in its social life had either died, moved away, or ceased to take much interest. The annual art exhibition, enlarged to accept pictures and sculpture from all of Berkshire, was the only event of importance that took place there. Behind its fine McKim façade with the three rounded arches, it put a brave face on its poverty and, like an aging gentleman who brushed the hair carefully over the bald spot, it paid its bills and reflected a little sadly on the past.

It was in 1926, when its fortunes were at their lowest ebb, that Miss Mabel Choate acquired John Sergeant's house and decided to move it down out of the wind and weather on the Hill to Main Street. She wished to make it a museum and a memorial to her father and mother, and restore it as nearly as possible to the house John and Abigail Sergeant had known. There, among other relics, she has recovered from the remnants of the tribe in Wisconsin the wonderful Bible that first came to Stockbridge in 1743, a present from the Court of St. James's to the Mahican Indians.

The obvious site for the Mission House was the land on which the Casino stood, and she was able to buy the property from the stockholders. The problem of what to do with the unwanted Casino building was solved by Walter L. Clark, a summer resident. He conceived the idea of moving it the length of the village street and starting a summer theater. Businessman and engineer through most of his life, Mr. Clark devoted his later years to the furtherance of artistic

projects. He had already started the Grand Central Art Galleries in New York, and at the age of seventy he did a bust of Duse which he presented to Mussolini. Large, bold schemes roused all his qualities of enthusiasm and ability. Miss Choate gave him the Casino, and he bought a property at the foot of Yale Hill for its accommodation. With Austen Riggs, Daniel French, Alexander Sedgwick, and Norman Davis, Walter Clark founded the Three Arts Society. Their object was to make it an educational and non-profit-making organization, which would provide a summer season of professional theater and music, and continue the annual art exhibition. Opening in 1928, with F. Cowles Strickland and Alexander Kirkland as co-directors, the theater gave its maiden performance with Eva Le Gallienne and her company in *Cradle Song*. After that a cast, resident for the summer, has usually supported a visiting star each week. Laurette Taylor, Osgood Perkins, Ina Claire, Katherine Hepburn, Ethel Barrymore, are a few of the players that have walked across the stage of The Berkshire Playhouse during the last ten years. In 1931 a school for drama was formed in connection with The Playhouse where young hopefuls received two months' training. The Playhouse is one of the oldest of the summer theaters.

The four hundred and fifty persons, who come nightly during the season to fill the theater, are negligible compared to the "unarmed army" of over five thousand who came to the National Assembly of the Oxford Group in May, 1936. "America Awake," they shouted from the ancient peaks of the Berkshire Hills, "to absolute honesty, absolute purity, absolute unselfishness, and absolute love." Early history was paradoxically pressed into the service of "religion in modern dress," in a cavalcade that marched the length of the village street. Uhm-pa-tuth, Chief of the Mahicans, had been imported from Wisconsin, and in Indian regalia that Konkapot would have envied led off the procession on horseback. It was said he never had ridden before. John Sergeant, Jonathan Edwards, and Mark Hopkins were followed by a covered wagon signifying Westward-ho, while a brand-new automobile bore the sign Eastward-ho. Then came the Oxford Group itself, 5,000 strong, and a grand finale of the flags of all nations borne aloft, preceded by no less than three brigadier generals.

If music, the third art of the Three Arts Society, never bloomed with the brilliance of the others, perhaps this can be accounted for by the establishment of music elsewhere. Elizabeth Sprague Coolidge's Temple of Music at South Mountain, in Pittsfield, and the Sunday afternoon concerts during the summer, had given an impetus to the growth of musical culture from the public point of view. Even so, Henry Hadley's dream in the May of 1934 of a series of symphony concerts, enjoyed in a setting of moonlight and stars, seemed fantastic. Dr. Hadley was guest conductor of the New York Philharmonic Orchestra. He suggested the details of the dream to Miss Gertrude Robinson-Smith: sixty-five members of the orchestra to be imported from New York, and the whole countryside to be offered the opportunity of enjoying the concerts in an open-air amphitheater. Miss Robinson-Smith, with the assistance of Mrs. Owen Johnson and Mrs. William Felton Barrett, undertook and performed in a few weeks the herculean task of the organization of committees and sub-committees throughout the county to make such a dream come true.

Grave apprehensions were felt beforehand by the committees as to the success of the three concerts that took place in August on the unoccupied Dan R. Hanna estate. But as the thousands of automobiles turned their headlights into the Hanna driveway that first evening, everyone drew a breath of relief. After another season at the Hanna farm under Hadley's leadership, he resigned because of failing health, and The Berkshire Symphonic Festival felt firmly enough ensconced in the public favor to approach Serge Koussevitzky and The Boston Symphony Orchestra. The summer of 1936 saw Dr. Koussevitzky's distinguished back presented to a capacity audience in a large circus tent on the Margaret Emerson estate. And the following year the Festival was established permanently at Tanglewood, not far from where Hawthorne's red cottage had once stood. But the elements proved refractory that summer and, after an evening in which a Berkshire thunderstorm competed with Wagner's *Ride of the Walkyrie,* and won, it seemed imperative that the Festival be provided with a building.

Eliel Saarinen drew the tentative plans for the music shed, but it was Joseph Franz of Stockbridge, a member of the Board of Trustees and an engineer, who adapted his drawings to the plan that was actually used in building it. Fan-shaped and covering an acre and a half of land, the shed seats 5,700 people. While the roof, supported by slender steel columns, protects the audience from sun and rain, the sides are open, so that the illusion of being out-of-doors is preserved. It is the largest structure in the world having natural acoustics, so that sound travels without the use of amplifiers.

The Berkshire Symphonic Festival has established Stockbridge as the site of a summer music festival for a national—even an international—audience, and its publicity carries the name of the Berkshire Hills and its advantages—"cultural, historical, educational, and scenic"—all over the world. Notices of the Festival, inviting the world to Stockbridge, appear in the symphony orchestra programs of Chicago, Cincinnati, Minneapolis, Cleveland, San Francisco and Montreal, to mention only a few. Thomas Cook and The American Express Company enclose with their own "literature" folders of the Festival. "The trip is worth the trouble," says *The New Yorker*, "because the Berkshires are all they are supposed to be, and so is the Symphonic Festival." Thirty-six thousand people attended the concerts in 1938.

The Boost-the-Berkshires motif, first sounded in the Jubilee of 1844, again taken up in the railway advertisement in the 1880's, has now reached its full crescendo. At the Jubilee it was the industrial success of the Berkshires, its institutions and its scenery that were matters of self-congratulation. In the later period the comforts and amenities of the not-too-high hills, the conservatively purling streams were stressed. But the twentieth century has thrown itself into a very frenzy of boosting. The buildings and even the former actors in the drama itself have become copy. Fanny Kemble compared the scenery to Italy, but a modern commentator compares the Chimes Tower to the *Campanile* in Venice. Simple-hearted John Sergeant preaching to his Indians, unpretentious Catherine Sedgwick and her long-forgotten novels, and Mark Hopkins's rugged simplicity—all clearly labeled history, culture, education—are grist for the mill of publicity.

On the other hand, there still exist some of the crotchets that have always distinguished the town. There is the same intolerance of innovation. Each new venture meets the old cat-and-dog-fountain clash of opinion. When the American Legion put up signs at the entrance of the main roads into the village saying, "Welcome to Stockbridge," an old lady was heard to remark with finality: "There isn't any use putting those signs up. We never *have* liked strangers in Stockbridge, and we never will."

The same strands twist in and out of the fabric of two hundred years of life. There is always the link with the outside world, always a core of village integrity kept intact. In the eighteenth century it was the Indians who caused a flutter in London drawing-rooms; in the nineteenth century

EPILOGUE

Cyrus Field linked the two continents; in the twentieth century it is The Berkshire Symphonic Festival. A refreshing breeze from outside forever blows into the valley. Williamses, Dwights, Lynches, Sedgwicks, Carters, Palmers, Fields and Choates still take their parts in the play against the eternal backdrop of Monument, Bear, and West Stockbridge Mountains. There is nothing new under the sun.

Notes

CHAPTER I

Page 1

JOHN SERGEANT'S GRANDFATHER, JONATHAN SERGEANT, was a native of New Haven. He was one of a group of men to oppose the union of the two colonies of New Haven and Connecticut, because Connecticut allowed the more liberal church membership of the Halfway Covenant. Connecticut even went a step further and allowed men not connected with the church to vote in civil affairs. To Jonathan Sergeant and his friends this seemed like a fatal compromise and they moved to New Jersey to settle the town of Newark. Here Jonathan became a boatman on the shores of the Passaic River. The Sergeants were humble people and do not figure among the elders, deacons, or ministers of the new settlement. John Sergeant was born in 1710. His father dying while he was very young, his mother married a Colonel John Cooper, who provided for his education and sent him to Yale College in 1725.

Page 12

WHEN SERGEANT AND BULL MADE THE TRIP TO HOUSATONIC there was no road at all, but only an Indian trail. The following year, 1735, a rough road was laid out by the colony of Massachusetts from Westfield through Blandford, Otis, Monterey and Great Barrington, to the New York line. This was known as the Albany road. The new road led to the settlement the same year of the townships of Tyringham, New Marlborough, Sandisfield, and Becket. Until 1738 this road was passable only on horseback, but in that year John Sergeant and Timothy Woodbridge, with eight other settlers on the Housatonic, at their own expense and with great difficulty, succeeded in getting the road to Westfield improved to a point where sleighs could travel over it in winter.

Page 19

MR. SAMUEL HOPKINS's *Historical Memoirs Relating to the Housatonic Indians* (1753) gives the first known account of the making of maple syrup. He described in detail the Indian method of getting their sugar from the trees and suggested it as a possible American industry. (See Bibliography.)

Page 22

EPHRAIM WILLIAMS was descended from Robert Williams, probably a Welshman, although on this point there is some divergence of opinion. We know certainly that he sailed from Norwich in 1638. His wife, Elizabeth Stratton, was at first unwilling to come to the new country, but it is said she had a strangely vivid dream—that if she came she would be the mother of a line of powerful and influential men. That her dream came true is evidenced in the history of western Massachusetts, for in every new enterprise we find the hand of at least one member of this energetic family. Robert Williams settled in Roxbury and his son, Isaac—the father of our Ephraim—seems to have been a man of substance, for he lived on an estate of 500 acres in what is now the town of Newton. He had eight children by his first wife, and married again in 1680 Judith Cooper, to whom he was greatly devoted. She seems to have been a most unscrupulous character. He had four children by this second marriage, the youngest of whom, his mother's favorite, was Ephraim. She persuaded Isaac to draw a most outrageous will leaving the bulk of his large estate to Ephraim, and almost entirely ignoring the other eleven children. This was the more unfair as most of Isaac's property had come to him through his first wife's father. Naturally the other children protested this will, and Judith lived to see it ruled as invalid by the judge of the Probate Court, and her beloved Ephraim left with only the old homestead and 100 acres of land. At the time he enters this history, in 1737, he was a man in the full vigor of middle age. He married twice. His first wife, Elizabeth Jackson, had borne him two sons, Ephraim and Thomas, and she dying in childbirth with Thomas, he had married Abigail Jones, by whom he had seven more children. He must have made a good thing out of the 100 acres of his inheritance, for we know that he was a man of some means when he arrived in Stockbridge in 1737.

CHAPTER II

Page 29

Mr. Frank Parker Stockbridge tells of a tradition in his family, that the name of the town came from his ancestor, Charles Stockbridge. The story goes that he set out from Scituate in 1680 and established a trading post with the Mahican Indians on the banks of the Housatonic River in that year. So that when John Sergeant arrived some fifty-odd years later, the Indians whom he found called themselves "Stockbridge Indians," and when the town was incorporated it adopted the name of Stockbridge. Although Deane's *History of Scituate* establishes Charles Stockbridge as being an Indian trader with posts strung throughout the New England wilderness, there is no contemporary record that mentions him as having one on the Housatonic River. Indeed, we have found no mention of his name at all. Therefore, after an examination of all available documents, the Timothy Woodbridge theory, while based only upon probability, is a far more convincing explanation to the present writers.

CHAPTER V

Page 101

THE EXACT DERIVATION OF LARRYWAUG OR LARRYWANG has never been finally settled. The Larry, of course, is from Larry Lynch. The *waug* is believed to have been corrupted from *wang*. Mr. Walter Prichard Eaton in the magazine *Stockbridge* (Vol. I, No. 7, p. 8) suggested that *wang*, a middle English word meaning *meadow* or *large field,* was applied to Larry's piece of land by the first English settlers. In the next issue of the magazine, Mr. Walter Patterson contributed to the discussion. He had heard from an old man, when he himself was a small boy, that the name came from the Indian word *wang*, meaning *store*. Mr. Eaton concludes, there is a word, *wangin*, said to be of Indian derivation, meaning *supply magazine* or *store of the camp*.

CHAPTER VII

Page 156

IT WAS WILLIAM EDWARDS, SON OF TIMOTHY, who planted the great elm tree in front of his house, now the house of Mr. Allen T. Treadway.

Page 158

A YARN BEAM is a beam upon which the warp threads in weaving are wound.

Page 160

EDWARD BELLAMY in his historical novel *The Duke of Stockbridge* placed Perez Hamlin as the son of a Stockbridge farmer, but the standard histories go no further than mentioning his name.

Page 161

MUMBET was an institution in the Sedgwick family. Her real name was Elizabeth Freeman and she and her younger sisters had formerly been slaves in the household of John Ashley in Sheffield. One day their mistress, in a fit of temper, had flung a heated fire iron at the younger girl. Elizabeth, to shield her, put a protecting arm out and received the full force of the blow. After this she left John Ashley, who went to law to recover his property. Such presumption, he considered, was clearly outrageous, since slavery was a well-recognized institution. Elizabeth asked Theodore Sedgwick to defend her. He won her case by appealing to the authority of the new Bill of Rights recently adopted by the state, which contained the pregnant phrase, "All men are created free and equal." His contention was that as there were no slaves in Massachusetts, Ashley could neither own one, nor collect indemnity upon one.

Historians have commonly cited Mumbet's case as the deathblow to slavery in Massachusetts, but George H. Moore, LL.D., in his *Notes on the History of Slavery* (New York, 1866), awards this palm to the case of Nathaniel Jennison *vs* Quock Walker, where the slave sued his master for assault. In 1874, Chief Justice Gray, of the Supreme Judicial Court of Massachusetts, in citing Dr. Belknap's opinion (given in Massachusetts Historical Collections, Series 1, Vol. IV) before the Massachusetts Historical Society upholds Mr. Moore's contention.

After gaining her freedom, Elizabeth spent the rest of her life in the Sedgwick household, brought up the children and nursed their mother when she was ill. Her epitaph, written by Catherine Sedgwick, expresses what she meant to them:

> "She was born a slave and remained a slave for nearly thirty years. She could neither read nor write, yet in her own sphere she had no superior nor equal. She neither wasted time, nor property. She never violated a trust, nor failed to perform a duty. In every situation of domestic trial, she was the most efficient helper, and the tenderest friend. Good Mother, farewell."

Page 163

MINOT SPEAKS OF "THE BARBAROUS PRACTICE" adopted by the rebels in deliberately putting their captives in front of them. David Dudley Field and Electa Jones, however, who quote from a man present at the encounter, maintain that Hamlin's party did not have time to reason such a plan out. They were surprised by the government forces, hid behind their prisoners to load their muskets and, overcome with terror, ran away instead of coming forward as they had intended.

CHAPTER VIII

Page 167

The Western Star was removed to Lenox in 1828 and named *The Berkshire Star and County Republican.* In 1851, it moved to Pittsfield as *The Massachusetts Eagle* and is the paper that is known today as *The Berkshire Evening Eagle.* From 1841 to 1843 another paper was published in Stockbridge called *The Weekly Visitor* and for a while a temperance paper was brought out at the same time.

Page 178

BERKSHIRE MEN SAW SERVICE during the War of 1812 in the Ninth and Twenty-first Regiments, of which the former was called the "Bloody Ninth."

Page 180

THE CONNECTICUT WESTERN RESERVE was a tract of land granted to the natives of Connecticut.

HIRAM H. PEASE was something of a wag and asked that the following verse be inscribed upon his tombstone:

> "Under this sod and under these trees,
> Lies the body of Hiram H. Pease.
> The Pease are not here, but only the pod,
> He has shelled out his soul and gone up to God."

CHAPTER IX

Page 184

A SEPARATE SCHOOL DISTRICT for Curtisville was established in 1837 and a "select school" started there several times.

Page 193

THE VILLAGE REWARDED DAVID DUDLEY FIELD'S PHILOSOPHY on the occasion of the burning of his house and gave him $1,400 for a new one which he built upon the site of that which had been destroyed.

Page 196

HARRY HOPKINS accepted a position as engineer to survey a railroad in Pennsylvania. He died in 1834, at Richmond, Virginia; all his charming brilliance snuffed out before its time.

CHAPTER X

Page 221

G. P. R. JAMES gave a clock to the Episcopal Church which was the first public timepiece in the town. In 1932, The Reverend George Grenville Merrill had its works renewed by the same company which had originally installed them.

CHAPTER XI

Page 226

THE CHAPEL OF THE GOOD SHEPHERD at South Lee is part of the Episcopal parish and has been supplied by rectors of St. Paul's Church in Stockbridge since 1856.

The non-sectarian Union Chapel in Glendale was organized in 1876 and has been supplied ever since by ministers of the different Stockbridge churches.

Page 227

ABOUT 1812 THE NAME OF THE RED LION INN WAS CHANGED to Stockbridge House. In 1897, when the present building was erected, it was known alternately as Plumb's Hotel, the Stockbridge Inn, as just The Inn, but eventually resumed its original designation. Among its owners were Jonathan Hicks, Eliada Kingsley, and Robert E. Galpin. Henry L. Plumb bought it in 1862, and since then it has remained almost entirely in the Plumb family. Today it is owned by Allen T. Treadway, Mrs. Charles Plumb's nephew, and is operated by his son, Heaton I. Treadway.

Page 229

OTHER SIMILAR CONCERNS were the Hunter Paper Company and their successors, Messrs. Chaffee & Callender, who employed forty hands in 1885 and turned out 12,000 tons of jute valued at $150,000.

Page 232

THE CATHOLIC CHURCH was actually erected in 1860.

CHAPTER XII

Page 237

THE WOOLEN MILLS AT GLENDALE were run by J. Z. Goodrich for many years. In 1880, F. W. Adams bought them from him and in 1885 they were still doing a thriving business.

Page 250

DANIEL WILLIAMS moved from Groton to Stockbridge in 1776, as is testified by the special permit quoted in Chapter VI. His son was Cyrus who kept the store. Daniel Williams was Cyrus Williams's nephew. This family is not to be confused with the Ephraim Williams family.

Page 252

ALTHOUGH MR. NATHAN JACKSON originally came from Tyringham and he had passed his life in New York amassing a handsome fortune, still a number of strings tied him up with Stockbridge history. At the time he offered the town the money to start a library, he was at the age when elderly gentlemen like to reflect upon the past. His great aunt had been the mother of Ephraim Williams (founder of Williams College) and his great grandfather had had the early training of that genial and promising child in the years before the family left Newton and came to Stockbridge. Moreover, when Mr. Jackson himself was a small boy and had been sent over from Tyringham to enjoy the superior educational advantages of the East Street school, he had attracted the favorable attention of that great democrat, Barnabas Bidwell. He patted the child on the head and presented him with the bewildering sum of one dollar. This he invested in sheep and his flock grew and prospered until in 1832 he sold it for $1,596. With this money he hastened to New York and invested in uptown lots in the city, whence sprang the Jackson fortune, the story of the famous "Bidwell dollar," and indirectly the Stockbridge Library.

In 1937, Miss Mary V. Bement gave a new wing to the Library. She is a direct descendant of Asa Bement who came to the village in the revolutionary era. The family moved west about the middle of the nineteenth century and lived for many years in Evansville, Indiana. The new wing is connected to the old by an entrance hall, the money for which was left in a bequest to the Library by Joseph H. Choate. The work undertaken in 1937 was under the direction of the office of Ralph Adams Cram.

Page 256

STEPHEN FIELD'S NAME was well known in the U. S. Patent Office where more than two hundred of his inventions were listed. The hotel annunciator, the electric elevator, the first central station for light and power, the police patrol telegraph, and electrical stage illumination were a few of his outstanding inventions.

Page 257

IN ADDITION TO THE BUILDINGS AND MONUMENTS mentioned in this chapter, the Soldiers monument was erected in 1866, and the Jonathan Edwards monument in 1872.

EPILOGUE

Page 269

STOCKBRIDGE WAS THE LINK between Lee and Great Barrington, and the natural route was down the Main Street to the Red Lion Inn and then south across the river. The route which the trolley line eventually took left the main highway a quarter of a mile west of the Lee-Stockbridge boundary, crossed the river and ran along to Laurel Hill, where it crossed the river again, making the trolley accessible to the village near the station.

Page 273

IT IS IMPOSSIBLE TO ASCERTAIN how many Stockbridge men actually saw fighting in France during the World War, but 101 were enlisted in the service.

Page 274
Population figures:

1800 population 1,261
1860 population 2,058
1905 population 2,077
1925 population 1,830
1936 population 1,921 (latest definite figure)

Bibliography

The following books have been the chief sources used in the preparation of this history:—

Stockbridge, Past and Present, by Electa F. Jones, Springfield, 1854.

History of Berkshire County, Massachusetts, revised and corrected by J. E. A. Smith, New York, 1885.

A History of the County of Berkshire, by Gentlemen of the County, Pittsfield, 1829.

Life and Letters of Catherine M. Sedgwick, edited by Mary E. Dewey, New York, 1871.

Origins in Williamstown, by Arthur Latham Perry, LL.D., New York, 1896.

R. H. W. Dwight Collection.

Historical Memoirs Relating to the Housatonic Indians, by The Reverend Samuel Hopkins, Boston, 1753. Reprinted 1911. (Extra No. 17 of the Magazine of History, with notes and queries.)

Mark Hopkins, by J. H. Denison, New York, 1935.

Acts and Resolves of the Province of Massachusetts Bay.

The rest of the material used is listed under separate chapter headings:

CHAPTER I

Gazetteer of Berkshire County, Massachusetts, Part First, Syracuse, 1885.

A History of Deerfield, Massachusetts, Vol. I, by George Sheldon, Deerfield, 1895.

Historical Discourses Relating to the First Presbyterian Church in Newark, by Jonathan F. Stearns, D.D., Newark, 1853.

Lee, A Centennial and A Century, compiled by The Reverend C. M. Hyde and Alexander Hyde, Springfield, 1878.

A Sermon Preached at Deerfield, August 31st, 1735, by Nathaniel Appleton, M.A., Boston, 1735.

The History of the Colony and Province of Massachusetts Bay, by Thomas Hutchinson, edited by Lawrence Shaw Mayo, Cambridge, 1936.

CHAPTER II

Memoirs of The Reverend David Brainerd, by Jonathan Edwards, New Haven, 1822.

Correspondence of Isaac Watts, Massachusetts Historical Society Proceedings, Series 2, Vol. IX.

Tour of the American Lakes and among the Indians of the Northwest Territory in 1830, by C. Colton, London, 1833.

Life of Jonathan Edwards, by Sereno E. Dwight, New York, 1830.

Sketch of Ephraim Williams, by President Ebenezer Fitch, Massachusetts Historical Collections, Series 1, Vol. VIII.

CHAPTER III

Archives at the Boston State House, Vol. XXXII.

Enfield Sermon, by Jonathan Edwards, contained in The American Mind, edited by Harry R. Warfel, Ralph H. Gabriel, Stanley T. Williams, New York, 1937.

A Narrative of the Surprising Work of God in Northampton, Massachusetts, 1735, by Jonathan Edwards, New York.

Jonathan Edwards, The Fiery Puritan, by Henry Bamford Parkes, New York, 1930.

Life of Jonathan Edwards, by Sereno E. Dwight. (See Bibliography, Chapter II.)

BIBLIOGRAPHY

Letter of The Reverend G. Hawley, Massachusetts Historical Society Collections, Series 1, Vol. IV.
Some Old Letters Relating to Early Stockbridge, 1749-1754, reprinted by permission from Scribner's Magazine, 1895.
Evolution of Beautiful Stockbridge, by Mrs. H. M. Plunkett.
New England Magazine, new series, Vol. V, October, 1901.

CHAPTER IV

Archives at the Boston State House, Vol. CVII.
Life of Jonathan Edwards, by Sereno E. Dwight. (See Bibliography, Chapters II and III.)
A History of Williams College, by Leverett Wilson Spring, Boston, 1917.
Muh-he-ka-ne-ok, by J. N. Davidson, A.M., Milwaukee, 1893.
The History of the Propagation of Christianity among the Heathen since the Reformation, by The Reverend William Brown, M.D., Vol. II, London, 1816.

CHAPTER V.

Proceedings at Centennial Commemoration held at Stockbridge. Historical discourse by Albert Hopkins.
The Minister's Wooing, by Harriet Beecher Stowe, Boston, 1896.
Orthodoxy in Massachusetts, by Perry Miller, Cambridge, 1933.
Records of the Congregational Church at Stockbridge, compiled by R. H. Cooke. (Berkshire Athenaeum, Pittsfield, Massachusetts.)
A Vindication of the Principles and Conduct of the Church in Stockbridge, by Stephen West, Hartford, 1780.
History of Pittsfield, by J. E. A. Smith, Boston, 1869.
Stockbridge Town Records.
In Memoriam, by N. H. Eggleston. (A discourse preached November 21, 1868, on the occasion of the erection of tab-

lets in the old church in Stockbridge in memory of its former pastors.)

Inquiry into the Grounds and Import of Infant Baptism, by Stephen West, D.D., printed at Stockbridge by Loring Andrews, 1794.

William Williams Collection, compiled by Thomas Colt. (Berkshire Athenaeum, Pittsfield, Massachusetts.)

Collections of Berkshire Historical & Scientific Society, Vol. III, Pittsfield, 1899-1913.

Berkshire Book, by its Historical & Scientific Society, Pittsfield, 1892.

CHAPTER VI

The American Revolution, by John Fiske, Cambridge, 1891.

Commonwealth History of Massachusetts, by Albert Bushnell Hart, New York, 1930.

The Massacre of the Stockbridge Indians, 1778, by Thomas F. DeVoe, Magazine of American History, 1880.

History of Great Barrington, by Charles J. Taylor, Great Barrington, 1928.

History of Pittsfield, by J. E. A. Smith. (See Bibliography, Chapter V.)

The Stockbridge Indians During the American Revolution, by Isaac J. Greenwood. New England Historical and Genealogical Register, Vol. LIV, Boston, 1900.

American Archives, by Peter Force. Prepared and Published under the authority of an Act of Congress, 1833 and 1843.

CHAPTER VII

The History of the Insurrections in Massachusetts, by George Richards Minot, Worcester, 1788.

History of Western Massachusetts, by Josiah Gilbert Holland, Springfield, 1855.

Porcupine's Works, by William Cobbett, London, 1801.

History of Massachusetts, by J. C. Barry, Boston, 1855.

An Episode of Shays' Rebellion, Magazine of History, Vol. XXII, 1916.
The Duke of Stockbridge, by Edward Bellamy, New York, 1901.
Autobiography of a Blind Minister, by Timothy Woodbridge, D.D., Boston, 1856.

CHAPTER VIII

Files of The Western Star. (Worcester Athenaeum.)
Stockbridge Library Papers.
Stockbridge Miscellany. (Berkshire Athenaeum, Pittsfield, Massachusetts.)
Unpublished letters of Judge Theodore Sedgwick. (At the Massachusetts Historical Society, Boston.)
Unpublished letters of Pamela Sedgwick. (At the Massachusetts Historical Society, Boston.)
The Federalist Party in Massachusetts, by A. E. Morse, Trenton, N. J., 1909.
Hamilton and Jefferson, by Claude Bowers, Cambridge, 1925.
Jefferson in Power, by Claude Bowers, Cambridge, 1936.
The Oxford History of the United States, by Samuel E. Morison, Oxford University Press, 1927.
The Expansion of New England, by Lois Kimball Matthews, Boston and New York, 1909.
Biographical Sketches Graduates Yale College, by F. P. Dexter, New York, 1903.
James Harris Fairchild, by Albert Temple Swing, London and Edinburgh, 1907.

CHAPTER IX

Life of Cyrus W. Field, by Isabella Field Judson, New York, 1896.
Files of the magazine, Stockbridge, edited by Walter Prichard Eaton, 1914-1915. (Stockbridge Library.)

Early Letters of Mark Hopkins, edited by S. S. H. (Susan S. Hopkins), Rahway, N. J., 1929.
Life of Henry Obookiah, by Edwin Welles Dwight, New Haven, 1819.
The Field Family Book, compiled and edited by Emilia R. Field, Denver, 1931.
The Life of David Dudley Field, by Henry M. Field, New York, 1898.
Story of the Atlantic Telegraph, by Henry M. Field, New York, 1866.
Dictionary of American Biography, New York, 1935.

CHAPTER X

Society in America, by Harriet Martineau, London, 1837.
A New England Tale, by Catherine M. Sedgwick, New York, 1854.
Hope Leslie, by Catherine M. Sedgwick, New York, 1842.
At the Library Table, by Adrian Hoffman Joline, Boston, 1910.
Records of Later Life, by Frances Ann Kemble, London, 1882.
Star Papers, by Henry Ward Beecher, Boston, 1855.
American Notebooks, by Nathaniel Hawthorne, 1883.
Memories of Hawthorne, by Rose Hawthorne Lathrop, Cambridge, 1897.
Article III, by H. M., The Westminster Review, October, 1837.
Travels in North America, by Capt. Basil Hall, London, 1829.
The Aristocratic Journey, by Mrs. Basil Hall, New York and London, 1931.
Harriet Martineau, by Theodora Bosanquet, London, 1928.
Literary Associations of Berkshire, by J. F. Cutler, New England Magazine, 1893.

BIBLIOGRAPHY

The Flowering of New England, by Van Wyck Brooks, New York, 1936.
Reminiscences of Literary Berkshire, by H. D. Sedgwick, Century Magazine, 1897.
De Tocqueville and Beaumont in America, by George Wilson Pierson, New York, 1938.
Lenox and the Berkshire Highlands, by R. DeWitt Mallary, New York and London, 1902.
Harriet Martineau's Autobiography, Memorials by M. W. Chapman, Vol. I, Cambridge, 1879.
Means and Ends, by Catherine M. Sedgwick, Boston, 1839.
Memories of Many Men, by Maunsell B. Field, New York, 1875.
The Democratic Review, by S. D. Langtree, Washington, D. C., 1840.
Political Portraits, No. XVII, Theodore Sedgwick. The United States Magazine and the Democratic Review, February, 1840.

CHAPTER XI

The Great Berkshire Jubilee, by N. S. D., Pittsfield, 1845.
Stockbridge Library Papers.
Stockbridge Town Records.
Statistics on the Condition and Products of Certain Branches of Industry in Massachusetts, by John G. Palfrey, Boston, 1846.

CHAPTER XII

Lenox and the Berkshire Highlands, by R. DeWitt Mallary. (See Bibliography, Chapter X.)
Matthew Arnold Letters, 1848-1888, collected and arranged by George W. E. Russell, New York, 1905.
Joseph H. Choate, by Theron G. Strong, New York, 1917.
Records of the Laurel Hill Association.

The Turn of the Century, by Mark Sullivan, New York, 1926.
Mary Jane Goodrich's Scrap-book. (Stockbridge Library.)
Minutes of the Stockbridge Library Association.
Stockbridge Library Papers.
Newspaper clippings and papers found in the Stockbridge Library.
Files of the magazine, Stockbridge. (See Bibliography, Chapter IX.)

EPILOGUE
Records of the Casino. (Stockbridge Library.)

Index

Agricultural Society, 207
Albinola, G., 219
Allen, Rev. Henry Freeman, 226, 230
Allen, Thomas, 127, 141-142, 146-147, 172
Andrews, Loring, 167-168, 175
Arnold, Benedict, 135-136, 149
Arnold, Matthew, 239, 242-243
Ashburner, Anne, 205-206, 217, 219, 225
Ashburner, William, 205-207
Ashley, John, 105, 127-128, 287
Atlantic Cable, 201-203
Austen Riggs Foundation, Inc., 270-271, 274-275
Ayscough, Rev. Francis, his Bible, 38, 276

Bacon, John, 113, 120, 168, 175, 208
Battle of Bennington, 145-147
Battle of Lexington, 133
Battle of Sheffield, 163-164
Battle of White Plains, 136, 139
Beecher, Henry Ward, 223
Belcher, Governor, 10, 16, 25, 37
Bement, Asa, 102, 163
Bement, Mary V., 291
Berkshire County, division from Hampshire County, 99
Berkshire Jubilee, 229-231, 280
Berkshire Medical Association, 153
Berkshire Missionary Society, 190
Berkshire Playhouse, The, 276-277
Berkshire Republican Library, 169
Berkshire Symphonic Festival, The, 278-279
Bernard, Governor, 105, 126
Bidwell, Barnabas, 172-176, 291
Bingham, Anna, 152, 157, 162
Bishop, Elkanah, 135
Bishop, Jared, 135
Bliss, Lucy, 232
Bombay Hill, 206
Bowdoin, Governor, 156
Bowker, Richard Rogers, 268
Brainerd, David, 33-34, 96
Bremer, Frederika, 216
Brewer, Adele, 259-261, 266
Brewer, David Jonathan, 199
Brewer, Emelia, 260-261
Brewer, Emilia Field, 198, 204
Brewer, Josiah, 198, 204
Brown, Ephraim, 23
Brown, Henry, 180
Brown, Samuel, 54, 91, 105, 115, 141, 180
Bryant, William Cullen, 209, 219-220
Buck, Jeremiah, 167
Buhler, Ulysse, 265
Bull, Nehemiah, 1, 11
Burgoyne, General John, 134, 144, 146-148
Burr, Aaron, 83
Burr, Esther, 83-84

Butler, Charles E, 239-241
Butler, Mrs. Charles E., 240
Butler, Fanny Kemble. (See Fanny Kemble.)
Butler, Rosalie, 241
Butler, Virginia, 241
Byington, Alice, 260-261
Byington, Cyrus, 190-191
Byington, Judge Horatio, 219, 225

Caffrey, James, 248
Canning, Agnes, 243, 266
Canning, E. W. B., 232
Carey, Thomas, Foreword xvii, 275
Carter, Edward, 196, 231
Carter, Henry J., 226, 233
Casino, 258, 264-266, 273, 276-277
Cat-and-Dog Fountain, 250, 269, 280
Catholic Church. (See St. Joseph's.)
Channing, William Ellery, 85, 123, 195, 211, 224, 232
Cherry Cottage, 91, 176, 195, 207
Chimes Tower, 254, 266
Choate, Joseph Hodges, Foreword xix, 242, 272
Choate, Joseph Hodges, Jr., 259
Churchill, Lyman, 194
Civil War, 233-236
Clark, Walter L., 276
Colman, Benjamin, 26-28, 36
Cone, Henry D., 257-258
Congress, Provincial, 132, 138
Congress, State, 125, 128-130
Congregational Church, first church, 25, 100-101; second church, 101-103; third church, 193-194; North Congregational Church, 193-194

Cooper, Jemima, 75
Courts, 130-132, 152-153, 155
Crowninshield, Frederic, 243
Crowninshield, Mrs. Frederic, 267
Crown Point Expedition, 77-82
Curtis, Abel, 156
Curtis, Alva, 180
Curtis, David, 234
Curtis, Elnathan, 54, 105, 136, 146, 151
Curtis, Jared, 169, 177, 183
Curtis, Mary. (See Mary Hopkins.)

Davis, Norman H., 277
Deane, Lavinia, 116-120
de Beaumont, Gustave, 194, 208
Debating Society, 169
Dieskau, Baron, 80-81
de Tocqueville, Alexis, 208
Draper, Ruth, 265-266
Dwight, Abigail. (See Abigail Sergeant.)
Dwight, Edwin Welles, 122, 187, 189-190
Dwight, Elijah, 127
Dwight, Henry W., 136, 171
Dwight, Senator Henry W., 218
Dwight, James, 235
Dwight, Joseph, 54-55, 60, 64-66, 69-71, 86

Eaton, Walter Prichard, 265
Ebenezer, 1-4, 6, 11, 18
Edwards, Jonathan, 22-23, 56-74, 83-88, 111, 253
Edwards, Sarah Pierpont, 60
Edwards, Timothy, 91, 100, 105, 128, 130, 132, 141, 145, 155-157, 162, 180
Edwards, William, 156-157, 286
Emmet, Lydia Field, 264

INDEX

Episcopal Church. (See St. Paul's.)

Fairchild, Daniel, 194
Fairchild, James Harris, 180
Fellowes, Colonel, 134-136
Fern, Fanny, 216-217
Field, Cyrus West, 192, 196-197, 201-203, 281
Field, David Dudley, 191, 192-193, 202, 204, 231
Field, David Dudley, Jr., 192, 196, 197-198, 199, 200-201, 204, 231, 254-255
Field, Emelia Ann, 192, 198-199, 204
Field, Henriette Desportes, 200-201, 204
Field, Henry Martyn, 192, 199-200, 202, 204, 255
Field, Jonathan Edwards, 192, 204
Field, Lucinda Hopkins, 200
Field, Mary Elizabeth, 192, 204
Field, Mary Stone, 197
Field, Matthew Dickinson, 192, 204
Field, Rachel, 259
Field, Stephen Johnson, 192, 199, 204
Field, Stephen Dudley, 203, 255-256, 291
Field, Submit Dickinson, 191, 204
Field, Timothy Beals, 192, 204
Fisk, John, 116-120
Follen, Charles, 226
Fort Massachusetts, 40, 42-45, 50
Franz, Joseph, 279
Freeman, Elizabeth. (See Mumbet.)
French, Daniel Chester, 264

French and Indian War, 7-8, 36, 39-45, 73-82, 88, 98
Gage, Governor, 132, 139
Gentleman Burglar, 260-261
Glezen, Solomon, 164
Golden Wedding, Field, 204
Golf Club, 259
Goodrich, J. Z., 251, 252, 290
Goodrich, Mrs. J. Z., 243-245
Gourlie, J. H., 250-251, 258
Goodwin, Agnes, 266
Grant of township, 24
Gray, Mary, 173
Hadley, Henry, 278
Hall, Basil, 206-208, 214, 228
Hall, Mrs. Basil, 206
Hawthorne, Nathaniel, 220-221, 223
Hawthorne, Sophia, 227
Hawley, Gideon, 63-64
Hendrick, 62-63, 77, 80-81
Hessians, 148
Hicks, Jonathan, 183, 205, 227, 290
Hoffman, Ferdinand, 233
Hollis, Isaac, 27, 35, 37-38, 39, 70
Holmes, Oliver Wendell, 222, 231
Hopkins, Albert, 113, 186, 187, 195
Hopkins, Archibald, 176-177, 187
Hopkins, Harry, 186, 187, 195, 196, 289
Hopkins, John, 177, 187
Hopkins, Mark, of Great Barrington, 129, 136
Hopkins, Mark, President of Williams College, 137, 185, 187-188, 195, 211, 230, 280
Hopkins, Mary, 176, 184, 186
Hopkins, Mary. (See Mrs. J. Z. Goodrich.)
Hopkins, Samuel, of Great Barrington, 40, 56, 111, 113

Hopkins, Samuel, of West Springfield, 10, 284
Hopkins, Sewall, 186
Housatonic National Bank, 232
Housatonic Townships, purchase of, 9
Hull, Agrippa, 145, 170
Huntington, Joseph, 119
Hyde, Caleb, 225

Ice Glen Parade, Foreword xviii, 227
Indian Boarding School, 34-37, 39, 47, 54, 59-60, 63-64, 69
Indian Monument, 245
Ingersoll, David, 132
Ingersoll, Deacon, 160, 231

Jackson, Nathan, 252, 291
James, G. P. R., 221-222, 289
Jameson, Anna, 216
Johnson, Owen, 265
Johnson, Sir William, 77, 80
Jones, Josiah, 23, 103, 105

Kellog, Martin, 39, 56, 60, 63, 64, 70
Kemble, Fanny, Foreword xviii, 212-215, 220, 231, 257, 280
King Ben, 91, 176
King Philip's War, 7
King Solomon, 91
Kobbé, Marie, 264
Konkapot, 1, 2, 3, 9, 10, 11, 13, 24, 46, 277
Kossuth, 233, 272
Kosciusko, 145, 170
Koussevitzsky, Serge, 279

Ladies' Sewing Society, 194
Larrywaug, 101, 157, 160, 286
Laurel Cottage, 225, 242
Laurel Hill Association, Foreword xvii, 243-246

Lawrence, Rev. Arthur, Foreword xiv, 241
Lincoln, General, 156, 158
Linwood, 239
Longfellow, Henry W., 222-223
Lukeman, Augustus, 265
Lynch, Charles, 235
Lynch, John C., 270
Lynch, Lawrence, 54, 74, 101

Mahicans, 5-7
Manufactures, 151, 229, 237
Marsh, Cutting, 96
Marsh, Perez, 78
Martineau, Harriet, 214-216, 234
McBurney, Dr. Charles, 268
McKim, Charles, 240, 258
Melville, Herman, 222
Metcalfe, Susan, 264
Methodist Church, 257
Metoxin, Johannes, 26, 88, 94, 137
Mills, 46, 151, 229, 290
Mission House, 31, 276
Mohawks, 5, 54, 56
Morpeth, Lord, 208
Morrissey, Dennis, 268
Muh-he-ka-neew, 5
Mumbet, 161-162, 286-287
Music Hall, 247

Nettleton, Walter, 265, 273
Nimham, Abraham, 138-139
North Congregational Church, 193-194
Norton, Lizzie, 266
Obookiah, Henry, 189-190
Old Place, the Dwight house, 150
Oneidas, 5, 92
Oxford Group, 277-278

Pagenstecher, Albert, 254
Palmer, Roswell, 208
Palmer, William Pitt, 219, 230-231, 266

INDEX

Parker, Samuel P., 225-227
Parton, Sara. (See Fanny Fern.)
Partridge, Dr. Oliver, 103, 153
Patterson, Colonel, 134, 158
Pease, Hiram H., 180, 288
Petition of Peace, 234
Pepoon, Silas, 100, 113
Pitkin, Mrs. Mary Jane, 266
Pixley, David, 54, 115
Plumb, Henry, 249
Plumb, Mrs. Charles H., 258, 266, 290
Porcupine, 154

Railroads, 228, 230, 238-239
Red Lion Inn, Foreword xiii, 100, 125, 140, 152, 182, 205, 258, 290
Riggs, Dr. Austen Fox, 270-271, 274-275
Riggs Foundation. (See Austen Riggs Foundation, Inc.)
Roads, 12, 46, 99-100, 182, 283
Robinson-Smith, Gertrude, 278

Schaghticokes, 71-74
Schilling, Mrs. Joseph, 266
Schools, English, 91, 103-104, 183-185, 232-233, 259-260
Schools, Indian. (See Indian Boarding School.)
Schuyler, Philip, 144-145
Sedgwick, Alexander, Foreword xv, 258-259, 267-268
Sedgwick, Catherine, 55, 112, 185, 208-212, 215-216, 219-220, 232, 235, 237, 280
Sedgwick, Charles, 218
Sedgwick, Mrs. Charles, 218, 221, 227
Sedgwick, Henry Dwight, 196, 218
Sedgwick, Henry Dwight II, 246-247

Sedgwick house, 150, 247, 267
Sedgwick, Pamela, 74, 150, 171, 173-174
Sedgwick, Robert, 196, 218
Sedgwick, Susan Ridley, 217
Sedgwick, Susan. (See Mrs. Charles E. Butler.)
Sedgwick, Judge Theodore, 123, 129, 133, 136, 141, 150, 157-158, 165, 172-176
Sedgwick, Theodore, 174, 184, 217, 218, 228
Sergeant, Abigail, 30-31, 42, 46, 49-50, 51, 54-55, 65, 67, 74, 81-82, 102, 151-152, 166
Sergeant, Electa, 32, 91, 174, 176
Sergeant, Dr. Erastus, 32, 129, 130, 153
Sergeant, John, 1-5, 11-20, 23, 25, 27, 30, 32-33, 34-35, 47-49, 181, 280, 283
Sergeant, John, 32, 91, 94
Seymour, George, 249
Seymour, Ira, 160
Shays, Daniel, 156
Shirley, Governor, 71, 77
Siege of Boston, 134-135
Six Nations, 5, 16-17
Society for the Preservation of Christian Morals, 188
Society for the Propagation of the Gospel, The, 10
Southmayd, Charles F., 241, 261
Stafford, Jesse, 167
Stage Coaches, 182-183
Stark, General John, 134, 146
Stockbridge Academy, 183, 232
Stockbridge Band, 257
Stockbridge House. (See Red Lion Inn.)
Stockbridge Indians. (See Mahicans.)
Stockbridge Library, 252-253, 291

Stockbridge, Emigrations from, 179-181
Stockbridge, name of, 29, 285
Stockbridge, raid of, 159-162
Stoddard, John, 8-11, 20-22, 41, 59
St. Joseph's Church, 232, 290
St. Paul's Church, 226, 240-241, 289
Strickland, F. Cowles, 277
Sunrise Prayer Meeting, Foreword xiv-xv, 192-193
Swann, John, 268
Swann, Mrs. John, 260-261
Swift, Seth, 121-122, 123

Thoreau, Henry, 223
Three Arts Society, 277
Town Hall, 232
Town Offices, 257
Town poor, 151-152
Treadway, Allen T., 270, 290
Trolley, 268-269, 292
Tuckerman, Emily, 266
Tuckerman, Lucius, 243

Umpachene, 1, 11, 18, 19, 20-21, 46, 53

Waumpaumcorse, 72-73
War of 1812, 177-179, 288
Watts, Isaac, 27-28
Wells, Carrie, Foreword xiv, 261
Wells, Thomas, 223, 243
West, Stephen, 90, 91, 110-114, 117, 118-124, 127, 128, 146, 161, 168, 178-179, 181, 191, 192, 223, 225, 232, 253
West, Mrs. Stephen, 121-122
Western Star, The, 167-168, 179, 288
Williams, Abigail. (See Abigail Sergeant.)
Williams Academy, 232-233

Williams College, 42, 79, 187
Williams, Cyrus, 192, 229, 232, 290
Williams, Daniel, 143-144, 290
Williams, Daniel, 250, 290
Williams, Elijah, 63, 86, 105-109, 131-132, 141-142, 229, 258
Williams, Elisha, 54
Williams, Elizabeth, 79
Williams, Ephraim, 22-24, 29, 36, 40-41, 50-53, 66-68, 76, 98, 284-285
Williams, Ephraim, Jr., 41-45, 61-62, 76-81
Williams, Israel, 59, 70, 74
Williams, Josiah, 78, 86
Williams, Stephen, of Longmeadow, 78
Williams, Dr. Thomas, 42-43, 78, 81
Williams, Thomas, 132, 135
Williams, William, 40, 42, 98-99, 126-128
Willis, N. P., 217
Willson, Mary, 109
Woodbridge, Jahleel, 129, 145, 151, 156, 160
Woodbridge, Joseph, 23, 99
Woodbridge, Timothy, 14, 19, 24, 29, 56, 62, 64, 87, 88-89
Wood-pulp industry, 253-254
World War, 271-274, 292
Wurtzbach, Frederick, 254

Van Deusen, John M., Foreword xiii, 251
Van Rensselaer, Cortlandt, 259, 265
Van Schaack, David, 106-107
Van Schaack, Henry, 106-107, 173
Van Valkenburgh, Jehoiakim, 3, 4, 10, 11, 18-19, 20-23